Streams in the Desert

ZONDERKIDZ

Streams in the Desert® for Kids
Copyright © 2009 by Zondervan

Requests for information should be addressed to:

Zonderkidz, *Grand Rapids, Michigan 49530*

Library of Congress Cataloging-in-Publication Data

Streams in the desert : 366 daily devotions for children / based on the original book by L.B. Cowman.
    p.   cm.
Originally published: Los Angeles, Calif. : Oriental Missionary Society, 1925. Includes bibliographical references.
ISBN 978-0-310-71600-6 (softcover : alk. paper)
1. Christian children — Prayers and devotions. 2. Devotional calendars — Juvenile literature.
I. Cowman, Charles E., Mrs., 1870-1960.
BV4870.S83 2009
242'.62—dc2   2009015222

Art direction: Sarah Molegraaf
Interior composition and design: Carlos Eluterio Estrada and Luke Daab

Printed in the United States of America

09 10 11 12 13 14 • 22 21 20 19 18 17 16 15 14 13 12 11 10 9 8 7 6 5 4 3 2 1

STREAMS
in the DESERT

366 Daily Devotions for Children
Based on the original book by L. B. Cowman

ZONDER**kidz**

ZONDERVAN.com/
AUTHOR**TRACKER**
follow your favorite authors

To all those who have found inspiration in the words of the original *Streams in the Desert* book, may this book be a similar inspiration to a new generation.

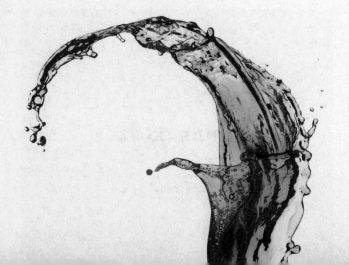

God is in Control

The land ... is a land the Lord your God cares for; the eyes of the Lord your God are continually on it from the beginning of the year to its end.
Deuteronomy 11:11-12

Happy New Year! What will your family do today? Do you usually watch the Rose Bowl Parade? Are there any football fans at your house? Perhaps you are one. Do you like to control the TV remote when watching the games and parades today so that you can switch back and forth or stay on the program you like?

Don't we all wish we could be in control, not just of the remote but of everything that happens in our life? We wish we could control our grades. We wish we could control our friends so they would always be good to us. We wish we could control how we play sports so that we could always be in first place. But we can't control very much about our lives because we don't know what's going to happen in the future. The good news is that there is Someone who knows everything. He knows all about what's going to happen, when it will happen, and to whom. That Someone is God.

In the scripture at the beginning of this devotion, we read that the eyes of the Lord God are always on the land. That means God is not only watching over the earth, but he is watching us. God loves us. Nothing can happen to us without him knowing about it. He cares about us more than we can imagine.

Dear Lord, Thank you that your eyes are always on us and on our land. Please help us to trust you, even when we feel as if everything is out of control. Thank you for loving us so much that you never take your eyes off of us. Amen.

Knowing God

*The side rooms all around the temple were wider at each successive level.
The structure surrounding the temple was built in ascending stages, so that
the rooms widened as one went upward. A stairway went up from the
lowest floor to the top floor through the middle floor.*
Ezekiel 41:7

If you have ever climbed stairs to look out of a high window, you
know there can be a lot to see. You discover things from high places
that you never see if you stay on the ground. And the higher you go,
the better the view.

In Paris, France, people buy tickets to get to the highest spot
around — the top of the Eiffel Tower. From there they can see over
buildings, rivers and entire cities. But to get to the top, they have to
climb almost 1,700 steps. (If you had 80 floors in your house, you
might have 1,700 stairs!) You can imagine how tiring it is to climb
all the way to the top. Leg muscles burn. Breathing becomes loud
and labored. Many people have to rest several times. But those who
keep trying and keep going get to see farther and wider than anyone
who stops halfway.

God invites us to live on the high places, where our lives and our
problems can be seen from a heavenly perspective. There are blessings we might never realize if we don't draw nearer to him. But it
can be a difficult climb. Praising God in hard times isn't easy. Standing up for what is right instead of what's popular takes courage and
strength. Remembering Jesus every day may seem tiring. But if we
give up too early, we could miss the grander life God has planned
for us.

So keep climbing. The Bible assures us that the view is worth it!

Dear Father, Help me follow your ways so that I can live closer to you.
Even though it takes a lot of effort and commitment, I know that's the
best place to be. Amen.

God Leads Us Gently

Jacob said to Esau, "I must care for the ewes and cows that are nursing their young. If they are driven hard just one day, all the animals will die. So let my lord go on ahead... while I move along slowly at the pace... of the children.
Genesis 33:12,14

Long ago, a man in the Bible named Jacob had a huge family as well as many servants, cattle, sheep, and camels. One day he decided to move the whole lot of them across some of the worst desert terrain in the world to his homeland in Israel. No moving vans or buses here. The people had to walk. Can you imagine the braying and baaing of the animals? Can you imagine the whining and crying of the babies? It wasn't a very pleasant trip.

The Bible tells us that Jacob realized how young and weak many of the children and animals were. He decided not to force them to go too far in one day. He was gentle with them. That's why he told his brother Esau to go on ahead of him, and he would only go as fast as the youngest and weakest of his tribe could go.

And that's the way God leads us. He takes us tenderly through the hard times in our lives. He is gentle with us, especially when we have failed. Sometimes we get so mad at ourselves when we just can't get it right. So we have to learn to be gentle with ourselves in the same way God is. It's important to treat yourself the way Jacob treated his family ... the way God treats us ... gently.

Dear Lord, Help me to be patient with myself. Help me remember that every day is a new day and you are in it. Lord, I pray for my friends who feel like failures. Help me to help them. Amen.

Finding God's Help

Therefore I tell you, whatever you ask for in prayer, believe that you have received it, and it will be yours.
Mark 11:24

Have you ever wanted something so much that you kept begging and begging your parents to get it for you? Perhaps they think you are not quite ready for whatever it is. But you want it so much you keep on bugging them for it. Finally, after a long while, you give up and figure you are never going to get it. You have lost hope. You have lost faith that what you want will ever be yours.

Sometimes the same thing happens when we pray to God. We want something so much that we beg him for it. When God doesn't grant us our request, we think he's not listening. We think he doesn't care. We pray so long and so hard that we pray ourselves right out of faith. But the Bible teaches that God always hears our prayers. Like your parents, he may not think you're ready for whatever you are asking. Or maybe he knows it would not be best for you. Or maybe he fully intends to answer your prayer, but it just isn't the right time.

Now is the time to simply trust God and believe he knows what he's doing. We have to let our prayer rest with him until he is ready to make it happen.

Dear Lord, I believe that you will answer my prayers in your way and your time. Help me to learn what it means to let my prayer rest in your hands. Amen.

Stuck Between a Rock and a Hard Place

Then Asa called to the Lord his God and said, "Lord, there is no one like you to help the powerless against the mighty."
2 Chronicles 14:11

Talk about being in a tough place! King Asa certainly was. Asa was one of the good guys. He listened to God. He did what he should. Then a huge army of Ethiopians, people from an African nation, began to gather in preparation for fighting and wiping out King Asa and his country of Judah. Well, Asa wasn't the kind of guy who just sat there waiting for something bad to happen to him. He gathered his own army. He called up 300,000 troops from one part of his country and 280,000 troops from another part of his kingdom. That seems like a lot of soldiers until you realize that the Ethiopians probably had closer to a million soldiers. That means Asa's enemies had nearly twice as many soldiers as he did.

On the day of the battle, King Asa stood with his troops and looked out at the huge army of the enemy. Then he did something we can do when we are facing an impossible problem and there seems to be no way out. He called to God. "Help!" he said. "Lord, there is no one like you to help us. We're depending on you to get us out of this mess. We've come against this vast army in your name. Now please help us!"

And God certainly did help. The enemy was "crushed before the Lord and his forces" (vs. 12). What a wonderful, encouraging story! When we are in the worst place of all our life, we need to call out to God. We need to tell God, and remind ourselves, that God is the one who stands protectively between us and our biggest problems.

Dear Lord, I'm going through a tough time now. I don't know where to turn or what to do. I need you to help me and lead me. You can do what I can't do and protect me from my enemies. I know that you are a God who cares for me. Amen.

Don't Worry, Be Happy

When you pass through the waters, I will be with you; and when you pass through the rivers, they will not sweep over you. When you walk through the fire, you will not be burned; the flames will not set you ablaze, for I am the Lord, your God.
Isaiah 43:2–3a

Do you know what a worrywart is? It's someone who worries about everything all the time. He worries about failing a test, even when he's studied. She worries it's going to rain when the sun's shining bright. Worrywarts worry about getting sick, about accidents, about every bad thing they can think of to worry about. But worry is not good for the worrier. Worry can make you sick. There is nothing that can be changed by worrying. And most of what we worry about never happens anyway. The Bible tells us not to be anxious — that means, don't worry.

Bad things do sometimes happen to people, but God has promised to be with us in the bad times. Corrie ten Boom, a Dutch lady whose family hid and saved Jewish people during World War II, was frightened and worried that her family might get caught. Her father said to her, "When we are going on a train ride, when do I give you the ticket?" "When we are ready to get on," she answered. "Yes," he told her, "and God will come to help you when you need him and not before." And God did help Corrie when she needed him.

You can choose to worry or choose to trust, and trusting is what God asks his children to do. Jesus said we should let tomorrow take care of itself. That means we can't do anything about what will happen tomorrow, so don't worry about it today (see Matthew 6:34).

Dear Lord, Help me not to worry about things I can't change. Help me to choose to trust you every day of my life. I know you will give me what I need to get through tough times. I'm going to choose to trust a lot more and worry a lot less. Amen.

Happy Just to Be ... Myself

I have learned to be content, whatever the circumstances.
Philippians 4:11

Have you ever noticed how easy it is to compare yourself to others? Even if we know better, we look at someone else and think he or she has it better. How many times have you thought: If only I had the right hair or clothes or shape ... If only I were taller or faster or bolder or funnier ...

There's an old story of a king who went to his garden and found everything withered and dying. He asked the oak tree what was wrong. The oak tree said it was sick of living because it was not as tall and beautiful as the pine tree. The pine was dropping needles because it couldn't grow grapes like the grapevine. And the grapevine let itself shrivel up because it couldn't stand straight and tall like the peach tree. Every plant in the garden was discontented and wanted to be something different, except the violet. There it stood with its happy face turned toward the sun. The king asked the little flower why it was so happy and content when every other plant in the garden was so miserable. "Well," said the flower, "I figured that if you had wanted a big oak tree or a pine tree or a peach tree in my spot, you would have planted one; but you planted me—a violet. Since I knew you wanted a violet, I've made up my mind to be the best little violet I can be."

You were made by the almighty Creator with a purpose in mind. Wishing to be anything other than who you are does nothing more than steal your time, energy and joy. But when you see yourself how God does, you realize how great you really are. So you can stop concentrating on other people and instead focus on your own blessings. Only then will you find you are ready for all the plans and adventures God has for you.

Dear Lord, Help me stop comparing myself to other people and worrying about the things I think I lack. Thank you for all of the gifts you have given me. Show me how I can best use them for your glory. Amen.

Let it Rain, Let it Pour

I will bless them ... I will send down showers in season; there will be showers of blessing.
Ezekiel 34:26

Without water there is no life, and with a tiny amount of water, there is a tiny bit of life. Death Valley is one of the driest places in North America. It gets only about two inches of rain a year, and it gets very hot: in the summer temperatures often rise above 120 degrees. Because of lack of rain and extreme heat, not much grows there. But a few years ago it rained and rained and rained all winter. When spring came every seed that had been lying dormant in the soil came to life and began to grow. Soon the hillsides and valleys were full of desert flowers. There were millions of them. Water and life had come to the desert!

Sometimes our hearts can get dried up. We may feel as dry inside as Death Valley. When that happens, God seems far away. It's easier then to do what we know is wrong. It's easier to be angry. Our souls shrivel up. But God wants to bring life to our souls. He promises showers of blessings. He wants to fill up every dry valley in our life with his living water. And when he does, God will cause good things to grow in our lives. We just have to get to a place where his rain can fall on us. Sometimes that place is beside our bed when we pray. Sometimes it's in church when God comes to us. And sometimes it's when we are alone outdoors that God speaks.

Dear Lord, Please send your showers of blessings to me. Please let good things grow in my life—things that will bless others. Fill up the dry deserts of my life with your love. Amen.

The Reason Why

I consider that our present sufferings are not worth comparing with the glory that will be revealed in us.
Romans 8:18

Each year in Grand Rapids, Michigan, the Frederick Meijer Garden has a butterfly exhibit. Part of the garden is a huge glass structure with tropical plants, waterfalls, birds, and, for a short time each spring, thousands of butterflies. When you come into the glass structure from the cold of early March, it's like stepping into a tropical paradise. Butterflies of all shapes, sizes, and colors flutter from feeder to feeder. Off to one side of the indoor garden is a case in which thousands of cocoons are hanging from pins. Some of the cocoons are empty. The butterflies that were once inside have come out and are drying their wings. Other cocoons are split open and butterflies are struggling to get out: it's a slow process that sometimes takes hours. The opening in the cocoon is so tiny that it looks like it might hurt to squeeze out of it. The butterflies look as if they need help, but none of the attendants help them. The struggle they are going through is actually what's best for them. Squeezing through the tiny hole is part of what helps make the butterflies' wings healthy and strong. If the attendants were to try to help, the butterflies would not develop properly. Their wings would be weak and they probably would never fly.

Struggle is part of life for butterflies. And struggle is part of our lives too. As young people, there is so much to learn and a lot of it is just plain hard. We struggle. We work. We get frustrated. We're sure we're never going to get it. But God knows that through your struggle you will grow strong. He knows that whatever you are going through now can't even begin to compare with the wonderful things he has planned for your future. So don't give up. Keep struggling and one day you, too, will fly!

Dear Lord, I am so glad to know that you understand I am struggling. I'm glad you have a plan, even though I can't see it. Help me to trust you. Help me not to give up. Help me to learn all I can as I pass through these tough times. Amen.

Go Where?

When Paul and his companions came to the border of Mysia, they tried
to enter Bithynia, but the Spirit of Jesus would not allow them to.
Acts 16:7

Have you ever played a game where you were blindfolded and your
friends shouted directions about which way you should go? If you
have, you know it's scary. It's hard to trust that your friend will
keep you safe. They might let you walk into a wall. They might not
see a curb you could trip over. You might not understand their
directions and ram into something. Often when we are trying to
figure out what God wants us to do, we might feel blindfolded.
We may have to just listen to his directions and keep walking even
though we can't see where we are going. Is it scary? You bet!

But God will guide us and keep us safe in his care. He's promised.
Our job is to pray, trust in God's wisdom, and listen for his direction.
So if we have to change schools or don't make a team we tried out
for, it doesn't have to discourage us. Often God closes doors to lead
us in a different direction, meet a new person, or offer us a new
opportunity that will help us to grow and change. It might be scary
at first, but we're never alone.

Dear Lord, Help me believe that you will guide me even when I can't
see anything ahead. Help me to keep walking and listening until you
show me the next path to take. Amen.

Comfort

Comfort my people, says your God.
Isaiah 40:1

Do you have something that gives you comfort — a blanket you've had since you were a baby, a special stuffed animal, a familiar place in your house? Maybe you have someone you go to when you especially need a hug, kind words and thoughtful reassurance.

Have you ever felt that you needed Jesus to comfort you with a big hug? When you are discouraged, you can turn to Jesus. Jesus promised to be with us right up to the end of the world. He promised he would never leave us or abandon us. So the next time you are feeling lonely or sad or discouraged, pray and tell Jesus everything that is troubling you. Then you will be able to say, "Shout for joy, O heavens' rejoice, O earth; burst into song, O mountains! For the Lord comforts his people ..." (Isaiah 49:13).

And when you have come through your struggle, friends will see that you understand and know what real comfort is. Then you will be the one who can be counted on for the hug, words of encouragement and comfort of Jesus.

Dear Lord, I feel so alone and I need you to comfort me. Please stay close beside me. Amen.

Hedges

Consider it pure joy, my brothers, whenever you face trials of many kinds.
James 1:2-3

In England one farm is often divided from the next either by a stone wall or a thick, thorny hedge. Hedges and walls have two purposes: to keep things in and to keep things out. The farmers want their cows to stay close to home, so they put them inside a hedge or wall. Shepherds, on the other hand, don't want dogs, wolves, coyotes, or lions to carry off their lambs, so they put up hedges or walls to keep them out and away from their sheep. If the sheep or cows find a way out of the enclosure, they are in great danger. It's better to stay where the farmer puts them.

God wants to put a hedge around your life. He wants to protect you from anything that might hurt you. God's hedge is made up of rules to keep. God doesn't give us a lot of rules to make us unhappy. He gives us rules to keep us safe. And God has appointed your parents to give you rules to keep you safe too. If you keep your parents' rules and God's rules, you will be safe. But if you jump over the rules you will be in dangerous territory. What dangerous territory might you be tempted to jump into?

Dear Lord, Put a hedge of protection around my life. Help me keep the rules you gave us and the rules my parents have set up for our family. Help me stay close to you. Amen.

Winning with God

In all these things we are more than conquerors through him who loved us.
Romans 8:37

There were some ancient people known as Phrygians who lived in what is now the country of Turkey. They believed that when you conquered an enemy, some of the enemy's physical strength passed into you. That's just a myth, of course. But when we Christians struggle against sin and win, we grow stronger. We grow more powerful not from the enemy, but from Christ's strength. Then we can face the next battle stronger. We become more than conquerors because we have Jesus fighting with us against the enemy.

God knows that every day that we try to live for him, we are fighting a war with an enemy. Satan doesn't want us serving God. He'd rather hurt us than see us become conquerors with Christ. But through the mighty powers of God's son, we can defeat the enemy and become great warriors in God's kingdom.

Dear Lord, I know that with you all things are possible. Please give me your strength to help me beat the enemy. Amen.

Follow the Shepherd

When he has brought out all his own, he goes on ahead of them, and his sheep follow him because they know his voice.
John 10:4

Sheep are animals that need constant protection from wild animals and from getting themselves into situations that can hurt them. Many people who have sheep keep them in pens to protect them, but there are other people who actually live with the sheep and guide them from one pasture to the next. They're called shepherds, and they usually have a sheep-herding type of dog to help them round up strays and keep the animals going in the right direction.

In Biblical times, the shepherd walked in front of his sheep and they followed him. Stories are told that several shepherds could mix their flocks at a watering hole, and when they were ready to move on each shepherd would give a particular call and his band of sheep would separate themselves from the others to follow their own master. The sheep knew their shepherd's voice.

And that's how we follow our Good Shepherd, Jesus. First we spend time with him so we get to know his voice. Then, when he calls to us, we follow him. We do exactly what he wants us to do. Jesus wants to keep his flock, his sheep — all of us — safe. We have to make the choice to stay close to him. What will you choose?

Dear Lord, Sometimes I'm like a headstrong sheep, butting my way into all kinds of things that aren't good for me. Help me to stay close to you and to listen for your voice all the rest of my life. Amen.

Be Still and Know

The Lord appeared to Isaac and said, "I am the God of your father Abraham. Do not be afraid, for I am with you."
Genesis 26:24

Have you ever fought with a friend at school and then spent the day feeling lousy? Or argued with a brother or sister and stayed upset even after you had gone to bed? When conflict, stress and worry pile up, it's easy to keep carrying around the anxiety.

During Jesus' time on earth, he drew crowds filled with people who loved him and people who hated him. The truth he spoke eventually upset enough people that they plotted to get rid of Jesus any way they could. Sounds pretty stressful, doesn't it? The Bible tells how Jesus deliberately took time to be alone with his father, away from his disciples, away from the crowds. In the quiet times and in his quiet heart, Jesus could listen, be renewed, and prepare for what was coming next.

When you are anxious because of disagreements, unfair treatment or other unsettling situations, it makes it difficult to hear God's voice. But be still and know that God is with you. Step back and rest quietly, so you can hear what God wants to say. Even Jesus did this.

Dear Father, You know the conflicts I've been having and the things that are bothering me. I know you are with me. Help me to first listen to you so I can handle the situation. Amen.

When Life Gets Tough — Hang On!

A furious squall came up, and the waves broke over the boat, so that it was nearly swamped.

Mark 4:37

Storms are scary. They are destructive and they can threaten life. When a huge hurricane named Katrina swept ashore in New Orleans, it just about ruined the city. Jesus' disciples knew all about storms, so when they got caught in a furious squall on the Sea of Galilee, they were sure they were about to die. They expected their boat to be demolished by the storm. Jesus was asleep in their boat, so they woke him up and asked him to save them. And that's what Jesus did. He spoke to the storm and told it to be quiet.

Tough times come to everyone. Sometimes someone we love gets sick. Sometimes a friend betrays us. Sometimes there are real storms like hurricane Katrina. There are lots of scary things that can happen, but just like the disciples, we have Jesus in the boat of our life. We just have to call out to him. He will help us find a way through the worst problems we could ever have.

Dear Lord, Thank you for being there through the good times as well as the bad. I know that with your help I can overcome anything that comes into my life. Help me trust you more. Amen.

God Is Alive!

He called to Daniel in an anguished voice, "Daniel, servant of the living
God, whom you serve continually, been able to rescue you
from the lions?"
Daniel 6:20

The Bible tells a story about a man named Daniel who was punished
by being thrown into a lion's den. That's a pretty big punishment,
so you might think Daniel had done something really bad, right?
Here's what he did: he prayed to the living God. That's it! But in
doing so, he broke a law that made it illegal for people to pray to
anyone but the king. The day after Daniel had been thrown into the
lion's den, the king came to see if the living God had saved Daniel.
Daniel was still alive. The lions had not been able to bite him because
God had sent an angel to shut their mouths.

After this miracle, even the godless king understood that Daniel's
God was alive. And Daniel's God is our God, and he is still alive!
So if God is alive, what does it mean for us? It means God can help
us every day. It means we can talk with him about any problem we
have. We can pray to him when we need something. We can ask
him to help people who are sick or sad or poor. We tell God about
our own problems and then listen for his answers. Our living God
wants to help us with our problems. He cares about what we need.
He wants us to do what is right and good.

Dear Lord, I am so glad you are alive and that you know all about me.
Help me remember to talk with you about everything that happens
in my life. Help me live so close to you that I can hear you when you
whisper. Amen.

Victory!

But thanks be to God, who always leads us in triumphal procession in Christ.
2 Corinthians 2:14

At some point everyone has to face great disappointment. Maybe you didn't get the part in a play you had your heart set on, or your parents are talking about divorce, or you had to move from a school you like. Situations like these feel like defeat, leaving behind pain, loss, and uncertainty about the future. Consider the defeat the three Hebrew prisoners in Babylon felt moments before they were thrown into a blazing furnace. Ever wonder how the Israelites felt just outside of Egypt—cornered by the Red Sea on one side and their enemy on the other? Think about how hopeless the disciples felt when they saw Jesus taken to the cross.

Now consider the rest of the stories.

The three prisoners, Shadrach, Meshach, and Abednego, declared their faith to their enemies, saying, "If we are thrown into the blazing furnace, the God we serve is able to save us from it, and he will rescue us from your hand, O King. But even if he does not, we want you to know that we will not serve your gods." Then the king watched them go into the flames and come out uninjured. In Exodus, when the Israelites saw the Egyptians coming to bring them back to captivity and were ready to surrender in defeat, they witnessed God's spectacular miracle of the parting of the Red Sea. And after three days of mourning, pain and confusion, the disciples met the risen Christ face to face.

Nobody likes to go through serious disappointment. But defeat is never the end of God's story. Stand in the faith that victory and goodness are in your future, even if you can't imagine it now.

Dear Lord, Even though I feel defeated, I know you have a plan. Please be with me in my sadness. And help me walk faithfully as I look forward to the victory. Amen.

Determined

You should always pray and not give up.
Luke 18:1

David Livingstone was one of the greatest missionary doctors who ever lived. But when he was struggling on his expeditions, he didn't look so great. His exploration of the River Zambezi was a failure —the river could not be navigated. He kept trying to find a way until the British government ordered him home. After that, no one wanted to give him more money to return for more explorations.

After a while, he somehow found the money to return to Africa. Once he got there, no one heard from him for six years. Many thought he was dead, but he was not. Although he was seriously ill, he was determined to stay in Africa until his mission was complete. He stubbornly continued to explore. Finally, he died and his friends carried his body a thousand miles to the coast so that he could be returned to England and honored with a proper burial.

At the time he died, many people thought Livingstone's whole life was a failure. But now, many years later, we know he traveled 29,000 miles in Africa, and that he made important geographical discoveries for Great Britain, such as Victoria Falls and four important lakes. He explored Central Africa so missionaries could go there. He was honored by African chiefs. He spoke out against slavery. And others who knew him were inspired to build schools to educate African children. Much good has come of his life.

One of the things Livingstone said was, "I determined never to stop until I had come to the end and achieved my purpose." That means he decided he would never give up, and it explains a lot about who he was. It also helps us understand that we must not give up praying for whatever it is we want and need from God.

Dear Lord, First help me know what I should pray for, and then make me determined never to stop praying and talking with you. Amen.

Crying Beats Laughing

Crying is better than laughing. It blotches the face but it scours the heart.
Ecclesiastes 7:3, The Message

Okay ... so what does that verse mean? How can crying be better than laughing, and who wants their heart scoured anyway? Have you ever been really, really sad? So sad you thought you couldn't breathe? What did you do?

That kind of deep sadness is sometimes called "sorrow." Nobody wants sorrow — not ever, but sorrow has a purpose. Think about Joseph in the Bible. He had some very sorrowful times. His mother died when he was very young. His brothers hated him and threw him in a pit, planning to kill him. Then, in a change of heart, they sold him. They sold their own brother to be a slave! And that's just the beginning the story. Many more sorrows followed, but God ultimately used all of them to help Joseph become a wise and powerful ruler, second only to the king over all of Egypt.

While the bad news is that there are going to be times when you will be sad, the good news is that God wants to comfort you, and he will use your sorrow to make you stronger. The sadness will pass (sometime it passes quickly and sometimes it takes a long time) and you will be happy again. Another verse in the Bible says: "Weeping may remain for a night, but rejoicing comes in the morning" (Psalm 30:5). That's a promise you can count on. Sadness will eventually pass and you will be a wiser, stronger person afterward — just like Joseph.

Dear Lord, I hate being sad. It doesn't feel good. It doesn't feel like it's doing anything good for me. Help me to learn from my sadness. Help me be a better person when it is all over. Teach me through my sadness to be what you want me to be. Amen.

You Have a Purpose

However, I consider my life worth nothing to me, if only I may finish the race and complete the task the Lord Jesus has given me.
Acts 20:24

When something makes us feel badly about ourselves — that we aren't very smart, or good looking, or talented — it's easy to forget how much God values us. We start to think that maybe we really aren't worth very much after all. We know such thoughts aren't from the God who loves us; instead, they come from Satan, who wants to destroy us. When we are down or depressed, he whispers that no one loves us or cares about us, that we aren't good enough, and we'll never amount to anything. But we know that's not true.

Remember this: Satan is a liar. You are loved. You are loved by God. God loves you no matter what you say, think, or do. He will never turn away from you.

No matter what you're struggling with, never doubt that God has a bright future for you. He has a plan and a purpose for your life, even if it's hard for you to see it right now. He wants to use you make a difference and to change our world. God wants you to follow the example of the Apostle Paul, whose goal was to finish the race and complete the task — the purpose — God had given him. God is your biggest fan as you run your race. He loves you and he's cheering you on.

Dear Lord, Help me to really believe down deep in my heart how much you love me. Help me to value my life the way you do. Show me the plan you have for my life. Help me to believe in my future even when it's hard to imagine. Amen.

Take a Deep Breath

When Jesus heard what had happened, he withdrew by boat privately to a solitary place.
Matthew 14:13

Musicians know that a song isn't merely a series of notes. Deliberate beats of silence, called rests, make up the melody as well. Blending notes with rests, the musician creates a unique composition of harmony, melody and depth.

As we go through our unique life, sometimes we are actively "playing notes" and sometimes we are obligated to take rests. Consider the times when we don't get to do what we want, but instead have to take a break. God is still with us. Even unexpected disappointments are part of his plan. Just like rests in a song, they have a purpose. If we're sidelined by a coach, we can accept the rest with the attitude that we will be ready when we're called on again. If we miss a field trip because of the flu, we can still appreciate the quiet time that our body requires to get healthy again. If you are forced to rest, don't let a bad attitude get in the way of the future notes you are to play.

Dear Lord, Even though I know you measure out the rests and the notes, I am still disappointed when I can't participate where I want. Please help me get through it so that I will be ready when I can. Amen.

Lord, What Are You Waiting For?

Why, O Lord, do you stand far off? Why do you hide yourself in times of trouble?
Psalm 10:1

Do you like to wait for stuff to happen? If you say yes, you are one in a million. Most people don't like to wait for anything, especially during serious and troubling times. Have you ever prayed for something and it seems as if God isn't listening because you're still waiting for an answer?

There is a Bible verse that says about God, "How impossible it is for us to understand his decisions and methods!" (Romans 11:33 NLT). Sometimes we must simply trust what God says: He is listening; he is with us even in the darkest of times; he loves us immeasurably; he will answer big and small requests. So if you are discouraged because something you are praying about seems unchanged, don't give up.

Dear Lord, Help me because I am impatient waiting for you to answer my prayer. Help me to believe you want what's best for me. Help me to wait and trust you. Amen.

At Last!

But the dove could find no place to set its feet because there was water over all the surface of the earth; so it returned to Noah in the ark ... He waited seven more days and again sent out the dove from the ark. When the dove returned to him in the evening, there in its beak was a freshly plucked olive leaf!
Genesis 8:9–11

Have you ever thought about what it was like on the ark? Imagine the smell of the animals. Imagine the endless work of feeding them and cleaning up after them. Imagine how tired Noah and his family were and how eager they were to get off that boat. And imagine the disappointment they all must have felt when the dove came back to the boat because there was "no place to set its feet." Then, seven long days later, Noah sent the bird out again. The family waited ... and waited ... and finally, along toward evening, the dove returned to the ark again. Perhaps they were a little disappointed when they saw it returning, until they saw something in its mouth — a new green leaf. They had not seen anything green and growing for a year. They knew that their long ordeal was almost over. Noah waited seven more days and sent the dove out again. This time it didn't come back. Now it was time for his family and all the animals to come out — at last!

In every person's life there are times when we have to go through something that seems to take forever for it to happen. It could be getting over an illness. It could be studying for an exam. It could be waiting to have enough money to buy something we want. It could be something you've been praying about. And then — at last — what you've been waiting for comes. And that makes all the waiting worthwhile. It's time now to be happy!

Dear Lord, Sometimes I find myself saying, "I can't wait until ..." But the truth is, I can wait, and sometimes I learn a lot while I'm waiting. When the waiting ends, I am so happy. There is such joy in my heart. Help me to remember that waiting can be good. Amen.

Tools of the Shepherd

Your rod and your staff, they comfort me.
Psalm 23:4

The rod and staff are tools of the shepherd. The rod is a club that the shepherd has carved from the root of a tree and fitted to his hand. The shepherd keeps the rod with him at all times and uses it as a weapon. When wild animals or snakes threaten the sheep, the shepherd takes aim and uses the rod to kill or drive off the intruder.

The staff is a useful and essential tool for the shepherd. Many staffs had hooks at the end for catching sheep that were wandering off, for lifting a lamb and putting it back beside its mother, and for pulling away thorny bushes the sheep might wander into and get caught in. Sheep fall over cliffs and have to be rescued. They get into weeds that will make them sick if they eat them. They must have a shepherd with them at all times to care for them and guide them. The shepherd uses his staff to assist the sheep. Sometimes he uses it to pull a sheep close to himself so he can inspect if for cuts and bruises.

So how are God's rod and staff a comfort to us? They comfort us because God is our shepherd, guiding us day by day. Some days we may feel the hook of the staff around our necks guiding us back to the right way. Sometimes we hear the rod as it flies past our head to chase away something that would have hurt us. And sometimes we feel the staff of God's love pulling us close to him.

Dear Lord, You are my Good Shepherd. Thank you for watching over me even when I am stubborn and foolish. Thank you for pulling me back in line and closer to you. Amen.

Go Get 'Em!

The Lord said to me, "See, I have begun to deliver ... Now begin to conquer and possess."
Deuteronomy 2:31

Have you ever picked green fruit from trees or sour berries from bushes? Kind of made your mouth pucker when you bit into it, didn't it? It wasn't ready yet. Have you ever picked fruit or berries that have been on the trees and bushes too long? Gross! They taste moldy and have the texture of a slushy. The best time to pick fruit is when it is ripe and sweet, but not overripe and falling on the ground.

We've talked a lot about waiting for God to answer our prayers and about being patient while we wait for him to answer. If we move ahead of his plan, it's like eating unripe fruit. But there is another side to this story. We can wait too long to move when God says "Go." And that can be as bad as moving too soon. There are lots of times in the Bible when God didn't do anything until his people took the first step. One of those times was when God's people needed to cross the Jordan River to get into the Promised Land. They stood at the river's edge and nothing was happening. God had told them to step out into the water and believe him. So that's what they did. They stepped into the water and whoosh, the water rolled back and a dry path appeared in the bottom of a muddy river. The point here is that God waited for them to get moving—to show their trust in him—before he began to move.

Is there something you know God wants you to do? Do you know he wants you to step out in faith? Then that's probably what you need to do, and you will see God do great things. God will help you to keep moving forward. He has already begun to help you.

Dear Lord, Sometimes I'm being so careful not getting ahead of you that I don't do anything at all. Help me today to begin doing what I know you want me to do. Amen.

Getting It Together

It won't be long before this generous God who has great plans for us in Christ — eternal and glorious plans they are! — will have you put together and on your feet for good. He gets the last word; yes, he does.
1 Peter 5:10-11, The Message

Do you ever feel like you have too much to do? So much that you don't know where to start? There's soccer practice and homework and chores at home and church activities ... on and on it goes. You feel stretched in so many directions, with so many different expectations and responsibilities, that it's hard to find any time for yourself and for God.

Want to know the secret to moving from all the activity and confusion in your life to God's glorious plan for you? The secret is in getting to know God. Now, how do we do that? First we read God's Word, the Bible. The Bible is one of the best storybooks ever written, but it is more than that. It teaches us about God, about life, and about how God will help us in our life.

In addition to reading the Bible, we also get to know God by talking to him — prayer. Lots of people think prayer is telling God what you want. But it is more than that. It is talking to God and then listening to hear what he wants to tell us. We will probably not hear a voice out loud, but God will impress his word on our mind. We don't have to act right away on what we think God is saying. We can continue to pray and listen and see if that thought continues.

One good thing to know is that God wants to "put us together" and "set us on our feet" for good. You'll never go wrong reading the Bible and praying and listening for God's voice. God has a plan for you and it's a good one.

Dear Lord, Please teach me how to hear your voice. I know I can learn a lot about you by reading the Bible, and I know I can talk to you in prayer. Amen.

We Could Make Beautiful Music

I am jealous for you with a godly jealousy.
2 Corinthians 11:2

A young man carefully held his kora harp in his hands. "If I were marooned on a desert island, the one thing I'd want with me is this harp," he said.

The kora harp is a West African instrument and has 21 strings. Each string is attached to a tuning peg on a long neck of the harp. The young man held the instrument between his knees and with his hands on two handholds on either side of the neck, plucked the strings to make a beautiful sound. As he plucked the strings, he often stopped to tighten or loosen one of those 21 tuning pegs. He knew exactly which string was out of tune. Most who listened had no idea there was anything wrong with the string, but the young man who knows his instrument well, and who is a master at playing this instrument, knew the sound it made could be better than it was. He loved his harp. He understood it and he wanted its music to be perfect.

That's the way God is with us. He loves us so much, just like the kora harpist loves his instrument. He knows all about us. He knows when we are living a true life and when we are faking it. He knows what our lives can be if we let him correct us and tune us so we make music that is harmonious with his will for our lives. And he will never leave us. He'll be close by to help us, always.

Dear Lord, Help me to let you change me into who you want me to be. I want to make beautiful music with my life. Let my life be like a love song to you. Tune me up so no ugly or unkind words come from my mouth. Thank you, Father, for loving me so much. Amen.

A Place of Safety

God is our refuge and strength, an ever-present help in trouble. Therefore we will not fear, though the earth give way and the mountains fall into the heart of the sea, though its waters roar and foam and the mountains quake with their surging.

Psalm 46:1–3

There are lots of things that happen on earth that scare us. It is normal to be scared when we hear of devastating earthquakes, huge fires that wipe out homes and businesses, wars on the other side of the world, terrorist activities, and disease. Even grown-ups are scared by these things. So the big question is, what do we do when we are scared? We turn to God's Word. God has made many promises in his Word and he keeps them all. Psalm 46 promises that "God is our refuge and strength, an ever-present help in trouble." What do you suppose ever-present means? Just what it says: God is always with us. He knows what's going on everywhere and he knows when we are scared.

God did not promise that we would never have trouble. Lots of God's people have trouble. But he promises to be with us when we do have problems. We shouldn't be going to bed too afraid to go to sleep. The great writer William Shakespeare said, "Cowards die many times before their deaths. The valiant never taste of death but once." In other words, you can live your life scared of your own shadow and have a miserable life, or you can live with courage right up to the end of your life. What will you do?

Dear Lord, I admit that some of the things I hear on the news and from my friends really scare me. Help me get your Word down in my heart so that I'm not scared. Help me to live with courage because you have promised to be with me. Amen.

The Water of Life

I will be like the dew to Israel; he will blossom like a lily. Like a cedar of Lebanon he will send down his roots.
Hosea 14:5

In the country of Israel, where the air is hot all day during the summer, droplets of water, called "dew," fall during the night and bring life to the land. As low, wet clouds pass over the hot land, the moisture in the fog condenses and falls on the land. It nurtures every blade of grass, every flower, every tree. The plants must absorb the moisture quickly, because as soon as the sun comes out, the fog lifts and soon the dew is gone.

Flowers like lilies bloom quickly but briefly — some only last one day. Cedars of Lebanon, however, are strong, magnificent trees with a long lifespan. The trees themselves are of a rather unusual shape — quite wide with branches growing straight out, and a nearly flat top that often reaches a height of more than 100 feet. Both the lilies and the cedar are dependent on the dew for life.

God has promised to be like dew for us. That means he provides — daily and consistently. He alone can renew us emotionally and spiritually so that we can have abundant life.

Dear Lord, Help me stay close to you and to soak up all the life you give me. Amen.

Not Talking

If God is silent, what's that to you? If he turns his face away, what can you do about it? But whether silent or hidden, he's there, ruling, so that those who hate God won't take over and ruin people's lives.
Job 34:29–30, The Message

In the Old Testament there is a story about Daniel. Daniel was praying to God for help, but none came. God was silent — so it seemed. Daniel prayed and went without food for three weeks. Still nothing. Then one day he was standing on the bank of the Tigris River when an angel named Michael appeared before him. Daniel was scared nearly to death, and fell on his hands and knees. Then the angel spoke to him. "Daniel ... consider carefully the words I am about to speak to you, and stand up, for I have been sent to you." Daniel obeyed, standing but trembling like a leaf in the wind.

Then the angel said, "Since the first day ... your words were heard."

God heard Daniel the first time he called out to God in prayer. Even though God didn't respond right away, God heard Daniel. God hears us in the very same way, always listening to our prayers. He'll answer when the time is right.

Dear Lord, I'm not always patient when I'm asking you for something I need. Help me to learn that you always hear me — even when there seems to be no answer. Amen.

It's Under Control

This is what the Lord says: "Do not go up to fight against your brothers, the Israelites. Go home, every one of you, for this is my doing."
1 Kings 12:24

When Jesus was unjustly arrested in the Garden of Gethsemane, he was not panicked or even surprised. His entire life had a mission — to be sacrificed as the perfect lamb for all of our sins. But at the arrest even Jesus' devoted disciples didn't really get it. They didn't understand that God's plan was coming to its climax. They only saw their beloved Christ being betrayed, falsely accused, and treated criminally. And so one of them drew his sword in defense and cut off the ear of a soldier. Sounds pretty reasonable.

But Jesus, who understood the full picture, stopped the disciple and healed the soldier's ear. Can you imagine the surprise of everyone standing near?

When you face injustices, betrayals, or accidents, it's reasonable to feel intense emotions and ask unanswerable questions. But then you realize that the same Jesus who knew about his crucifixion to the last detail also knows every detail of your life. He's not surprised. He's not wondering what to do next. He is still the one who loved you enough to live and die for you. Isn't there a sense of security in that knowledge — that God is not only all-knowing and all-powerful but all-loving?

Dear Lord, Thank you that we can rely on you, both because you know things we don't and because you love us more than we can understand. When things look bleak to us, help us remember who you are and have peace. Amen.

Ready for Action, Ready for Service

In the shadow of his hand he hid me; he made me into a polished arrow and concealed me in his quiver.
Isaiah 49:2

In our time there are a few people who use bows and arrows for hunting, but most people who shoot arrows do it as a sport. These athletes — called archers — compete to hit the center of a three-ring target called a bulls-eye. In Bible times arrows were not just for games, they were an essential part of a warrior's equipment. His life and the lives of others depended on his skill with a bow and arrow. Arrows were carefully made and were kept in a long slender container known as a "quiver." The warrior carried the quiver on his shoulder so that he could quickly reach back, grab an arrow, and in one motion have it in the bow and on its way to defeat the enemy.

God wants us to be like arrows in his quiver. That means he keeps us very close to him so that he can quickly send us out to do his work in the world. What is that work? It might take different forms for different people, but there are two things God wants all of us to do: to love him and to love others. Even on days when we may not feel like we're doing much for God, we are doing very important work when we love God and love others.

Maybe you feel as if you are stuck in a dark quiver and not much is happening. Maybe you wish you could just fly out on your own. But God has a plan and he wants you to stay close to him and be ready to do his work — to show your love for him by loving others. He'll call on you when he needs you.

Dear Lord, I want to be an arrow in your hands. I want you to use me to do your work in the world. Please help me stay ready and help me to stay close. Thank you for loving me and for using me to show your love to others. Amen.

We Win!

At once the Spirit sent him [Jesus] out into the desert, and he was in the desert forty days being tempted by Satan.
Mark 1:12

It happens to everyone—being tempted. It even happened to Jesus. No sooner had Jesus been baptized by his cousin John in the Jordan River than God's Spirit led him into the desert. There the devil came to him and tormented him, tempting him to use his power for his own glory instead of good. It was so bad that when it was over, angels had to come and take care of him.

If Jesus was tempted, you can be sure that you will be too. But here's the good news. God made a promise about how he will help us. Here it is: "No test or temptation that comes your way is beyond the course of what others have had to face. All you need to remember is that God will never let you down; he'll never let you be pushed past your limit; he'll always be there to help you come through it" (1 Corinthians 10:13, The Message).

There's more good news. Being tempted is not sin. As long as we don't give in to the temptation we have not sinned. And one more piece of good news is that if we "submit ourselves to God and resist the devil, he will flee from us (James 4:7). We will always win because God is with us.

Dear Lord, Thank you for making a way for us to escape sin when we are tempted. Help me when I am tempted to remember that Jesus was tempted too and he came through it without sinning. I know Jesus can help me when I am tempted. Amen.

Riding the Wind

You will find your joy in the Lord, and I will cause you to ride on the heights of the land.
Isaiah 58:14

Humans were fascinated by flight long before there were airplanes. Scientists and dreamers watched birds fly and wondered if humans could ever join them in the air. They were particularly interested in the flight of hawks and eagles and other soaring birds that could ride the warm thermal air currents rising from the earth. These birds seem to fly with no effort at all, banking into the wind to get the lift they need to climb to higher altitudes.

Wilbur and Orville Wright built the first successful airplane. One of their key discoveries was that a plane must face into the wind in order for it to be lifted into the air. In 1903 at Kitty Hawk, North Carolina, the Wright brothers turned their homemade airplane into the wind and it lifted off! Although the plane flew less than 100 feet that day, it was an important beginning that eventually enabled people to fly safely all over the world.

To succeed, you have to face into the wind, too. You have to face the tough stuff in life. As you do, you will learn to solve problems and use what you've learned to get to the next level. A really good time to learn how to solve problems and work out solutions in your life is right now. Face into the wind of peer pressure and the rest of the struggles in your life and you will grow stronger.

Dear Lord, Please give me the strength to face into the winds. I trust that you will use those things to teach me to fly. Please give me strong wings so I can be ready for the winds that come my way. Amen.

What's the Rush?

You will not leave in haste or go in flight.
Isaiah 52:12

Think about how many hours you spend being active and how many hours you spend quiet (sleeping doesn't count!). With school, homework, practice, friends, and chores, it takes serious effort to jam in a little silence when the music is turned down, the TV is turned off, and the telephone isn't ringing. Even when you are productive or spend your days doing good deeds, there comes a time when we need to pause and enjoy the stillness.

What would happen if you spent just ten minutes every day being absolutely quiet? What wonderful ideas might come to your mind? What would God say to you if he could get your attention? What encouraging thoughts might come to mind if you stopped talking and doing stuff long enough to listen to God instead? Give it a try today and see what happens!

Dear Lord, Help me slow down. Help me realize you might have something you want to say to me. I'm going to listen and see what you will teach me. Amen.

They Didn't Even Get Their Feet Wet!

Shout with joy to God, all the earth! Sing the glory of his name, make his praise glorious! Say to God, "How awesome are your deeds ... He turned the sea into dry land, they passed through the waters on foot—come, let us rejoice in him."
Psalm 66:1-2, 6

The Bible is full of stories about how God helped his people when they faced impossible obstacles. When God parted both the Jordan River and the Red Sea so his people could cross over, the pathway through was completely dry. They didn't even get their sandals wet. When Jonah was thrown overboard, God sent the big fish to save him from drowning and get him to dry land. When Naaman faced a debilitating disease, God told his prophet Elisha how Naaman could be miraculously healed in the Jordan River.

Our God is one of miracles and grand gestures of love. Because he loved us first, we are privileged to love him back, even when facing big problems—especially when facing big problems. In the Bible Job faced exceptional pain and tragedy when he lost his home, his possessions, his health, and, worst of all, his family. And yet in his grief, he demonstrated love for the Lord who loved him first. "At this, Job got up and tore his robe and shaved his head. Then he fell to the ground in worship and said, "The Lord gave and the Lord has taken away; may the name of the Lord be praised (Job 1:20–21). The same God who chose to save his people with miracles didn't spare Job from his pain. But God still delighted in Job. And Job still rejoiced in God. Their relationship was deep and it helped Job face his tragedy.

Dear Lord, I don't know when I'll have to face something really hard. What I do know is that you go ahead of me and make it possible for me to pass through hardship. Thank you for loving me that much, Father. Amen.

Castaways

Why are you downcast, O my soul? Why so disturbed within me? Put your hope in God ... my Savior and my God.
Psalm 43:5

Sheep are funny creatures. They are very helpless and not terribly smart. They will go out to feed in the pasture, find a ditch, and topple over into it landing upside down. Once on their backs, they are stuck in that position and will die if the shepherd does not rescue them. They are called "cast" sheep. They are cast down in a ditch. They are cast over on their backs. They feel helpless and doomed ... until a shepherd rescues them.

We are like sheep. Sometimes (and it happens to everyone) we get cast down — or downcast — and we feel stuck and hopeless. We are sad over something that has happened, or maybe we don't know what has made us sad — we just are. We need a shepherd to rescue us. Jesus, the Good Shepherd, gives us hope. He takes us out of the ditch and sets us on our feet again, showing us the right way to go. We need to depend on him and trust in him, just like sheep trust their shepherd.

Dear Lord, Sometimes I feel cast down. I feel stuck in my sadness. I don't know how to lift myself out of the ditch, and that makes me feel hopeless. Please put your hope in my heart. Help me grab hold of your hand and hang on. Amen.

Fear of the Dark

"And surely I am with you always, to the very end of the age."
Matthew 28:20

Were you ever afraid of the dark? A lot of kids are. There's nothing harmful about darkness itself—it doesn't make us wet; it doesn't crush us; it doesn't suck the oxygen out of the room. It only hides something that could hurt us. So when we're afraid of the dark, we actually fear things that we imagine could be there. Turn on a nightlight and the fear melts away, because we can see when there is nothing to be afraid of.

Just like in the dark, fear and worry grow in uncertainty. If you don't know anything about a new school, you might worry about your upcoming year. If a parent goes to the doctor, you might fear the worst. But worrying about the future is like being scared of the dark—we're afraid of things we imagine could happen. That's when we turn on a nightlight. Jesus, the Light of the World, runs into the darkness to show us that there is nothing we need to worry about. God will shield us from any danger, and he will supply the strength and mercy to get through the worst.

So give up the fear and the worry. Hold onto him instead; he will take care of the rest.

Dear Lord, You are big enough and caring enough to take care of anything I'm anxious about. I would rather spend my time trusting in you than worrying about what could happen. Help me give up my fear, because I can't do it alone. Amen.

Help Me!

A ... woman from that vicinity came to him, crying out, "Lord, Son of David, have mercy on me! My daughter is suffering terribly from demon-possession." Jesus did not answer a word.
Matthew 15:22–23

A man once had a dream about Jesus who came upon three young men. As he came to the first of the three, he bent down to talk with him and smiled. He even gave a quick hug. Then he came to the second. He only put his hand on the young man's head and gave him a quick look. Then he came to the third young man. This time he just walked right past and didn't do or say anything.

Those who were watching wondered what that third young man had done to cause Jesus to ignore him. So they asked Jesus why he treated each young man so differently. Jesus said, "The first young man is a new Christian and he needs all the help I can give him. I wanted to encourage him, so I spent time with him. The second young man is a little stronger and loves me a little more. I can trust him and so I didn't spend as much time with him. I was not ignoring the third young man. I love him very much and I'm training him for a very important role in life. I want him to be able to trust me even when it seems I'm not paying attention. It's important for what I want him to do."

When you pray and it seems like your prayers are being ignored, know that God hears you. God's silence isn't anger or disapproval. In fact, he loves you very much and it could be that he is training you to trust him even when it feels like he's not paying attention. Perhaps he is preparing you for a greater role than you ever imagined.

Dear Lord, I still have a lot to learn about trusting you. Help me to believe you are at work no matter what I see. Amen.

Overcoming Evil with Good

Do not take revenge, my friends, but leave room for God's wrath, for it is written: "It is mine to avenge; I will repay," says the Lord.
Romans 12:19

Josh and Kevin were put together as partners for a class project. They had to write a report, create a poster, and give a presentation on the Civil War. Josh worked hard on the project. He went to the public library to do extra research and spent long hours perfecting the details on the poster. When the day came for the class presentation, Josh did almost everything. The whole time, Kevin had been too busy playing video games to help his partner. Josh was certain that Kevin would receive a lower grade for not participating in the project.

After school, however, he overheard Kevin telling the teacher that he had done exactly half the research and half the work and should receive the same grade. Josh was fuming mad. Kevin had lied!

Josh continued to think about revenge for the rest of the week. At church that weekend, the pastor spoke on Romans 12:19. "Vengeance must stay in God's hands," he said. "The Lord is the one who will repay. When God takes care of the wrongdoer he does it in a way that helps that person, not hurts him."

Josh knew that what the pastor said was true. He decided not to take revenge on Kevin. Rather, he would pray for him and he would look for ways to make Kevin his friend. He would overcome Kevin's evil act of lying by doing good to him.

Dear Lord, When someone tells lies about me or cheats me, I feel hurt and angry. It makes me want to hurt them like they hurt me. But I know that you want me to leave revenge to you. Help me remember that it's your job to avenge wrong and that it's my job to respond to evil by doing good. Amen.

Go Straight Forward

And as soon as the priests who carry the ark of the Lord ... set foot in the Jordan, its waters flowing downstream will be cut off.
Joshua 3:13

Persistence means that we keep going no matter how hard it is to make progress. It means that we won't quit no matter how much we want to. Everyone who has ever done anything important had to learn to be persistent. Christopher Columbus was persistent in his struggle to get money to fund his voyage to the new world. Later when he was sailing over the sea, he had to be persistent when his sailors wanted to turn back. Marie Curie was persistent in the scientific experiments that earned her two Nobel prizes, even though those experiments would eventually cause her death.

In our lives we have to be persistent. We must keep doing what we do, even if our progress is very slow. So if you are praying for something and haven't seen an answer yet, keep praying—you are making progress even if you can't see it. If you are trying to achieve something like better grades but getting better grades seems slow to come, keep going. Everyday you are learning something important and if you don't quit, you will see success.

Dear Lord, Help me never to give up, no matter what. Amen.

You Are Worth More than Flowers

If God gives such attention to the appearance of wildflowers—most of which are never even seen—don't you think he'll ... do his best for you?... Don't worry about missing out. You'll find all your everyday human concerns will be met.
Matthew 6:30–33, The Message

Have you ever wandered deep into the woods and found a beautiful flower blooming there? Ever wondered who, beside you, will ever see that beautiful flower? Jesus talked about that. He said that God gives a flower so much beauty and detail and then he may put it in a place where no one ever sees it. Why? It is because God makes everything perfect whether or not anyone notices. Everything he makes has a purpose. You have a purpose. And he didn't make any mistakes when he made you. Even if you sometimes feel like you are hidden in the woods where no one notices you, God has a purpose for your life.

Because you are his child, God will take care of all your needs. Jesus told the people of his time to stop worrying about everything. He told them that God knew they needed certain things to live. He said that if God dressed the flowers that are here today and gone tomorrow, God will certainly take care of his children—that includes you—who are much more important to him than flowers.

If you can understand that God loves you and wants to take care of you, life will be a lot easier. God knows what you need. God knows what your family needs. Count on the fact that God knows, and trust him.

Dear Lord, I know you love me and that you care about my needs. Help me to trust you to take care of me and my family. Amen.

Yes, I Can!

Joshua said to the house of Joseph ... You are numerous and very powerful.
You will have not only one allotment but the forested hill country as well.
Clear it, and its farthest limits will be yours.
Joshua 17:17-18

When the Israelite leader Joshua was handing out land to each tribe
of Israel, he gave more land to the family of Joseph. He told them,
"You are the ones who can conquer the hill country that is full of
forests and natural resources." He was handing them a great
opportunity — a land full of natural resources. But the decision to
actually go fight and conquer the high country was up to them.
They could fight till then won or they could waste the opportunity.

The world we live in today is full of opportunities. There are
opportunities for you to become a scientist, musician, athlete,
teacher, doctor, pastor, and researcher. We have unlimited opportunities to do more and be more than any generation who has ever
lived. But to take advantage of those opportunities we have to work
hard, study hard, and keep going.

Dear Lord, Sometimes it's easier to focus on what I don't have than
what I do have. You have entrusted me with gifts and talents and
resources. Help me to live up to the potential you have given me.
Give me the energy and motivation I need to make the most of all the
opportunities you bring my way. Amen.

A Heart that's Happy

Rejoice in the Lord always. I will say it again: Rejoice!

Philippians 4:4

Everyone has bad days. You know what it's like—you wake up late for school, can't find the clothes you wanted to wear, and miss the bus because you dawdled over breakfast. School isn't much better: you forgot to do the second half of the homework assignment, your mom packed a peanut butter and jelly sandwich *again*, and it's too cold and rainy to go outside for recess.

Some days it's easy to be happy and some days it's not. So how can the apostle Paul say "Rejoice in the Lord always"? How can we rejoice on the really hard days? Circumstances change, but here's the key: our Lord never does. He is always loving, always faithful, and full of grace and mercy. That's worth rejoicing in. A lasting invitation into a relationship with the King of Kings is worth rejoicing over.

Whether our day is good or bad, whether we have reason to be happy or angry, Jesus and our relationship with him is solid. This is our foundation. So set your mind on good things, reach out to friends, take a break and feed your soul. No matter what awful thing might be going on in our lives, we have the tools for peace that lasts.

Dear Lord, I know I can't control what happens in my life, but help me to keep my focus on the joy I have in my relationship with you. Whatever happens, I know that you will guard my heart and give me your peace. Amen.

Don't Fret

Do not fret because of evil men or be envious of those who do wrong.
Psalm 37:1

What in the world does "fret" mean? Here is a little word that doesn't have any positive definitions. It means "to worry, to be discontent, to have something be eaten away by something else." It means, "to torment or irritate or upset someone or yourself." So when the Bible says not to "fret" it means "quit worrying about it." That's not always easy to do, is it?

Here's another little word with a negative definition: Envy. Envy is a kind of jealousy. The dictionary defines it as the "resentful or unhappy feeling of wanting somebody else's success, good fortune, qualities or possessions." We can envy someone else's clothes, their looks, their friendships, their talents, or their achievements. For example, when a friend does well on an exam, instead of being happy for her, you feel jealous and you wish it could have been you instead. That's envy.

The Bible says that we shouldn't fret about or envy the apparent success of people who do wrong. Do you know someone who got rewarded for cheating? How did it make you feel? Did you fret and feel envious? Unfortunately, fretting and envy don't change the situation, but they do make us miserable. That's why the Bible says not to fret or envy. And although people who cheat to get ahead appear to be getting away with it, they're losers in the long run.

Dear Lord, I admit I have both fretted and been envious. Please help me to be content with doing honest work and to trust you with the rest. Amen.

Making Masterpieces

"I've afflicted you, Judah, true, but I won't afflict you again.... I'm cutting you free from the ropes of your bondage."
Nahum 1:12 The Message

If you played with play dough when you were younger, you know how great it feels to mold and fashion a masterpiece. But play dough has no staying power. If you want a finished product to last, you have to graduate to real potter's clay. And then the work begins. The clay has to be kneaded to soften it and get out bubbles. The piece also has to be painted with a dull glaze and then put into a firing kiln. Only after firing it will the bright colors come out and the piece become strong and durable. The entire process takes time, effort and intense heat.

God has been called a potter who molds us into masterpieces. With purposeful pressure and heat, he gives us shape and character. It takes time and energy, but he's willing to spend it. After all he's making something precious in our soul.

Tough circumstances train us and make us strong. It is good to know that there is a limit to how much tough stuff he will allow. He knows just how much we can take before we might crack. When his purposes are accomplished, he says, "Enough!" and it stops.

Dear Lord, Help me to trust you to know exactly what is good for me and exactly how much I can handle. Amen.

Following in Faith

Now then, you and all these people, get ready to cross ... into the land I am about to give ... to the Israelites.
Joshua 1:2

It's difficult to believe God is working for you when you can't see any action. But faith means going on even when you don't know where you're going. While some people say, "I'll believe it when I see it," true faith believes before it sees. It believes in a powerful God before we meet him face to face. It believes in heaven before we arrive. And it characterizes our ongoing walk with God.

True faith counts on our heavenly Father. It prays with confidence that he is who he says he is, even when we'd rather have him prove it by parting the Red Sea before our eyes. Our relationship with God will always require trust. Our walk of faith will always be connected to some uncertainty. But even in difficult times, we trust because God has revealed himself. And faith is how we respond.

Dear Lord, I want to learn your promises and trust you more. Teach me how to respond in faith. Amen.

Believe!

Therefore I tell you, whatever you ask for in prayer, believe that you have received it, and it will be yours.
Mark 11:24

A young boy who lived far away from his grandmother loved video games. His grandmother knew he loved to collect the different games and told him she would send him a special new game for his birthday. When his birthday came, there was no video game in the pile of gifts and no note from his grandmother saying she had changed her mind. When his friends asked him what he got for his birthday, he listed all the gifts he had opened and then he added, "And my grandma's going to send me a new video game."

His mother overheard him and asked him about it later, "The game from Grandma didn't come," she said. "Why did you tell your friends it was going to be here?"

"If Grandma said she would get it, she will. So it's just the same as if I had it now."

Days later when there still was no video game, he asked his mother, "Do you think it would do any good for me to email Grandma and ask her if it's still coming?" His mother encouraged him to give it a try.

Grandma wrote back the same day she got her grandson's message and said, "I haven't forgotten your game. I have been looking everywhere trying to get exactly the one you wanted, but have not been able to find it. I'm sending you some money so you can buy it in Chicago. Would that be all right?"

This boy believed in his gift when he could not see it. He knew his grandmother would not let him down. She would keep her promise. That is what faith in God is all about. We know him and we know he will not fail us. We know he will keep his promises, and we live waiting for him to give us what we need.

Dear Lord, Help me to believe that you are at work even when I can't see anything happening. I know you hear me when I pray. Thank you for listening. Amen.

Cut Back to Grow Forward

Jesus said, "I am the true vine, and my Father is the gardener. He cuts off every branch in me that bears no fruit, while every branch that does bear fruit he prunes so that it will be even more fruitful.
John 15:2

In the summer, grape vines in California's vineyards are full of long, leafy branches that grow in the hot sunshine. But in winter, the gardeners come into the vineyard with sharp tools called pruning sheers. They use the sheers to remove all the branches from the vines. When the pruning is done, the only things left are ugly stumps that look completely lifeless. Anyone who didn't know better might think, Oh, they've killed the plants. But the vines are not dead, and as soon as spring comes they will grow strong new branches that will bear huge bunches of grapes. Without the pruning, the vines would produce only a few small grape clusters as all the vine's strength would go to growing vines rather than fruit.

Gardeners have pruned in vineyards for thousands of years, and there are even stories about it in the Bible. Jesus uses the example of pruning to teach us that our hearts need to be pruned—cleaned up—from time to time. Perhaps we've become careless about telling lies, or maybe we say mean things to other kids. These are the kinds of things God wants to clean up in us. It's how he disciplines us and makes us more fruitful for his kingdom. It doesn't always feel good at the time, but this kind of heart pruning is something God uses to make us stronger.

Can you think of something God might want to clean up in your heart? Tell God what it is. Ask him to take the bad stuff away so that what comes out of your life is good and strong.

Dear Lord, It's so easy for me to slip into bad habits that drain your strength out of me. Please prune my heart so I can be who you want me to be. Amen.

Help Yourself

Nothing will be impossible for you.
Matthew 17:20

What if you found a locked chest filled with more money than you could count? And what if you were then given a key and invited to take all of the riches you wanted, how much would you take? Would you consider taking one penny, closing the chest and then returning the key? Of course not! What if the treasure chest was filled with immeasurable talent — that whatever you chose to do, you could walk away with enough talent to be the very best the world has ever known? Would you consider taking the smallest amount and turning down the rest? Absurd!

We can have as much of God as we want. He has invited us to know all about him, to understand his ways and his thoughts. We can chat, share our secrets, be his friend, confide in him. We can depend on him to never betray us, never leave us, know us completely and still love us. He can replace our worry with peace and replace our guilt with freedom.

Now that is treasure. You're invited to have as much as you want. How much will you take?

Dear Lord, Thank you for who you are, and thank you for sharing all these divine possibilities with us. Help me walk closer with you so that I can share in the treasure you are. Amen.

Be Patient!

Be still before the Lord and wait patiently for him.
Psalm 37:7

When we read the Bible, it seems like miracles happened every day, but it wasn't really that way. In the Old Testament, for example, God performed amazing miracles when he freed his people from slavery in Egypt. First there were ten plagues to convince Pharaoh to let God's people go. Then, when Paraoh sent his army after the slaves, God parted the Red Sea so his people could escape from the Egyptian soldiers. And if that weren't miracle enough, God closed the sea at just the right time so the entire army drowned!

That's a lot of miracles one right after the other, but God's people had waited 400 years for these miracles to begin. For four hundred years they were slaves and held onto God's promise that they would one day be free to go to their Promised Land. Four hundred years is nearly twice as long as the United States has existed as a country. It's a long, long time.

Not many people like to wait; and they especially don't like to wait a long time for something they really want. How about you? Do you get impatient when the Internet connection isn't fast enough or when the microwave seems to take too long? It can be even harder when God is the one we're waiting for, hoping he will do something.

What do you wish God would do for you? Are you praying about it? Are you waiting for an answer? God knows what you need better than you do. He cares about you. Patience helps us wait quietly knowing God is going to give us exactly what we need.

Dear Lord, I have a hard time waiting. I know you have plans that are much bigger than anything I can think of. Help me to wait patiently for you to answer my prayer. Amen.

Millions of Possibilities

"Everything is possible for him who believes."
Mark 9:23

Everything? Sure, everything is possible for Superman or Spiderman or Batman, but for me? Yes, everything is possible for you—at least that's what Jesus said. If we are going to believe what Jesus said, we have to believe it all and not just the parts we understand. Everybody knows you can't walk on water, but Jesus did and he helped his friend Peter walk on water too. Everyone knows you can't make a blind man see, but Jesus did it several times. And especially everyone knows you can't raise someone from the dead, but Jesus specialized in resurrection.

So what's happening in your life that seems impossible? "Im" (as in "im-possible") means "not," so when we stick it on the front of the word "possible" we change the possible to the impossible. If you could only get rid of the "im" part of that word, you'd have "possible." We need to knock "im" off the word impossible. The tool we must use to knock off "im" is the hammer of faith. You might pray, "I believe. Jesus, help me to believe even more."

God is mighty. He is all powerful. Superman, Spiderman, and Batman are all made up fictional characters, but God is real—and so is his son, Jesus Christ. What God wants to do most is help you turn impossibilities into possibilities. Will you let him?

Dear Lord, In my head I know that nothing is impossible with you, but when it comes right down to the day-to-day living it out stuff, I'm not so sure. Will you help me with my faith so that I know all things are possible for me because I believe? Amen.

Roaaaar!

A lion ... came and carried off a sheep from the flock.
1 Samuel 17:34

David was just a boy watching his father's flock of sheep when a lion crept up and snatched one of them. To the young shepherd, the lion could have been cause only for fear and panic. But to God it was an opportunity for David to call upon the Lord for strength and direction.

David didn't know it, but he was in training out there in the fields. God was going to use him very soon to rescue an entire nation from a giant named Goliath. And those sheep? God was teaching David how to lead those who don't really want to be led.

God may send some problems to you that seem as difficult to overcome as the lion did to David. God doesn't waste anything. Everything that happens to you happens for a reason. Not only will God help you now, but he will also use it as training for what will happen in your future. In temptation, trouble and problems, don't despair or run for cover. Those troubles are God's opportunities in disguise.

Dear Lord, Use whatever you need to in my life to make me ready for what you will call me to do in the future. Amen.

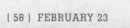

Pit Crew

Though John never performed a miraculous sign, all that John said about this man was true.
John 10:41

In the world of professional auto racing, only a few people get to be drivers and have their names splashed across the newspapers and TV. But for every successful racecar driver, there are dozens of back-up people, many of whom are called the "pit crew." Pit crews are vital to the success of any racer. When the driver comes off the track and heads to the pit, the crew springs into action. They fuel the car and change all the tires in seconds. They make minor adjustments and get the driver back out on the track. Time spent in the pit impacts the outcome of the race. A slow pit crew can cause a driver to lose.

In the Bible, John the Baptist is an example of someone who never got to be the "driver." He was more like part of Jesus' pit crew. John's role was to tell everyone that Jesus was coming and they should get ready. While John did not perform any miracles, he had an important job to do by alerting everyone that someone was coming soon who would take away the sin of the world. When some people asked John if he was the Christ, he simply replied, "I am the voice of one calling in the desert, 'Make straight the way for the Lord.'" It takes a really big person to step back and let someone else shine in the spotlight. But when we perform the most everyday, insignificant tasks, God still sees what we are doing.

Dear Lord, Sometimes I want to be the person everyone talks about and praises, but help me to be humble. Amen.

Take a Hike

"I will give you every place where you set your foot, as I promised Moses."
Joshua 1:3

Suppose someone brought you to a large, open field and said to you, "We know this piece of land has gold on it. I will give it to you if you will walk all the way around it." What would you say? "Gold? You're kidding! I'm supposed to believe there is gold in the ground?" Would you do nothing or would you believe and take a hike to make the land yours even though you couldn't see the gold yet?

The gold is like the promises of God, buried all over the pages of the Bible. This is your opportunity to stake your territory, dig for the nuggets and claim God's promises. To stop short would be to give up gold that was meant for you.

The Bible is our map to a wide land of promise. Explore it and know it so you will know the breadth of riches God has given to you.

Dear Lord, I don't want to miss out on your promises. Reveal them to me as I learn more about you. Amen.

There Will Be Enough

He said to me, "My grace is sufficient for you, for my power is made perfect in weakness."
2 Corinthians 12:9

Many people around the world today are concerned about running out of resources. There are discussions about not having enough fresh water on the planet. Government leaders talk about running out of oil and gasoline. Already there are a lot of people in the world who don't have enough to eat. The resource of food has just about run out for them. But there is one resource we will never run out of, and that is God's love and grace. God says that his grace is "sufficient" for us. That means there is enough of his grace for everyone and enough for any situation you get into.

And just what is this grace of God that is so sufficient? It is a lot of things: it is forgiveness for our sins; it is God's love for us; it is God giving us what we need when we ask; it is the gift of his patience when we mess up. (And we will mess up — everybody does.) Not only is God's grace sufficient for whatever is happening in our lives, he also promises that his power is made perfect in weakness. That means that when we feel too weak to do the right thing, God will give us the strength we need to succeed. This is a promise we can count on.

Dear Lord, Thank you for giving us your grace to help us. And thanks for giving us your power when we are weak and want to do the wrong thing. Help me learn how to ask for you grace and power before I do the wrong things rather than afterward. Amen.

All Alone

So Jacob was left alone, and a man wrestled with him till daybreak.
Genesis 32:24

Some kids love to be alone. They like to go into their rooms and read or think or play music. Other kids can't stand to be alone. The more company they have the better.

Being one way or another is not better or worse. We all have preferences. It is interesting, however, to think about some of the great characters of the Bible and their miracles. Many of their great miracles happened when they were alone. Jacob in the scripture above was alone when he met an angel who wrestled with him. Moses was by himself when he saw the burning bush. Peter was alone on a housetop when he had a vision giving him instruction about what he was to do next. Jesus often went off alone by himself to pray and think.

Maybe these people knew something we need to know, especially if you are one of those who likes lots of activity and company all the time. There is so much noise in our world coming into us that it can be very hard to hear God's voice telling us what to do. Once in a while we need to shut off the iPod, close down the computer, turn off the TV and the cell phone, and just listen to see if God might want to say something to us. You might be surprised at what he says to you.

Dear Lord, Sometimes I use all the noise in my life to keep me from talking to you and listening to see if you have something to say to me. Help me to listen for your voice. Amen.

A Different Kind of Sacrifice

Let us continually offer to God a sacrifice of praise.
Hebrews 13:15

A "sacrifice of praise" sounds a little weird, doesn't it? What kind of sacrifice is that? Is it like the kind of sacrifice that happens in baseball when one batter intentionally hits a ball that produces an out but advances another runner? Or is it like giving up something we really value, or selling something we have at less than its value? Those things are sacrifices, but they're not the kind of sacrifice the Bible verse describes. When we give God a sacrifice of praise, we praise God for everything he has done, no matter what we are going through and no matter how we feel that particular day.

No matter what's going on in our lives, God is doing something good. When your problems seem overwhelming and you feel sad, it's still possible to praise God for his goodness and for all the good things he has done for you. There is something about praising God and saying thanks out loud that helps us "get it" in our minds. Give thanks for everything God has done for you from giving you toothpaste to helping you get your homework done. And thank him for being our living God.

Dear Lord, Praising you changes me, so I'm going to try to thank and praise you today for how good you are and for all the good things you have done for me. I'm going to offer you a sacrifice of praise. Amen.

Dive In

When he had finished speaking, he said to Simon, "Put out into deep water, and let down the nets for a catch."
Luke 5:4

One early summer morning Tim asked his friend Jon if he would like to go fishing. "Sure," Jon agreed, so the boys gathered their equipment and headed to the lake. They chose a spot on the shore, baited their hooks, cast their lines into the water, and waited.

After an hour neither boy had gotten so much as a nibble on his line. They looked into the water near the shore and saw plenty of minnows swimming in the shallow water, but none of the big fish they were hoping for. Finally, Tim's father came by to see how the boys were doing. When they gave him their disappointing news, he chuckled. "You need to get out on the pier so you're fishing in deep water," he told them. "That's where the big fish live." Sure enough, as soon as the boys moved out to the pier they started getting bites on their hooks. After a short time they had both caught big fish.

Jesus told the disciples that if they wanted to catch a lot of big fish, they needed to get out into the deep water. They couldn't expect to catch anything worthwhile by hanging out on the shore. So Jesus invites them to take the risk of moving into deep waters.

We can keep it shallow with the one we know as Lord. Or we can have a deeper relationship where we can discover otherwise hidden riches of God.

Dear Lord, Help me to hear your voice and follow you closely so that I can have a deeper friendship and more adventurous, abundant life with you. Amen.

A-Mazed

Consider what God has done: Who can straighten what he has made crooked?
Ecclesiastes 7:13

Have you ever been in a maze—the real kind that's made out of hedges and paths? There's one at a palace in England called Chatsworth House. It is a very complicated maze. Every hedge is the same height so there are no identifying features to help you even go back the way you went in.

It could be frightening to get into a maze and not be able to find your way out. Life is like that sometimes. We find ourselves in situations where we don't know where to turn, and when we do make a choice of which way to go, it ends up being the wrong way. It's scary when our situation gets worse and worse. But there is someone who knows every turn, every path of our life. Jesus is that someone, and he came to guide us through life. When you are confused and don't know which way to turn or which decision is best, you can rely on Jesus to lead you. Isn't a relief to know you don't have to make decisions on your own? Ask for his guidance and wait patiently for him to show you the way out of your problems.

Dear Lord, Sometimes I really get mixed up when I'm trying to make decisions about my life. Please guide me and help me to listen for your voice telling me the right way to go. Amen.

Practice Makes Perfect

"Be ready in the morning, and then come up on Mount Sinai. Present yourself to me there on top of the mountain."
Exodus 34:2-3

How do you wake up in the morning? Are you ready to pop up the moment the sun comes through the window? Or do you pull your covers over your head so you can stay in bed a few more minutes? Do you wake up groggy, hungry, happy, chatty, quiet, rested? No matter what kind of mood you're in, wouldn't it be nice if you could start your day with a best friend? You could share your thoughts with each other, get some encouragement, remember that someone is pulling for you...

Consider meeting your closest friend in prayer every morning. Whether you're facing a hard day or a fun day, focusing first on God only makes the day better by helping you remember what is important and reassuring you that you're not alone.

You can start small. You don't have to pray on your knees or read the New Testament for an hour in order for your quiet time together to be worthwhile. Checking in with God right away might be just the start of the conversation, but your focus will already be on track.

Dear Lord, It's nice to know that I can talk to you at anytime. Help me develop the discipline of starting my day with you. Amen.

The Dark Side

The spirit shrieked, convulsed him violently and came out. The boy looked so much like a corpse that many said, "He's dead."
Mark 9:26

The verse above is taken from a story in Mark 9:14–26. A father brought a young boy to Jesus and said that the boy had an evil spirit living inside him. He had been that way since he was very young. Jesus commanded the spirit to come out and only then was the boy no longer tormented. Jesus took him by the hand and raised him up as a normal boy, finally at peace.

The devil is evil and very powerful—although not as powerful as God. Because he hates us, he tries to get us to do many things that will only harm us, but God is there to help us if we ask. He not only rescues us, he helps us make good choices. Sometimes we have to fight hard to resist what is wrong and do the right thing. To make that easier, don't entertain risky behavior. Instead, take a stand right away. For example, it is easier to hang out with friends who will steer you right than to continually resist joining friends who make wrong choices. Poor choices are much easier to resist if you never even toy with them from the beginning.

Don't let the devil get a foothold in your mind or in your actions. Keep your mind on whatever is true, noble, and right. And never forget that you know the all-powerful God who will help you.

Dear Lord, Please protect my mind and heart. Help me know when something is not good for me. Thank you for protecting me and helping me to make good choices. Amen.

Lazy Is as Lazy Does

We do not want you to become lazy, but to imitate those who through faith and patience inherit what has been promised.
Hebrews 6:12

Sometimes it's interesting to look up a word in the dictionary and see what it really means. "Lazy" means "not easily aroused to activity." A lazy person just doesn't want to try very hard. For example, lazy students don't make much effort in school; they don't study very hard or do their homework well. They might even try to get someone else to do it for them!

There is something inside all of us that wants to be lazy. But the Bible teaches that we must not be lazy when it comes to our faith. Instead, we need to be willing to make an effort. We are to follow the examples of people in the Bible who demonstrated faith and patience, even when they had problems. That's how they grew strong spiritually. It's good advice because being lazy — especially being lazy about prayer and reading our Bibles — in the long run doesn't feel good. There's nothing like jumping in, doing a task well, and then feeling the satisfaction of a job well done.

Dear Lord, Help me to be faithful to my work, both at home and in school and help be to remember to prayer and read the Bible so that I can be everything you want me to be. Amen.

Finish Well

We have come to share in Christ if we hold firmly till the end the confidence we had at first.
Hebrews 3:14

A basketball game is not won until the last ball goes in the basket before the closing buzzer. A football game is not won until the last play of the last quarter is complete — and it could be a touchdown. The winner of a hockey game might not be determined until a shoot out after two extra periods of play.

Our Christian life might be a little like a game. Our start on the Christian walk may be kind of slow. We might not get everything right at the beginning. Just like new players in a game have to learn how to play, so believers have to learn how to live our lives as followers of Christ. We learn to hang on in tough times. We learn to trust God with every detail. We learn to turn to him with our problems and needs. The goal is to finish well, ending the game with as much enthusiasm and focus as we started with. And when we come to the end of our life, we will be winners. We will be triumphant with Christ.

Dear Lord, Sometimes it seems progress is so slow. Help me to keep on playing the game of life until the end. Amen.

I Believe He Lives!

"We had hoped that he was the one who was going to redeem Israel."
Luke 24:21

After Jesus was raised from the dead, he appeared to many people. One day he joined some friends walking along the road. They didn't recognize him. They spoke about Jesus in the past tense, as if were dead. They said he was a prophet. They said they had hoped Jesus was the Messiah, the one who would overthrow the Roman rulers and establish a new government. They told him they had hoped he would rescue them from poverty and illness. Now it was all over. Jesus was dead and gone. Their dreams of a better life were dead and gone.

As he walked with these two disciples, Jesus listened patiently and then he began to explain what the Scriptures said about the Messiah. Still, they didn't recognize him. It wasn't until he sat down at the table with them and gave thanks for their food that they finally knew it was Jesus. He was alive! All was not lost! In a moment, Jesus disappeared, but the hope in their hearts did not go away.

We won't get to see Jesus until we are in heaven, we can still believe that he is alive. We can't see him but we know deep in our hearts that Jesus is with us and that he cares about us. Just as Jesus explained the Scriptures to his two disciples, we can learn more about Jesus and hear his voice by reading God's Word.

Dear Lord, I know you are alive, and that you love me and are with me. Help me to recognize your presence in my life, and to hear your voice when I read the Bible and pray. Amen.

Diamonds in the Making

For when we came into Macedonia, this body of ours had no rest, but we were harassed at every turn — conflicts on the outside, fears within.
2 Corinthians 7:5

Carbon is a soft natural material, but it is also the raw material from which diamonds — the hardest substance on Earth — are made. How does that happen? Diamonds are formed 75 to 120 miles below the earth's surface. When carbon buried deep in the earth is put under extreme pressure, and when the temperature is at least 192 degrees Fahrenheit, the carbon changes into diamonds. Scientists discovered that there have been only three times during Earth's history when diamonds were made, and the planet no longer makes diamonds as it once did. Diamonds are highly valued as jewelry. Maybe your mother or father has a diamond ring. Diamonds are also valued in industry. A diamond saw blade will cut through almost anything.

In the scripture verse for today, the Apostle Paul describes being harassed, or troubled, on every side. He was under extreme pressure, but God used that pressure to change Paul from an ordinary person into an extraordinary man of God. And God can do the same thing for us. When we feel like everything is pushing on us so hard we cannot stand it, it could be that God is changing us from soft material into a beautiful diamond that he can use.

Dear Lord, I hate to be under pressure. Help me to understand, though, that you can use my troubles to create something new and beautiful in my heart. Amen.

Do as You Promised

And now, Lord, let the promise you have made concerning your servant and his house be established forever. Do as you promised."
1 Chronicles 17:23-24

Sometimes when we pray, we ask God for things he has not promised us and then we wonder why we don't see an answer to our prayer. The way to be sure that what we are asking for is part of God's plan for us is by spending even more time in prayer. We might need to pray, "Dear God, I really want this, but I'm not sure it is what's best for me. I know you have a plan for my life. Show me if I am asking for the right thing." He will let you know what is best. There are other times when we know for sure that what we are asking for is what God has in mind. That's because we can read the promises of God right in the Bible.

Just remember that it is God's plan to give good gifts to us. He says that when we ask him for what we need, he will be a good father. He is not the kind of father whose child asks for bread and he gives him a stone. He's not the kind of father who gives his child a snake when the child asks for a fish. Our heavenly father is the only one who can keep every promise he has made—and he will.

Dear Lord, I'm so glad that you keep your promises to us. I know I can trust you. Amen.

Travel with God

Descend from the crest of Amana, from the top of Senir, the summit of Hermon.
Song of Solomon 4:8

An old book called Pilgrim's Progress tells the story of a pilgrim named Christian. Christian starts out on a long journey and on his back is a huge sack filled with burdens — all kinds of concerns and sins. Even though others encourage him to lay down the sack, Christian is determined to carry it. He trudges up one mountain and down another and through many hard places that have names like the Valley of Humiliation, the Valley of the Shadow of Death, and Doubting Castle. His goal is to make it to the Celestial City, the city where God lives. Christian struggles and struggles to make progress in his journey, but he is weighed down by the heavy load he carries. One day he comes to the cross where he asks Jesus for forgiveness for his sins. Finally, he is able to leave his huge sack of burdens at the cross and continue on his journey without it.

Have you ever felt like you were carrying around a huge sack of burdens? If you've done something wrong that makes your heart feel heavy, the good news is that you don't have to carry it around even one day longer. You can give your sins and burdens to Jesus and leave them with him. You can ask him to forgive you and to carry your concerns and he will.

Dear Lord, Please take from me everything that weighs me down — my load of sin, my worries, and my disobedience. I give myself and my burdens to you. Amen.

Facts vs. Feelings

But my righteous one will live by faith.
Hebrews 10:38

Suppose you were invited to stay in a palace for a week. You could take dips in the swimming pool, eat from a gigantic refrigerator, and sleep in king-sized featherbeds. You could do whatever you wanted in this palace, but for seven days you would be by yourself. "No problem," you might say. "I'm tired of sharing a room anyway." The first couple of days you might really enjoy the new place. But by day three or four, you might start to notice the silence. Without anyone to talk to or share with, the loneliness might become the only thing you could think about.

The facts of the situation didn't change, did they? The palace was the same. The arrangement was the same. Only your feelings changed. The problem when we rely on our feelings about God is that some days we'll feel secure in his presence and some days we'll feel like he's nowhere to be found. But has God changed? The Bible says no. Does God decide the days he'll be with us and the days he won't? The Bible says no.

In the face of problems and fears, if it seems like God isn't there, acknowledge your feelings and then look up the facts. The facts — God's Word — will bolster your faith and give you something solid to hang on to.

Dear Lord, Help me to walk by faith, not by feelings. Amen.

A Light in the Dark

After the death of Moses the servant of the Lord, the Lord said to Joshua
son of Nun, Moses' aide: "Moses my servant is dead. Now then, you and all
these people, get ready to cross the Jordan River into the land I am about to
give to them."
Joshua 1:1-2

Moses, the leader of the Jewish people, had died at the edge of the
Promised Land. The people no doubt felt sorrow and sadness. They
were probably fearful of their future without the leader they had
come to rely on so heavily. Now Joshua had the weight of filling
Moses' shoes and leading the people into the land that God gave
them. What if Joshua decided he was too sad to leave his tent?
What if he decided he couldn't imagine going into the land without
Moses? They would certainly be stuck, wouldn't they?

But Joshua, knowing God was with them, moved on even though
he was sad. He wouldn't allow any loss divert him from his calling.
We, too, can intentionally focus on the light of God instead of the
darkness around us. And when we surrender our troubles to him, we
find we are stronger and more prepared for whatever comes our way.

Dear Lord, Thank you for Jesus. Since he grieved on earth, he
understands my suffering and can comfort me. Please help me keep
moving even when I would rather just curl up in the dark. Amen.

Ugly Bugs

So Moses stretched out his staff over Egypt, and the Lord made an east wind blow across the land all that day and all that night. By morning the wind had brought the locusts ... And the Lord changed the wind to a very strong west wind, which caught up the locusts and carried them into the Red Sea. Not a locust was left anywhere in Egypt.
Exodus 10:13, 19

There are huge clouds of locusts that move in swarms. They are ugly bugs that eat everything in sight, completely stripping trees of every green leaf. Some species of locust are as much as six inches long. Imagine a swarm of millions of grasshoppers that might be up to six inches in length. What sound would their whirring wings make? Could you hear them chomping on plants? What if you stepped on them? Would they crunch and would you slip on them? Yuck.

God used a plague of horrible grasshoppers against the stubborn pharaoh of Egypt in an attempt to convince him to let God's people leave Egypt. Moses stretched out his staff and God filled the sky with flying, chomping insects. In order to get rid of the locusts, Pharaoh pretended to be sorry about keeping God's people captive. So Moses prayed and the wind shifted to the west and off flew the locusts. Not a single one was left in the land. And that's how quickly God can change our circumstances and answer our prayer. He's God and he can do it all.

God used the locusts to change Pharoah's mind and eventually let the Israelites out of Egypt. And God used the strong wind to take the locusts away. Stormy, difficult situations in life, like the swarms of locusts and the stiff wind, are still in God's control. They are tools he can use to bring us through to a better place.

Dear Lord, When I have a problem, it feels as if it will never end. Help me to remember that you are in control and you can make everything change in a moment when it is time. Amen.

Heavenly Music

"Just and true are your ways, King of the ages."
Revelation 15:3

We cannot even begin to understand what God is going to do in the future. The book of Revelation gives us a tiny peek into that time. People who are believers will stand beside a sea that looks like glass mixed with fire. These believers will be singing praises to God.

Here is the praise song that they will sing:

Great and marvelous are your deeds,
Lord God Almighty.
Just and true are your ways,
King of the ages.
Who will not fear you, O Lord,
and bring glory to your Name?
For you alone are holy.
All nations will come
and worship before you,
for your righteous acts have been revealed.

Revelation 15:3–4

On earth and in heaven we get to trust and praise God for who he is and what he has done for us. During good days or bad, peaceful times or stormy ones, God is always good, always in control, always with us.

Dear Lord, It is wonderful to know that we don't have to wait for heaven or even for good days to sing songs of praise to you. Thank you for saving us. Amen.

Our Rescuer

The people remained at a distance, while Moses approached the thick darkness where God was.

Exodus 20:21

A lot of people think that Christians must have easy lives — that God smoothes out our paths. But instead of taking away our troubles, God meets us there to lead us out. In times that are cloudy with uncertainty or stormy with fear, and we are surrounded by darkness, God's voice becomes clear. And as we draw near to him, he responds with a rescue.

Moses was on top of the mountain in the thick darkness of clouds in the middle of a desert. God was there. He invited his people to draw near so he could save them. In the valley of the shadow of death, we fear no evil, for God is with us (Psalm 23:4). When you're facing storms and trouble of your own, look for God. He'll meet you there.

Dear Lord, Thank you that you come in the clouds. Thank you that we don't have to stumble around in the dark wondering who to turn to. Draw me near. Amen.

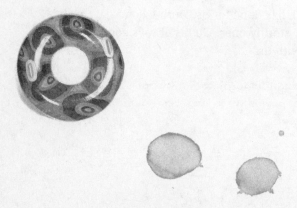

God's Butterflies

"Do not be afraid ... O little Israel, for I myself will help you," declares the
Lord, your Redeemer, the Holy One of Israel.
Isaiah 41:14-15

When you saw your first caterpillar, did you think that it could turn
into a butterfly? Who would imagine that a soft, wormy creepy crawler
could eventually fly? God's creativity and wildest dreams apply to his
beloved children as well. He takes thieves, failures, and outcasts and
transforms them into brave, charitable, strong followers of Christ.

Zacchaeus was despised by people because as a public official,
he took advantage of them and kept their money for himself. But after
encountering Jesus' love, Zacchaeus became an honest man who
gave money away. Rahab was rejected by society, but she risked her
life when Israelite spies needed a safe place to hide. Her faith in the
God of Israel gave her great courage that is still known today.

There is no life so broken that God can't restore it to a thing
of beauty. The great apostle Paul wrote, "I will boast all the more
gladly about my weaknesses so that Christ's power may rest on me.
That is why, for Christ's sake, I delight in weaknesses, in insults, in
hardships, in persecutions, in difficulties. For when I am weak, then
I am strong" (2 Corinthians 12:9 – 10). If you feel defeated, like a
worm on the ground, take heart. God is giving you wings.

Dear Lord, Help me remember that even when I feel broken, you love
me and can use me. Use my failures so that I can learn to fly. Amen.

For Our Own Good

Our fathers disciplined us for a little while as they thought best; but God disciplines us for our good, that we may share in his holiness.
Hebrews 12:10

Have you ever seen a ski jumper fly off the ramp and thought, "I could do that"? Of course not. You know it takes hours and hours of practice to pull off a stunt like that. When you start something new, like ski jumping, a coach doesn't just push you down a ramp and say, "Jump!" You first learn the basics. You practice fundamentals. You repeat what you learn over and over. And as you practice, you become a better jumper, eventually able to do things you thought you never could.

No matter what you pursue, practice takes time, energy, focus, and perseverance. As you pursue Jesus — talk to him, read what he said, consider what he did — you will eventually be able to do things you never thought you could. You might forgive a friend more easily than before. You might become more patient with a little sister who used to drive you nuts. You might be best able to comfort a new kid in school. Your practice and discipline will start to reflect your new heart and character borne through hour and hours of practice.

People will notice the changes in you — certainly your family will, everyone you show kindness to will, friends who are watching will. It may not be an Olympic sport, but your practice is enough to earn a medal.

Dear Lord, Help me pursue you with discipline. I want my character to reflect you. Amen.

Listen to Directions

When they had gone, an angel of the Lord appeared to Joseph in a dream.
"Get up," he said, "take the child and his mother and escape to Egypt. Stay
there until I tell you, for Herod is going to search for the child to kill him."
Matthew 2:13

When the angel said, "Stay in Egypt until I tell you," he meant, "Stay and trust." Trust God for your security. Trust as God prepares a way for you and prepares you for the way. Trust God for he has a plan.

As in this case, trust is often coupled with patience. Joseph and his family needed to wait on God, exercising patience even when they were restless to just do something. The angel of the Lord specifically said now is the time for patience — for their protection and for God's preparation. Their situation would change. Until then, stay and trust.

Do you feel stuck in a situation? Maybe it's time for you to exercise patience and trust God.

Dear God, Help me have patience. Let me hear your voice when I should patiently stay and when you are ready for me to do something different. Amen.

The Power of Silence

He answered nothing.
Mark 15:3

It's important to learn to be still inside. That's where God talks to us — in our hearts. If we stay busy and keep talking all the time, we can't hear his voice. There are lots of diversions in the world today to keep us so busy we are never still until we fall exhausted into bed. But great thinkers and followers of Christ have learned to keep quiet and listen.

Jesus learned to be quiet and listen to his heavenly Father God. He would go off by himself at night to pray and be quiet. All of that was good training for the day when he had to stand before Pilate and be questioned and accused of things he had not done or said. Using great judgment in this situation, Jesus said nothing. He had learned to have a quiet spirit. He had grown strong on the inside by spending time with God. He knew who he was — God's son — and he knew what was true.

God wants to have time with you too. It takes quite a bit of discipline to turn off the TV or shut down the video game to think and pray. That's how you will grow strong and become ready for whatever God has next for you in your life.

Dear Lord, Help me to be silent and trust in you for everything. Amen.

Walk with Jesus

Dear friends, do not be surprised at the painful trial you are suffering, as though something strange were happening to you. But rejoice that you participate in the sufferings of Christ.
1 Peter 4:12-13

Jesus paid a huge price so that you and I could live in heaven with him forever. We can't even begin to appreciate what he did for us — the suffering he endured, the lives that he changed — but we can be grateful for his love. This love gives us courage and strength to face hard times just like Jesus did as God's son.

No one likes to suffer, but remember that when you do, Jesus understands all about it, not just because he's God, but because he himself suffered on earth too. He understands when you're sad, lonely, angry, and depressed because he experienced every one of those emotions. He felt betrayed when his closest friends handed him over to the Pharisees and pretended not to know him. He felt pain when he suffered under the whip and on the cross. And because he knows what it's like to suffer on earth, Christ will be with you in your tough times.

Dear Lord, I'm so glad that Jesus knows everything about me. Thank you that he chose to endure the cross. Please help me endure the hard things I face. Amen.

Where Joy Can Be Found

Sorrowful, yet always rejoicing; poor, yet making many rich; having nothing, and yet possessing everything.

2 Corinthians 6:10

How can someone have nothing yet everything at the same time? Doesn't it seem impossible to be sorrowful yet rejoicing? If you have a relationship with the living God, then you have everything you need and that's worth rejoicing about.

People come in and out of our lives. Friends move away. Parents argue. Times get tough. And that's why we build a foundation on God, the solid rock. Where do we turn when our world is turned upside-down? To the unshakable, all-powerful God. Where do we turn when sorrow sweeps in? To the faithful, almighty comforter. Where do we turn when we lose everything? To the only one we can never lose. No matter what happens that makes us sad or scared or upset, we can have a deep undercurrent of joy, because we know we can always count on our good, loving God.

Dear Lord, Knowing that you are good and faithful helps me when I'm down. I want to have a deeper relationship with you, and I know you want that too. Thank you for always being with me. Amen.

Seeing Prayer Answered

Then he touched their eyes and said, "According to your faith will it be done to you."
Matthew 9:29

Long ago when people prayed for something that seemed impossible, they often talked about "praying through." "Praying through" meant praying until they believed that God had heard them and would answer in his own time. It wasn't so much about trying to change God's mind as it was a way to help the people who prayed believe God promises. These Christians would pray and pray and pray. Sometimes they went without food or sleep because what they were praying about was so important. They prayed through until their hearts were full of faith that God was at work. It's not such a bad plan — to pray until we believe with our whole heart that God is at work.

Whenever you pray, God hears you. He keeps each of your prayers like a treasure. God enjoys spending time with you, and loves to come near and listen. God answers your prayers in his own time — the right time.

Dear Lord, I know you hear me the first time I pray, but sometimes my problems feel so big it's hard to believe that my prayers really make a difference. Help me, Lord, to pray until I trust you. Amen.

A Good Lesson

After forty years had passed, an angel appeared to Moses in the flames of
a burning bush in the desert near Mount Sinai ... "I am the God of your
fathers, the God of Abraham, Isaac and Jacob ... I have indeed seen the
oppression of my people in Egypt. I have heard their groaning and have
come down to set them free. Now come, I will send you back to Egypt."
Acts 7:30, 32, 34

Does time seem to pass slower when you're at school? You're
watching the clock, waiting for recess or the end of the school day,
and the hands don't seem to be moving at all. It can be hard to pay
attention in school when you're focused on getting out of class as
quickly as possible. But remember: this is your learning time. Fill it
up with everything you can possibly learn. Then you will be ready
for whatever God calls you to do.

Jesus was 30 years old before he started his ministry. Before
that, he was learning. Before Moses led God's people out of Egypt,
he spent 40 years in the desert herding sheep — and learning. Your
days may seem hard. Or maybe school seems long and boring. But
don't be fooled — these are important times of learning. God has a
plan for you, and you want to be ready. Learn everything you can in
school so that you will be prepared to work in God's kingdom.

Dear Lord, Help me to use well this time while I'm growing up. Help
me to get ready for whatever you ask me to do. Amen.

Passing on our Plunder

Some of the plunder taken in battle they dedicated
for the repair of the temple of the Lord.
1 Chronicles 26:27

When God's people went to war and won, they got to take what they wanted from those they had defeated. What they took is called "plunder." The plunder was then divided among those who had fought in battle. In this story, some of the plunder was used to repair the temple of the Lord.

When the battle is emotional or spiritual, it is our hearts that have been wounded. This kind of battle is won when we come through a problem by God's grace. What we take from that battle is the lesson about the character of God and the nature of suffering that we learned. We can take these important lessons to show compassion for another person's heartache, to build up someone else who is suffering, and to become a better friend. That "plunder" pleases God and makes our battles worth the fight.

Dear Lord, Thank you that I can take my discouragements and learn from them. Allow me to encourage someone else from what I've gone through. Amen.

Who Are You Talking To?

Then Jacob prayed, "O God of my father Abraham, God of my father Isaac, O Lord, who said to me, 'Go back to your country and your relatives, and I will make you prosper.'
Genesis 32:9, 11

Praying is not a hard thing. There are no rules to follow. There is no length of time required. We don't have to be at the top of a mountain to be heard. Prayer is talking to a good friend and father who loves us. So why don't we do it more often?

Sometimes we get stuck, wondering where to start when there's so much to pray for. We start by remembering who God is. Jacob remembered that he is the faithful God of his fathers. Solomon remembered that God keeps his promises (1 Kings 8:23). King Hezekiah remembered that the one living God is Lord Almighty over all the kingdoms (Isaiah 37:16). When you are able to remind yourself of God's proven power, goodness and trustworthiness, your confidence grows and your relationship with him deepens.

It's like saying to your best friend, "You have always been there for me. You helped me feel better when my dog died. You brought me a present when I was sick. I'm so glad I can count on you. Now I have another problem. Listen to this...." The same friend of the kings of the Bible is your friend too. So don't be shy; he's always happy to hear from you.

Dear Lord, I believe you are who you say you are. Thank you that I can have a deep friendship with you. Amen.

How to Please God

And without faith it is impossible to please God, because anyone who comes to him must believe that he exists and that he rewards those who earnestly seek him.

Hebrews 11:6

When we are facing a tough, extreme, or tragic situation, our faith is either strengthened or destroyed. Consider the intensity of a fire. Most things can't withstand its heat, as it can consume entire forests and neighborhoods in a matter of days. But the same fire doesn't burn up gold. Instead, it purifies it.

When Shadrach, Meshach and Abednego faced the furnace, they confirmed they would praise only the living God. It was a death sentence. They could have decided to save themselves by doing what the king wanted, but their faith would have been unreliable — burned up in the midst of danger. Instead they went against the king by keeping their loyalty to the Lord. Their faith was purified. Whether God saved them or decided not to, their faith didn't waiver because the holy object of their faith never waivers. (And God did save them in the most dramatic way — after they were thrown into the fire, they walked out unharmed!)

In an impossible situation, faith recognizes that the only hope is in God. If you are facing a desperate time, remember that your faith is being purified. If you don't know all the answers, your faith is being developed. You may be overwhelmed by uncertainty and doubt, but your faith is being strengthened.

Dear Lord, Because you are trustworthy, I have faith in you. When I am desperate, I will turn to you. Amen.

No Limit

*The Lord said to Abram after Lot had parted from him, "Lift up your eyes
from where you are and look north and south, east and west ... All the
land that you see I will give to you and your offspring forever."*
Genesis 13:14-15

In today's Scripture, God is talking to Abram (later called Abraham)
about all the glorious plans he has for his people. Abram is looking
out at a beautiful country, and God tells him that his descendents
will someday live in this land. But his promise to Abram is also a
promise to us. We are also the offspring of Abram, and God has
wonderful things in store for our lives. Think about what
2 Corinthians 2:9 says:

It is written:
"No eye has seen,
no ear has heard,
no mind has conceived
what God has prepared for those who love him."

That doesn't just mean great things are in store someday in heaven. It means now. God has a plan for your life and his plans are
always good. Your job is to use the brain he's given you to learn all
you can. Your job is to live as a believer in Jesus Christ, to be obedient to all those in authority over you, and to take care of your body
so it is ready to do whatever job God gives you.

Dear Lord, Help me want the things you want. Help me move forward
as a follower of you. I'm so excited about your plan for me. Amen.

It Gets Better and Better

I consider that our present sufferings are not worth comparing with the glory that will be revealed in us.
Romans 8:18

Brian was eleven years old when he realized he was having trouble seeing. He sat near the back of the classroom in school and couldn't see the board. He asked his teacher if he could move closer to the front, but that didn't seem to help. Finally, his mother took him to see the eye doctor.

The doctor confirmed that Brian's eyes were not strong and told him he needed glasses. Brian picked out a pair with bright red frames, and as soon as he put them on he started seeing things he couldn't believe. It had been a long time since he had been able to see the individual leaves or twigs on a tree. He hadn't been able to see the shapes of clouds in the sky. He hadn't been able to see the names of streets on road signs. All of a sudden Brian could see things he hadn't even realized were there.

That's kind of like us with Jesus. We know about him, but we can't see him very well yet. We look forward with faith and hope because the day we can see Jesus face to face is coming. Someday there's going to be a great celebration when we will at last see him, not with our faulty human eyes but with eyes that have been made new by Christ's love.

Dear Lord, I love you and your Son, Jesus. I look forward to seeing you with my own eyes. Amen.

Water in a Pile

And as soon as the priests who carry the ark of the Lord—the Lord of all the earth—set foot in the Jordan, its waters flowing downstream will be cut off and stand up in a heap.
Joshua 3:13

The Jordan River was at flood stage. So did his people worry when God said, "Have the priests pick up the Ark of the Covenant and walk into the water"? Did the priests wonder if they could hold onto the Ark in the swirling water? Did they think they would be swept away and lose their lives? No matter, God told them what would happen when they did what he said. They had to have enough faith to put their feet in the water. And that's when the miracle happened. Somewhere way up stream the waters were cut off and piled up. Even more miraculous, the ground in the river bed was dry. The priests walked to the middle of the river and stood there until all the people crossed over into the Promised Land. When God is the architect, we are the workers, using our hands, our feet, our faith to help our heavenly father. God directed the priests. Because they had bold faith, they followed directions. And God's people passed safely, understanding his faithfulness and power.

As you carry your load, remember you have the living God with you. You are working for him. So be bold in your faith. Who knows what he will accomplish with it!

Dear Lord, I'm not sure what you can accomplish with me. But you are the master planner. Help me have enough faith to work for you through troubles. Amen.

He Knows What You Need

*"And why do you worry about clothes? See how the lilies of the field grow.
They do not labor or spin. I tell you that not even Solomon in all his
splendor was dressed like one of these."*
Matthew 6:28

The Bible often talks about lilies of the field. They grow everywhere
in the Mediterranean region where the Bible was written. The flowers
from this bulb are lavender, dark purple, red, white, and pink. The
inner part of the flower has a ring of black that looks like a crown.
It's easy to understand what the Bible meant about Solomon not
being as grandly dressed as these flowers are. The dark purple ones
look like velvet. They are unbelievably beautiful, and it is hard to
imagine that even King Solomon had a robe with such beautiful
color. The red ones are brilliant red, and the white are as white as
new snow. God carefully and lovingly made this flower of beauty.

If people, God's children — you! — are so much more important
to him than a flower, wouldn't he carefully and lovingly watch over
you that much more? You can trust your life to the one who made
you, delights in you and knows what's best for you.

Dear Lord, Sometimes I get really worried about things. Help me
remember that if you give the flowers what they need, then you will
certainly watch over me too. Teach me to trust you. Amen.

Safe Paths

But now, all you who light fires and provide yourselves with flaming torches,
go, walk in the light of your fires and of the torches you have set ablaze.
This is what you shall receive from my hand: You will lie down in torment.
Isaiah 50:11

Sometimes we want to go the same way God wants us to go. And
sometimes we think we know better than God. We think we've
found a shortcut or have a better way. We might choose to steal or
lie because it seems easier than what God would have us do. But
our way will only lead to misery as we cover up our sin or try to get
someone's trust back.

When times are hard for you, remember no one has done more
for you than Jesus. Every motive of his is out of love. So you don't
have to worry if he's going to take care of you and your needs. You
don't need to take matters in your own hands and look for shortcuts
when you don't understand why God is calling you to do something.
It will only lead to sin. But God's way will lead you to peace and
rest. Hold his hand; he will guide you through.

Dear Lord, I trust in you. Please change my desires and thoughts to
match yours. Amen.

In the Storms

But the boat was already a considerable distance from land, buffeted by the waves because the wind was against it.
Matthew 14:24

This wasn't the first storm the disciples been in. Jesus had stopped the wind and the waves before with just his word. But this time Jesus wasn't with them. The disciples were struggling alone.

And then Jesus came. Walking on water he said, "Take courage! It is I. Don't be afraid."

He says the same thing to us today when we are struggling during emotional storms of life. Jesus isn't our security against the storms, commanding every cloud to go away. He is our security in them. It is when we are struggling that his comfort is the sweetest.

When Jesus climbed in the boat, the wind died down. He came alongside his disciples and they worshiped him, saying, "Truly you are the Son of God."

Dear Lord, Thank you for your sweet comfort in hard times. Thank you for the security of Jesus. Come close. Amen.

How Far to Infinity?

Though he slay me, yet will I hope in him.
Job 13:15

Infinity is something without limits such as time, space, or distance. It is something too great to count. In math it is a number that is greater than any countable number, and it is shown by something that looks like a figure eight lying on its side. In space it is a place that cannot be reached it is so far away. It is "infinity."

So what does that mean when facing tough times like the biblical character Job? He had lost his family and all he owned then became very ill. Yet in the midst of his troubles, Job said, "Even if God kills me, I'm still going to hope in him. I'm not going to give up. My hope and trust will be to infinity and beyond." Wow, Job! Infinity is a long time.

It is, but God's love and care reaches into infinity. He will never stop taking care of us. Paul wrote to Timothy that he knew the one in whom he had put his trust — God. Paul was sure that God is able to keep whatever we entrust to him to infinity and even beyond.

What hard things do you need to entrust to God to care for into infinity? Even if your life is not hard right now, give your soul, your heart, your whole self to Jesus Christ, then one day, you will meet him in infinity and will stand by his side.

Dear Lord, Hold me safely into infinity. Right now I want to ask you to take care of me and help my heart to trust you always. Amen.

God's Awesome Love

While Aaron was speaking to the whole Israelite community, they looked toward the desert, and there was the glory of the Lord appearing in the cloud.
Exodus 16:10

Do you ever wonder if God is really around when you need him? Do you ever think that maybe he's looking the other way when you're down? Well, there is a story in the Old Testament about how much God wanted his people to know he was there for them. God had brought his people out of slavery in Egypt. Now they had to cross a desert to get to the Promised Land. It was blazing hot during the day and pitch black at night. God, in his great and tender love, gave them a towering cloud to lead them forward during the day. At night the towering cloud turned into a pillar of fire that gave them light so they could see and move around the camp at night. It was such a little thing for God to do, yet it showed his children that he was with them.

After a while, the people got used to the cloud and fire. It didn't seem so awesome anymore. The people stopped watching the cloud and the fire. They let themselves become distracted and discouraged by other things going on around them. They grumbled about having to stay in the desert. They complained about the food — the manna God sent every day. One day Moses called them together because God had heard their grumbling and wanted to deal with it. God showed up and displayed his glory in the cloud to remind them that he was still there. Then God spoke to them and said he would send them new food, meat, to eat since that was one of the things they had been grumbling about. God cared for them even when they forgot he was there.

Dear Lord, Sometimes I don't know what you are doing, so I grumble and complain. Send me a sign as clear as a cloud by day and a pillar of fire at night to help me know you are with me. Amen.

Shout for Joy

There are some who will break into glad song. Out of the west they'll shout
of God's majesty. Yes, from the east God's glory will ascend. Every island of
the sea will broadcast God's fame, the fame of the God of Israel. From the
four winds and the seven seas we hear the singing: "All praise to the
Righteous One!"
Isaiah 24:15, The Message

When your favorite team wins a huge victory, you just can't help
shouting for joy. When you are given an important award, you jump
up and down in happiness. When you get a gift you have been
wanting for a long time, you want to tell all your friends about it.
You want to broadcast the good news.

When we take the time to think about all God has done for us,
there is so much good stuff that we could certainly shout for joy
about it. What has God done for you that could make you jump for
joy? Has he healed a grandparent from a scary illness? Has he given
your mom or dad a job or a better job? Has he helped you improve
your grades or your basketball game when you prayed and asked
him?

Even if he hasn't done any of those things for you, he has made a
way for you to go to heaven with him. Also remember that in tough
situations, God is doing good things. He loves you even when you
act ugly. When you are sick, he may use it to help you rest or to
encourage someone else who is ill. Maybe you don't feel like yelling
out loud to God in all situations, but look for reasons to praise him.
Something about giving thanks and praise to God out loud makes us
feel better.

Dear Lord, As the writer of Isaiah said, "All praise to the Righteous
One!" You are my God, and you are mighty. Thank you for loving me.
Amen.

The Other Side

Elisha prayed, "O Lord, open his eyes so he may see." Then the Lord opened the servant's eyes, and he looked and saw the hills full of horses and chariots of fire all around Elisha.
2 Kings 6:17

Once in a while God pushes back the curtain of heaven and we get to see what we usually don't know is there. This was one of those times. When Elisha's servant got up one morning and looked outside, he saw that their city had been surrounded by an enemy army of horses and chariots. The servant was really scared. "What shall we do?" he asked Elisha.

Elisha was calm. He prayed, "O Lord, open his eyes so he may see." Suddenly, Elisha's servant saw that all the hills around the city were full of horses and chariots of fire. He and Elisha were in no danger at all because God's invisible heavenly army had come to defend them. As the human army came down the hills toward them, Elisha prayed and asked God to strike them blind. And that's what happened. That was the end of the battle.

Just because we can't see God's army around us doesn't mean it's not there. It is. God is always watching over those who love him. You can count on it.

Dear Lord, Even though I can't see you, I know you are there, defending me, protecting me, helping me. Open my eyes so I can see what you are doing around me. Amen.

More than Enough

Then go inside and shut the door behind you and your sons. Pour oil into
all the jars, and as each is filled, put it to one side.
2 Kings 4:4

When you are having a tough time because you don't have enough
money, what should you do? A wise person once said, "Don't ask
God for money to meet your needs. God has so many more ways
to take care of you than just giving you money." That's kind of
what happened in the Scripture above. Elisha the prophet came to a
woman's house. The woman's husband had died, and he had some
big debts that had to be paid. This woman had no money, so the
moneylenders were going to take her two boys and make slaves of
them to pay the debt. This mother was heartbroken.

Elisha had a creative solution. He told her to gather all the pots
she could find and borrow. Then he told her to begin filling the pots
with oil from a little jar she had. She poured and poured and kept
pouring until all the pots were full. God kept multiplying her small
supply of oil. Then she sold the oil and saved her sons from slavery.

What do you or your parents need? Tell God about what you
need, and ask him to provide for you. He may have an amazing
solution to your problem that you can't even imagine!

Dear Lord, You know what I need. I have been thinking and thinking
about how I could take care of this problem, but I should have come to
you first. Help me to wait for your solution. Amen.

Watch Out!

I will stand at my watch and station myself on the ramparts; I will look to see what he will say to me.
Habbakuk 2:1

In Bible times, one of the main defenses of the cities was a wall that extended around the perimeter of the town. Along the wall were watchtowers where watchmen stood guard. It was their duty to "watch" everything that went on both inside and outside the city. They were vital to the city because they were the first to spot messengers, visitors, good news and approaching danger. When a watchman saw danger, he blew a horn to sound an alarm. The gates could be closed to keep out the enemy. If an important visitor was coming to the city, then the watchman would quickly alert the right people.

Ezekiel, one of the great prophets of the Bible, had quite a bit to say about the responsibility of a watchman. He said, "But if the watchman sees war coming and doesn't blow the trumpet, warning the people, and war comes and takes anyone off, I'll hold the watchman responsible for the bloodshed of any unwarned sinner" (Ezekiel 33:6, The Message).

We are watchmen too. It is our job as Christians to watch for God's happenings and to tell people there is an enemy who wants to destroy our souls. The Bible says Satan roams around looking for someone to destroy. So we need to always be on the lookout for the good and the bad. When you tell others about what God is doing or to beware of approaching danger, then pray that they will listen.

Dear Lord, Help me to be a faithful watchman for my friends. There is so much bad stuff we can get into—stuff that can destroy us. I know the devil would like us to go that direction, but I also know you are stronger than he is. Please help me to see the things you are doing and share those as well. Amen.

Be Still

*"Be still, and know that I am God; I will be exalted among the nations,
I will be exalted in the earth"*
Psalm 46:10

Henry was a boy who couldn't be still for a minute. The moment he
was up in the morning until he went to bed at night, he was in
motion. That was fine when it was playtime outside, but it wasn't
so good at school and at church. He usually got into trouble for
wiggling and moving around.

Then one day Henry hurt his knee, and all of a sudden he
couldn't move around so fast anymore. While no one was happy
that he had hurt his knee, everyone, including his dog, was happy
that he had to sit still for a few days. His dog jumped up on his lap
and settled down with him. His brother came and asked if would
like to play a game. Mom baked his favorite cookies then sat with
him while he ate them. She told him about the time when she was
little and had hurt her knee too. In the evening his dad came to talk
to him and to carry him up to bed. At the end of the day, Henry
began to think what a nice day it had been, even though his knee
really hurt. What had made this day different from other days? Then
he realized that it was probably because he had to stop what he
usually did and sit still. Hmmm, he thought, maybe there is
something to this sitting still that everyone is always asking me to do.

You can't hear others — including God — if you are constantly
busy. Even if you're not active all the time but your insides feel
anxious or worried, it's hard to pay attention to God. It's in the
quiet times that we can understand what God wants us to do. But
it takes discipline to make your body and mind be still so you can
focus on God.

Dear Lord, I'm going to try to listen better. I know you have important
things to tell me, and I could miss them if I don't take time to be quiet
and listen to you. Amen.

Weak and Strong

That is why, for Christ's sake, I delight in weaknesses, in insults,
in hardships, in persecutions, in difficulties. For when I am weak,
then I am strong.
2 Corinthians 12:10

Maybe when you read the Scripture above you thought, "What, is he crazy? Who in his right mind would be happy about being in need, being picked on, being insulted, just for being a Christian?" When that Scripture was written, in some places it was illegal to be a Christian. It's not illegal today, but sometimes Christians are still bullied for what they believe.

But there is really good news in all of this. When we are at our weakest, God is at his strongest. That's why when you feel small and weak, you can be happy because the Bible says that we are truly strong when we have to rely the most on God to help us. We pray more often, we look to God for answers, we trust him. He comes and gives us power to live for him. So being weak can really be about getting strong in the Lord.

Dear Lord, Sometimes I do feel weak and need your help. You are a good God who always hears my prayers, and I know you will give me the strength I need to live for you. Even when I feel strong, help me to remember to rely on you. Amen.

It's All Good

*And we know that in all things God works for the good of those who love
him, who have been called according to his purpose.*
Romans 8:28

If ever there was a story of how God can take the worst stuff that
happens to us and turn it to good, it is the biblical story of Joseph.
Joseph was the second youngest son of Jacob. Jacob had twelve
sons and when Joseph, the little guy, said that one day he would
rule over his brothers, they got angry. They threw him in a pit then
sold him to the first caravan of traders that came along.

Those rotten brothers told their father that Joseph had been eaten
by wild animals. It broke Jacob's heart. But Joseph was not dead.
He was beginning a new life in Egypt. First, he was a lead servant in
the household of Potiphar. Potiphar's wife told lies about him, and
he wound up in prison. Then through an amazing series of divine
events, Joseph was taken from prison and made the ruler of the
land. And it all happened just in time to save Egypt from a
seven-year famine.

Oh, and those brothers who threw him in a pit? They came
begging for food in Egypt. Joseph gave it to them twice before he
told them that he was their little brother. They were really scared
that he was going to have them all killed for what they had done to
him. Instead, Joseph said, "You intended to harm me, but God
intended it for good to accomplish what is now being done, the
saving of many lives" (Genesis 45:3). Everything worked out for the
best because God was watching over them.

Dear Lord, Help me to trust you. Everything bad that happened to
Joseph turned out to be for the best. I know I belong to you and that
everything that happens is part of your plan for me. Amen.

Why?

I will say to God: Do not condemn me, but tell me what charges you have against me.
Job 10:2

The little three-letter word why can raise some of the biggest questions our minds will ever face. "Why did my dog die? Why is my grandpa sick? Why did I fail my test when I studied so hard?" Since the beginning of time, people have been asking God, "Why?" But let's look at it another way. Maybe God has a purpose for hard times. Some of the greatest music, stories, and experiments have come out of someone's hard times.

In the Bible we read that David wrote several of the Psalms when he was isolated with his sheep or running from his enemies. Many of the books of the New Testament were written by people who were in jail. A Jewish girl hiding from Nazi soldiers, Anne Frank, wrote a legendary diary when she was a prisoner in her own home before she died at the age of 14. Beethoven, a musician and writer, began going deaf in his twenties, yet he wrote wonderful music. The civil rights leader, Martin Luther King, Jr., spoke out against racism when it would have been easier not to. He died at a young age for his beliefs.

These are the people we remember. They went through hard times, yet God used those times to develop their gifts and their faith. They are role models for us because we can see that difficulties did not stop them from making a mark on the world. When hard times come and bad things happen, it doesn't mean God has forgotten us. It just means that he has a purpose in what he allows into our life. God uses hardship as a training camp for our souls.

Dear Lord, Help me to trust you even when the going gets tough. Help me to remember you are a loving Father and that you may have a bigger purpose in what I go through. Amen.

Tell the Good News

What I tell you in the dark, speak in the daylight; what is whispered in your ear, proclaim from the roofs.
Matthew 10:27

C.S. Lewis, who wrote the Chronicles of Narnia, called experience "that most brutal of teachers." There are many difficult lessons that we cannot learn from books or wise teachers. We cannot learn how to sympathize with someone who is in pain just by imagining what they must feel like: we have to actually experience that pain to know what it feels like. "You learn," Lewis continues. "My God, do you learn."

It is in our very darkest hours that we learn the most. If life were always easy — if our parents never worried or fought, if we always had the newest clothes and video games, if we had the most friends in school and got the best grades — we might not know very much about living. There might come a time in our lives when we realized that we didn't have the experience to help someone who was hurting.

In your times of darkness and difficulty, listen for the Lord's voice. Listen to what he might be saying to you and calling you to understand. Learn from the experience, especially if it's an experience that hurts, and you will be all the more prepared to work in God's kingdom.

Dear Lord, These hard times hurt, and I don't see how anything good could come out of it. Help me to learn from my experience and grow in my love for you. Amen.

High and Low

Jesus, full of the Holy Spirit, returned from the Jordan and was led by the Spirit in the desert, where for forty days he was tempted by the devil.
Luke 4:1–2

Have you ever noticed that after you've had a "high" day like a birthday or passing a test or a vacation, sometimes you have a "low" day? On high days everything seems to be going great and you are happy. On low days nothing seems to go right. You are grumpy and sad and you may not even know why.

Everyone has high days and low days. Jesus had a wonderful day when he was baptized by his cousin John in the Jordan River. The Bible says he was full of the Holy Spirit, and being full of the Holy Spirit makes you feel great. But immediately, the same Holy Spirit led him out into the desert, and there the devil came to visit him and to tempt him. It was an awful time for Jesus. So how did he get through it? He responded to every temptation by quoting God's Word, and the devil finally gave up and left him.

So when a high day comes your way, don't be surprised if a low day follows. And when the low day comes, believe that it will go away in time. Hide God's Word in your heart for those low days, and use it to help you resist the temptations that you face.

Dear Lord, I love high days, and I wish they could stay all the time. I hate low days, but help me to realize they won't last forever. Help me to hide your Word in my heart for those low days. Amen.

Listening for God's Voice

Then the Spirit was upon me there, and he said to me, "Get up and go out to the plain, and there I will speak to you.
Ezekiel 3:22

When we make up our minds to listen to God, we don't know what we might hear. God told Ezekiel the prophet to do a lot of strange things, like laying on one side for 390 days and then turning over and laying on the other side for 40 more days. Ezekiel knew God so well that he didn't question what God asked him to do. As a result, God showed this prophet many wonderful things. He got to have a peek into the future and saw the magnificence of God. Ezekiel even got to see what heaven looks like!

When we listen for God's voice, we don't know what we might hear. We also don't know how long we might have to wait for him to speak. God is looking for people who are willing to listen to what he tells them and who will do what God asks them to do, no matter how silly it might seem at the time. Do you think you could hear God's voice if he spoke to you? Do you know how to wait on God? It's a goal to work toward.

Dear Lord, I really hope I would hear your voice if you spoke to me. And I hope I would be ready to do what you ask. Help me to get to know you better every day so that when you call I'll know it's you, and when you ask me to do something, I won't be afraid to do it. Amen.

The Big Surprise!

For the Lord himself will come down from heaven, with a loud command,
with the voice of the archangel and with the trumpet call of God, and the
dead in Christ will rise first.
1 Thessalonians 4:16

You've heard a lot about the kingdom of God. If you've had a relative
die, you've heard a lot about the people we love going to heaven
to be with God. The verse above is describing the best day any of
us can imagine: the day when the dead will rise and the kingdom
of God will come down to earth. That will be the most triumphant
day in history — so triumphant that we can't even imagine all the
wonders it will hold.

When Christ comes again and establishes his kingdom on earth,
we will never be sick or get hurt again. All our tears of sadness will
be wiped away. And we will live with Christ forever — Christ who
loves us more than any parent, and who loved us enough to die
for us. That's a day worth being excited about. The best times will
begin, and they will last forever.

Dear Lord, Help me to always live for you and worship you as I wait
for your day of triumph! Amen.

I Know You

I trust in your word.
Psalm 119:42

Have you ever met someone who you are sure you've met before, but you can't remember when or where? Then all of a sudden, it comes to you and you say, "I know you!" You recognize the person. You remember where you met. That's a little bit like it is with God. You go along living your life day after day, then something happens that seems familiar. All at once you know. This is God at work. God has come to help.

What do you know about God? Where have you learned what you know? God's Word is the best place to learn about God. When we know God's Word, we get to know him too. We learn he is a good, kind, loving God who expects certain things from us. His Word also builds our faith and strength in him. It's not hard to trust and believe in him when we know him. So get acquainted with God in the pages of his book today.

Dear Lord, I want to know more about you. I want to recognize you when you speak to me. I want my faith in you to grow stronger. I want to love you more. Amen.

Where Am I Going?

By faith Abraham, when called to go to a place he would later receive
as his inheritance, obeyed and went, even though he did not know
where he was going.
Hebrews 11:8

Imagine that Abraham was your father. One day he comes into
the tent and says, "We need to start packing." "Packing?" you
ask. "Yes," he tells you. "Um, Dad, where are we going?" And just
imagine if your dad said, "I don't know." You would think he had
lost his mind or was starting to lose it. That's kind of what God did
to Abraham. God told him to get ready to move on, and all God told
him was, "Go to the land I will show you." No Mapquest directions.
No Google Earth. No atlas or map. Just start walking and as you
go, God will show you when you reach your destination. Talk about
having faith! Abraham had to have a ton of it. He was no kid either.
He was seventy-five years old when he started out.

When God calls and we answer, the only thing that matters is
that we are following him. That is enough. Our lives are a lot like
the journey Abraham made. We don't know where we are going,
we don't know when we are going to get there, and we don't know
what's going to happen on the way. We just know who is leading
us — God — and that is enough.

Dear Lord, I'm just going to put my hand into yours. Hold it tightly and
lead me in the best way for me. Amen.

Who Did That?

Which of all these does not know that the hand of the Lord has done this?
Job 12:9

Many years ago, a magnificent diamond was found in a mine in Africa. It was shipped to England so it could be placed in the king's crown. Before the stone could be placed in the crown, it needed to be cut and polished so that its true beauty would show. The king sent it to an expert diamond cutter in Amsterdam. The diamond cutter first cut a small notch in the top of the diamond. Then he struck it hard with hammer and it split into two pieces. Had he ruined it? Not at all. The diamond cutter had studied the diamond very carefully, and he knew exactly how to cut the stone for its greatest brilliance and beauty. Two gorgeous stones were cut from that huge diamond, and they can still be seen in the royal crown now worn by the present Queen of England, Elizabeth.

Have you ever experienced a heavy blow you weren't expecting? A big disappointment or something that made you very sad or angry? These are the kinds of things that hit our lives like the diamond cutter's hammer; they're also the kinds of things God uses to create something beautiful in our lives. Our job is to trust God to do his job. You are a precious jewel in God's hands, and he is a master diamond cutter. You can trust him to use the hard things in your life to make your heart shine with brilliance.

Dear Lord, Keep cutting away the junk in my life so that I can be a beautiful person in you. I trust you to do what needs to be done to make me like you. Amen.

I Trust You

Commit your way to the Lord; trust in him and he will do this.
Psalm 37:5

"Stop struggling," the lifeguard yelled at the drowning victim. "I can't help you if you try to save yourself. Relax!" The young boy finally relaxed, and in a minute the lifeguard had him ashore and to safety. There are some situations where struggling and trying to fix things ourselves only gets us in deeper trouble. God knows that, so he says, "Give me your troubles and your struggles." That means that when we tell Jesus about our problems, we can relax and let him carry them. We don't have to worry about them anymore. Most struggles we have in life will pass after a while, so there's no point worrying about them. We might just as well give them to Jesus.

It might take a while to see God doing anything about what we've given to him. He takes time to answer our prayers in just the right way. And even when we can't see God doing anything, he is. So if you feel like you are drowning in trouble and questions and sadness, call for the lifeguard — Jesus — to see how he comes to your rescue.

Dear Lord, Sometimes I feel like I'm drowning in problems and sorrows. Come rescue me, and I will let you carry me and my troubles to a safe place. Amen.

Stand Still

Moses answered the people, "Do not be afraid. Stand firm and you will see the deliverance the Lord will bring you today.

Exodus 14:13

Over and over God tells us to stop trying to fix things in our own strength. He tells us to be still and see what he will do. There are some things in life that are not a do-it-yourself project. When the sea is in front of you and Pharaoh's army is behind you, what can you do but stand still to see if God will rescue you? He will.

There was a man named George Muller who had an orphanage in England. George rarely knew where the next meal to feed the orphans would come from. It was his idea never to ask a human being for help, no matter how great the need might be. Instead, he would make his wants known to God who has promised to care for his servants and to hear their prayers. God did not disappoint George or the orphans. They always had food to eat and clothing to wear at their warm orphanage in Bristol, England. Sometimes it didn't come until the last possible moment, but it did come. George knew God's timing was always right. And he never let worry or fear drive him to panic and get ahead of God.

Remember, just when things seem darkest God can show up with a miracle. Pray and let God work within your heart and life, or you will never know what he can do.

Dear Lord, I like to get things done for myself. The idea of waiting for you to do things is difficult. Teach me to stand still. Amen.

Power Enough

"Not by might nor by power, but by my Spirit," says the Lord Almighty.
Zechariah 4:6

A boy was pedaling uphill against the wind, and found it very hard work. Just as he working the hardest and doing his best painfully, a trolley car came by going in the same direction as the boy. It wasn't going too fast, so the boy got behind it and grabbed on with one hand. Then he went up the hill like a bird.

Many times, we are like that boy on the bicycle. We are trying to do something on our own so hard that we are weary and weak, pushing ourselves uphill against all kinds of opposition. But all we have to do is grab onto the great power and strength of the Lord Jesus through his Holy Spirit.

The Holy Spirit is the most powerful force on earth. The Holy Spirit is part of God's family, and he is the part that is here on earth to help us every day. The scripture says that it is not by might (physical strength) that God helps us. It is not by power, which is the strength that is within something. No, the Holy Spirit is stronger than that.

What do you need God's power to do? The Holy Spirit will help you and show you the answers to your situation. You just have to let him. God loves you, and he will work for you.

Dear Lord, Help me to understand you better through the working of your Holy Spirit. Amen.

He Can Do It

Yet Abraham did not waver through unbelief regarding the promise of God, but was strengthened in his faith and gave glory to God, being fully persuaded that God had power to do what he had promised.
Romans 4:20-21

There is an old song that says God has promised us strength, rest, light, grace, help, sympathy, and love. Those are things we can count on. In addition God grants many of our requests by his power.

> God hath not promised
> Skies always blue
> Flower-strewn pathways
> All our lives through
> God hath not promised
> Sun without rain
> Joy without sorrow
> Peace without pain
> But God hath promised
> Strength for the day
> Rest for the labor
> Light for the way
> Grace for the trials
> Help from above
> Unfailing sympathy
> Undying Love
>
> Annie Johnson Flint (1862–1932)

Like the song says, God's resources are unlimited. He will take care of us and keep his promises. He will give us strength, rest, light, grace, help and love.

Dear Lord, There isn't anyone else I can count on to never fail me. You are our good God who has promised to care for us. Amen.

Pure Gold

But he knows the way that I take.
Job 23:10

Some of us make some bad choices, then we pay the consequences of those choices. If you choose to do drugs, you can be certain you will be ill and get into trouble for drug possession. If you choose to smoke, that will have consequences too. If you continue to smoke, eventually your body will react. You may get a lung disease or heart trouble. If you choose not to wear a seat belt, there could be serious consequences if you get in an accident.

These are problems we bring on ourselves, but poor old Job didn't make bad choices. God allowed Satan to test Job to see what he was really made of. Satan thought Job was protected and spoiled by God and wanted to prove it. So God allowed Satan to test Job. Later on Job says, "God knows the way I am taking and when he is finished testing me, I will come forth as pure as gold." Job had a lot of faith that God would bring him through the testing and that he, Job, would pass the test. He knew God was watching him.

God promises to be with us in everything we have to go through. God is right there beside you — always! — whether you've made a poor choice, are facing a test, or have found a situation confusing. God is in control, and he's promised not to put us through more than we can stand.

Dear Lord, When times are hard, help me to pass all the way through and come out like gold. Remind me, when I need it, that you know everything about my life and will help me. Amen.

Save Me!

Though I walk in the midst of trouble, you preserve my life you stretch out your hand against the anger of my foes, with your right hand you save me.
Psalm 138:7

Hurricanes are fear-producing storms. Winds filled with rain and lightning whirl with ever-increasing speed of up to 200 miles an hour. If hurricanes come ashore, terrible destruction happens. Maybe you've seen the destruction caused by a hurricane on television.

When the writer of the Psalm above says he walks in the midst of trouble, it is something like walking in a hurricane. Trouble will come and it could come from someplace we did not expect. It's important to take shelter when a hurricane comes. And in times of trouble, we can take shelter in Jesus. Go to him in prayer and keep praying until the problem ends. It will end in God's time. Storms always pass.

Dear Lord, Sometimes I feel like I have problems swirling all around me, just a like a hurricane. It's scary and I feel afraid. Thank you for your promise that you are with me in my storms, and that you will protect me. Amen.

I Know for Sure

Now faith is being sure of what we hope for and certain of what we do not see.
Hebrews 11:1

Mark was a young boy whose grandmother told him he could ask for one thing for his birthday from a catalogue. Mark spent the next few days pouring over the catalogue, looking at all the different things he could ask for. Should he ask for a new ski coat or new running shoes? Should he ask for a new book or a DVD? Should he ask for new swimming gear for the summer or a video game?

It took a long time, but Mark finally decided. He wrote a letter to his grandmother telling her that he wanted a brand new swim suit that he could use at her cottage on the lake that summer. He went to the mailbox to mail his letter, but instead of letting it go he held onto the end of it. He stood there for quite a while, thinking, *Did I really ask for what I wanted most? Should I think some more about what to ask for? Maybe I want a red swim suit instead of the green one. Did my grandmother really mean it when she told me to ask for a present?*

Finally, Mark pulled the letter out of the box and put it in his pocket and went home to worry about it some more. Guess what? He didn't get a gift from his grandmother until he finally made up his mind to let the letter go. Then soon there was a package from her with his gift inside.

Having faith in God is something like that. If we trust God completely, we tell him what we need then we let it go. We go on about our business and see what he will do for us. That is what it means to be certain about what we do not see.

Dear Lord, I'm going to ask for something I really need. Then I'm going to let go and wait to see what you will do. Amen.

Wait and See

Mary Magdalene and the other Mary were sitting there opposite the tomb.
Matthew 27:61

Hold up your hands in front of your eyes. What do you see? Your hands. Can you see anything else? No, not unless you are peeking around your hands. That's kind of what happened to the disciples after Jesus died on the cross. They couldn't see beyond the sad events that were right in front of them.

Jesus was crucified, dead, and buried. And that was all that the disciples could think about. They couldn't see the bigger picture because they thought Jesus had come to be a king who would set them free from the Roman rule. Now that he was gone, they forgot all the miracles of the Old Testament and all the miracles Jesus had done. They forgot that Jesus promised them he would rise from the dead. That's why the two Marys were crying their eyes out at the tomb. They couldn't see beyond Jesus being dead and buried. But what they thought was the end of all their hopes and plans was really just the beginning of God's bigger plan — to raise Jesus from the dead!

Sometimes it's hard for us to see beyond the sad events that are right in front of us. We have hopes and dreams, then something happens and it feels like nothing will ever be the same again. Our dreams have died. That's one of God's favorite times to come alongside and whisper to our hearts, "This isn't the end; it's just the beginning of my bigger plans for you. Trust me. I will give you new life." What may seem like the end may really be a new start that God has been planning all along.

Dear Lord, Sometimes I can't see beyond today. I can't see what you are doing. I just have to remember that everything you plan for me is good. Amen.

What a Waste!

What is more, I consider everything a loss compared to the surpassing greatness of knowing Christ Jesus my Lord, for whose sake I have lost all things. I consider them rubbish, that I may gain Christ.
Philippians 3:8

There is a plant that blooms only once in its lifetime. It is called the "Century Plant" because for many years people thought it bloomed only once in a hundred years. The truth is that in most cases is doesn't take a hundred years for it to bloom. It probably takes fifteen to twenty-five years to bloom. The plant has pointed leaves spreading out from the center in a rosette. After many years, it gains enough strength to bloom and puts up a flower stalk as thick as a small tree trunk. The stalk grows about an inch an hour. The stalk of the flower can grow as tall as forty feet. Then it blooms a huge cluster of white or yellow flowers. The flowers last for a month. After the blossoms die, so does the whole plant. That's it. It's done.

Does it all seem a waste — that the plant can bloom all by itself in the desert where no one ever sees it? Nothing is a waste in God's plan. Everything on this planet is here for a reason. And we fit into that plan too. If we spend our lives doing God's will, living the best life we can for Jesus, we will be a blessing to others even when it doesn't seem that way to us. We will bloom just when God wants us to bloom. It's part of his purpose for each of us. When the end of our life comes, we will have gained the best. We will gain Christ and will be with him forever.

Dear Lord, Teach me to be a blessing to others and to focus on your purpose alone. Help me not to keep back things for my own life, but to trust you and give and give. Amen.

The Living One

I am the Living One; I was dead, and behold I am alive for ever and ever!
And I hold the keys of death and Hades.
Revelation 1:18

Have you ever been to a funeral? They are very sad times. There is a finality to funerals that is difficult for us to understand. One moment the person we love is with us on earth, and the next he or she is gone. A funeral is a way for us to say goodbye to that person. We know that we will meet him or her again in heaven, but it's still hard without him or her here on earth. We won't be able to make any more memories with that person. We won't be able to laugh with him or her about a funny joke. Death is the end of everything we know here on earth. We will all die someday and leave our life here behind.

But there is one person who lives forever. Christ died on the cross, but three days later he burst the chains of death and rose victoriously. Christ conquered death and lives in heaven, at the right hand of God the Father. And Christ also lives within us, working within your heart to bring his kingdom to earth. Because Christ lives, we don't have to fear death. We don't have to worry when our loved ones pass away. Someday we will all share in Christ's eternal, heavenly glory!

Dear Lord, The best news of all is that you are alive today and that you love me. I know that someday I'll be able to see you and everyone I love here on earth! Amen.

A True Judge

But when they cried out to the Lord, he raised up for them a deliverer,
Othniel son of Kenaz, Caleb's younger brother, who saved them. The Spirit
of the Lord came upon him.
Judges 3:9-10

God is always looking for people he can use to be his heroes. In the
verse above, when God's people needed someone to deliver them,
there was Othniel, prepared and waiting. It's interesting that God's
people weren't living such great lives when all this happened and
God was angry with them. Yet after eight years under the control
of the king of Aram, when they begged God for help, he sent them
Othniel. The Bible says that the Spirit of the Lord came upon
Othniel and he saved them. After that the people lived in peace for
forty years.

What would happen if we all lived as close to God as possible
and made ourselves available to God to use? Would some of us end
up being heroes? Maybe. But to be a hero, we have to be prepared
and ready, just like Othniel. There are a lot of things that need to be
done in the world. Stay ready to do God's will and he can use you
to work out his plan for the world.

Dear Lord, I'm here if you need me. I believe one person can make
a difference in the world today. Help me be ready for whatever you
might call me to do. Amen.

Just Like Us?

Elijah was a man just like us. He prayed earnestly.
James 5:17

Elijah was a prophet who did many miracles over his lifetime. He was the one who told King Ahab it wasn't going to rain again for several years ... not until Elijah prayed for the rains to come. Elijah was the one who built an altar on the top of the mountain and teased the king's evil prophets when their prayers were unanswered. Then Elijah prayed and God sent fire on the altar Elijah built. It burned up the offering, the stones, and all the water that had been poured over the altar. Elijah was the prophet who asked a widow to bake him a cake even though she had only enough flour for one cake and not enough to feed her son. Then God multiplied her flour throughout the entire time of no food. Elijah raised this same woman's son from the dead. And finally Elijah went to heaven in a whirlwind. All of that happened to God's prophet and the Bible says he was a human being — just like us.

For all those events, Elijah prayed before each one until he heard from God. He was known for praying without giving up. God answered all his prayers. You, too, can learn to pray earnestly. If God could use Elijah to be his helper on earth, he can use us too. No one knows what he or she can do for God until the time comes when God asks you to help him.

Dear Lord, I can't imagine doing the awesome miracles that Elijah did, but if he was just like us, then perhaps it can happen. I want to learn to pray like Elijah. Teach me to be persistent in prayer. Amen.

A Wild Dream

And the cows that were ugly and gaunt ate up the seven sleek, fat cows.
Then Pharaoh woke up ... The thin heads of grain swallowed up the seven
healthy, full heads. Then Pharaoh woke up; it had been a dream.
Genesis 41:4, 7

Pharaoh had a really bad dream. He saw skinny ugly cows gobble
up fat healthy cows. Shortly afterward, he had a second dream of
seven heads of thin sickly grain swallowing up seven healthy heads
of grain. When he called Joseph to come tell him what the awful
dreams meant, he probably did not expect what Joseph told him.
Joseph said that there would be seven years with good harvests, but
right after that there would be seven years of famine, hard times,
and hungry people — unless they prepared. God was good to the
Egyptian king and all the people who lived in his land when he gave
them an opportunity to get ready for the hard times that
were coming.

   God tells us that we will have hard times, but we can be prepared
by staying close to God and his love. He will care for us in tough
times.

Dear Lord, I know that tough times happen in everyone's life. Help me
to be ready by staying very close to you every day. Amen.

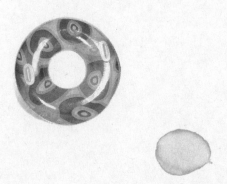

God Cannot Lie

A faith and knowledge resting on the hope of eternal life, which God, who does not lie, promised before the beginning of time.
Titus 1:2

At some time in our lives, most of us say something that is not true. We may flatter someone with compliments we don't really believe. We promise to do something when we know we won't actually do it. And sometimes we tell out-and-out lies to avoid getting in trouble. But did you know that God cannot lie? Cannot lie! Since that is true, we can look at the promises he makes in the Bible and know that he will do exactly what he promises. He promises that if we ask for forgiveness through Jesus Christ his Son, he will grant us forgiveness. He promises us eternal — unending — life with himself. He promises to meet our needs — not all our wants, but our needs.

This is what Paul the apostle taught the church in Corinth about God's promises: "Since we have these promises, dear friends, let us purify ourselves from everything that contaminates body and spirit, perfecting holiness out of reverence for God (2 Corinthians 7:1). We must believe what God promises, and we must live clean lives.

Dear Lord, Thank you for being a God I can count on. I know your promises are true, every one of them. Amen.

If I Ruled the World

The Lord has established his throne in heaven, and his kingdom rules over all.
Psalm 103:19

If you were all-powerful and could change something about the world, what would you change? And if you changed that one thing, what would happen? Would everything be better or worse—or do you really know what might be the result? For example, if you like to play outside a lot, you might want to change the weather so it never rained. Everyone loves a sunshiny day. But if it never rained, what would happen to all the trees and plants where you live? How long would they survive without water? What would your neighborhood look like if all the trees and plants died? It probably wouldn't be so fun to play outside anymore, which is the very thing you would have wanted in the first place!

When people take action because they think they know what's best for our world, often they don't know and problems result from their decisions. But God knows everything. He knows the beginning and the ending for everything—especially your life. You can trust him to guide you.

Dear Lord, Help me to know what you want me to do every day and to turn to you before I make decisions. Amen.

Everyone, Come Now!

And everyone who calls on the name of the Lord will be saved.
Joel 2:32

Jeremy was just about the meanest kid in town. He beat up smaller kids. He stole candy from the store. He picked on animals. He had even been in trouble with the law for some of the things he had done. Some people called him "incorrigible." Incorrigible means that a person is impossible to correct. They are incurably bad, and punishment doesn't seem to make any difference.

There have been some real bad guys in history, but even they are included when God said, "Everyone who calls on the name of the Lord will be saved." If they had asked God to forgive their sins, he would have. Wow! Every single person who asks God to save him will be saved.

So when you are in a bad situation or facing a tough time, remember that you, too, can call on the Lord. He answers anyone —bad guys, good guys, in easy times, in hard times. There is never a reason to keep you from asking God for his salvation and help.

Dear Lord, You answer prayers, even from people who are so bad it seems they can't be saved. But your Word says that anyone can come to you for help and salvation. Please remind me of that promise whenever I am in a tough spot. Amen.

God's Discipline

"What a blessing when God steps in and corrects you! Mind you, don't despise the discipline of Almighty God! True, he wounds, but he also dresses the wound; the same hand that hurts you, heals you. From one disaster after another he delivers you; no matter what the calamity, the evil can't touch you."
Job 5:17–19, The Message

Do you like to be disciplined? What about time-outs and being grounded? Not much fun, are they? Sometimes God, just like our parents, has to discipline us to get our attention. We are doing something wrong or are weak in some area, and he wants to correct us and make us stronger. We can be stubborn and resist God's work in our lives, just like sheep who don't always follow their shepherd. But a shepherd will always go after that lamb and bring it back to the flock, even if it doesn't want to return.

God might allow something painful to happen to you as a way to teach you something or draw you closer to him. But if God allows something like that to happen to you, he will also be there to help you. God loves you more than you can understand and what he wants most is for you to follow him.

Dear Lord, Help me to stay close and listen to what you say. But if I wander too far from you, bring me back to you. Amen.

A Praise a Day

As they began to sing and praise, the Lord set ambushes against the men of Ammon and Moab and Mount Seir who were invading Judah, and they were defeated.
2 Chronicles 20:22

Do you ever wish there was a magic button you could push to help you stop worrying? Well, the Bible talks about something kind of like that — praise.

The Bible is full of praises to God — even from people who had lots to worry about. In the above Scripture passage, King Jehoshaphat of Judah heard the news that a huge, mighty army was coming to destroy his kingdom. But what did he do? Instead of worrying, Jehoshaphat and all his people bowed on the ground and had a worship service.

The next time something worries you — maybe a fight with a friend, a bad grade or a bully at school — try singing to God. A song of praise will help you remember that God is in control. He will take care of you. He will use the problems in your life for his glory, so why not praise him even before anything changes?

When we praise God, we have more hope and faith. We stop being sad and can live life with joy. And, as with Jehoshaphat, when we begin to sing and praise, God goes to work to help us when we are in need.

Dear Lord, My first thought when I'm in trouble is *Oh, boy. How do I get out of this?* Help me to turn my problems over to you, and help me to praise you and sing songs of worship no matter what's going on around me. Amen.

God's Secrets

The Lord confides in those who fear him;
he makes his covenant known to them.
Psalm 25:14

Paleontologists study prehistoric life — that is, life that came before
recorded history. They labor under harsh conditions, digging up
ancient bones and fossils that help scientists understand more about
God's amazing diversity of creatures. This work isn't easy:
paleontologists work in the dust and the heat, digging slowly and
carefully so they won't damage any specimens. Because of this
painstaking work, we have learned a great deal about life that came
before us.

There are wonders and mysteries about God that we only get to
know by being determined to learn about him. Those who fear God,
dig deep into study about him, and pray and listen for his voice are
the ones who get to know those secret mysteries and wonders. It's
like uncovering ancient bones or fossils that we didn't even know
existed until we started searching for them. Often people learn the
most about God in hard times. What would you like to know about
God and his great love?

Dear Lord, As I grow up, I want to know more about you. Please share
your secrets, mysteries, and wonders with me. Amen.

Never Give Up

Then Jesus told his disciples a parable to show them that they should always pray and not give up.
Luke 18:1

Pray always? You've got to be kidding! How can anyone do that? Jesus probably didn't mean for us to go around reciting prayers all day long. He meant that we should go on praying even when we don't see anything happening. We are not to give up.

Jesus told his disciples a story to help them understand. This is what he told them. A widow wanted justice for a problem in her life. She went to the judge and asked him to do something. The judge didn't care about her or anyone else. He didn't even care about or fear God. He refused to help her. The woman, however, wouldn't give up. She kept asking and asking and asking until finally he said, "Even though I don't fear God or care about men, yet because this widow keeps bothering me, I will see that she gets justice, so that she won't eventually wear me out with her coming" (Luke 18:1–8).

That widow got what she wanted because she wouldn't give up. When we are praying about something important, we can never give up until we know God has answered or is going to answer our prayer. Even when we haven't seen an answer, in our heart we believe that God will answer us.

By persisting in prayer, we learn patience, and God teaches us what faith really is. Our prayers are also a tool to defeat Satan, so we must not give up. There is so much more to prayer than just getting an answer.

Dear Lord, I know that sometimes when I'm praying about something, I give up if I don't get an answer quickly. Help me to never give up until you answer. Amen.

Walking through Fire

He said, "Look! I see four men walking around in the fire, unbound and unharmed, and the fourth looks like a son of the gods."
Daniel 3:25

This is one of the most amazing stories in the Bible. King Nebuchadnezzar built a statue that was ten stories tall and nine feet wide. Everyone in his kingdom was to bow down and worship the statue. But there were three Hebrew young men who refused to do so. They knew God's commandment about not worshipping idols, and they would not bow down to the king's statue. Their punishment was a death sentence. They were thrown into a blazing hot furnace — heated seven times hotter than ever before. Immediately, the ropes that tied their hands and feet burned off, but nothing else was burned — not even one hair on their heads! In fact, they were so safe and comfortable in the furnace that they were up walking around. Then they were joined by a fourth man that the king's people said looked like the son of a god.

When the king saw that the fire hadn't harmed the three young men, he called them to come out. Then the king understood that these men didn't serve a dead god like the huge statue he'd built, but a living God — a God who could rescue them.

Only God can do a miracle like that. In the hardest, most trying times, God will free us from the sorrows that accompany these situations. We can walk around in the "fire" when we know he is there too. Since he is a living God, he can still rescue us when we get in trouble. We just have to call out to him.

Dear Lord, A story like this helps me know that you never change and you can do anything. Amen.

God's Friend

Abraham remained standing before the Lord.
Genesis 18:22

Can you imagine what it would be like to be so close to God you were called "God's friend"? That's what Abraham was called. When God said to Abraham, "Take your family and leave the land of Ur," Abraham gathered everybody up and started off to ... well, he didn't really know where. When he got to the land we now call Israel, he stopped and built an altar (which was often just a pile of rocks) to his Friend, God. God spoke to him and said, "I'm going to give you this land." Then Abraham went on to other places and built more altars to his Friend.

Sometimes Abraham had a hard time trusting God, such as when God told him he'd become a dad at 100 years old. But Abraham's faith grew until he trusted God completely. By the time God asked Abraham to sacrifice his son Isaac — the one God had promised him for such a long time — Abraham did not doubt God. He prepared to sacrifice his only son. Of course, God was only testing Abraham. The angel of God stopped Abraham from hurting his son.

Abraham was God's friend. Would you like to be God's friend? Friends of God can do mighty things for him. Friends of God can pray for others and see their lives changed. Friends of God trust him completely. Are you a friend of God?

Dear Lord, I'd like to be your friend. I know I will never be perfect, but I'd like to know you a lot better and I want my faith to grow. Teach me how. Amen.

Wind, Fire, and Water

I am still confident of this: I will see the goodness of the Lord in the land of the living. Wait for the Lord; be strong and take heart and wait for the Lord.
Psalm 27:13

A couple had a farm that lay right in the path of a California wildfire. As the fire roared toward their buildings, they got the horses out of the barn. Moments later the hay inside the barn caught fire and flames leaped to the heavens. Then the fire moved toward their house, closer and closer. About that time, the owner decided she didn't want to lose her home. Standing in the middle of a field she cried out to God and God heard her. She could have fallen apart as she saw the fire coming closer to her house. But she didn't. She turned to God. She knew he would be with her. The fire stopped six feet from her home. God had saved her house. That is the goodness of the Lord to one of his children.

Some awful things happen on our planet. Winds, fires, earthquakes, tsunamis, hunger, war, and on and on. There are problems and illnesses and concerns in our families too. It would be easy to feel down or sad all the time. What we have to remember when bad things happen is that God is still good and he is with us. When we get to heaven, our eternal home, we will not have all these tragedies. Heaven will be a place of absolute peace and happiness. We have hope—hope in a future both here on earth and hope for heaven. God will help us get through the worst of the worst.

Dear Lord, Please help me to have hope when everything seems pretty black and I can't see where my life is going. You are the God of hope. Amen.

Getting Strong in Tough Places

We went through fire and water, but you brought us to a place
of abundance.
Psalm 66:12

When people go through difficult circumstances, they sometimes
say, "I've been through hell and high water." What they've endured
has been so hard, they feel as if their lives have been burned by fire
and overcome by flood. But there is something else that's interesting
about this phrase — it also describes the process used to create steel.

Making steel involves heating iron and carbon to a near-molten
(liquid) state. Once the steel is formed into whatever it's going to
be, it is then plunged into clean cold water. Fire heats steel to the
point where it can be shaped; cold water sets the shape so it stays
in place, and the whole process tempers the steel. Tempering makes
the steel strong and keeps it from being brittle. Going from fire to
water and sometimes repeating the process is essential if the steel is
going to be used to make a tool or construct a building. Who would
want to use a brittle screwdriver that breaks apart, or be in a
building constructed of weak steel?

Have you ever felt as if your life was on fire or that you were
in water over your head? It's at these times that God can use our
circumstances to make us spiritually strong. When we are tempered
like steel, we become tools God can use to accomplish his work in
the world.

Dear Lord, I don't like hard times. It's good to know that you can use
hard times to make me strong. Help me to trust you and rely on your
strength when I'm facing tough times. Amen.

Every Single Thing

"If you can?" said Jesus. "Everything is possible for him who believes."
Mark 9:23

Everything? Wow! That's some promise, Jesus! The promise was given when a man brought his son to Jesus. The boy had an evil spirit living inside him. It made the boy do strange and sometimes dangerous things. The father said to Jesus, "If you can do anything, take pity on us, and help us." That's when Jesus answered with a question, "If you can?" and then said, "Everything is possible for him who believes."

So what do you want from Jesus? Would it be good to pray for something then add, "If it is your will"? That's the hard part of knowing how to pray — are we praying the way God wants us to pray.

Understanding that Jesus can do everything is easy because God's Word says it is true. But that doesn't mean God will automatically do everything you ask. Even though he can, he may delay an answer — or do something else — to develop your faith. For example, God told Joseph that Joseph would rule in Egypt one day. But many years passed before God put Joseph on a throne. During that time, God tried Joseph's soul but developed his faith.

The challenge for us is to believe God's Word that says he can do anything, but then trust that if doesn't do what we ask, he is up to something else for our good.

Dear Lord, I believe it. You are the one who can do everything. I trust you and whatever answers you give me. Amen.

Watch Out What You Pray For

We do not know what we ought to pray for.
Romans 8:26

If you pray for patience, watch out! You'll probably get a bunch of trouble to teach you patience. Pray for riches and you'll probably get a job and have to work for your riches. Pray for good health and you may have to stop eating junk food and start eating healthy. Pray for more friends and you may find yourself in a new school or church where you have to work to make friends. But the good news is that God loves us and when we pray to him, he gives us only what is best for us.

By now you are probably thinking, Why bother praying for anything? We pray because Jesus told us to pray. Let's see what he said.

"Ask and it will be given to you; seek and you will find; knock and the door will be opened to you." (Matthew 7:7)

"If you believe, you will receive whatever you ask for in prayer." (Matthew 21:22)

"If you remain in me and my words remain in you, ask whatever you wish, and it will be given you." (John 15:7)

We pray because Jesus told us to pray and what happens after that is up to him. We don't know how he will answer. It may be by testing us in the areas that we've asked for his help. He will help us through whatever comes next.

Dear Lord, Thank you for the gift of prayer. Help me to pray more often and to believe you will answer. Amen.

Hop to It

On that very day Abraham [did] ... as God told him.
Genesis 17:23

A woman had five children. Her husband was away one night, and she was in her house when it caught fire. She awoke to a smoke-filled house. Quickly, she went to her children's bedrooms and one by one she put them outside on the roof of the porch. She told them not to move until the firemen could get them off the roof. She went back again and again until she had all the children out on the roof and the firemen had arrived. Her quick action and the instant obedience of her children saved them all.

The Scripture above says that Abraham acted as soon as God gave him an instruction. We should learn to respond immediately as well. Sometimes the difference between being saved from a disaster and not surviving is simple, immediate obedience. That's what God wants from us. When he tells us to do something, the sooner we do it the better. When he says for us to stop doing something, we'd better stop right now.

Dear Lord, I know sometimes I don't obey immediately. Help me to do what you ask as soon as you tell me. Amen.

Above the Clouds

Now no one can look at the sun, bright as it is in the skies after the wind has swept them clean.
Job 37:21

When you read a verse like the one above from Job, you may begin to wonder what was going on with Job and his friends to bring up such a conversation.

These guys said to Job, "Do you know how God controls the clouds and makes his lightning flash? Do you know how the clouds hang poised? . . . Can you join him in spreading out the skies, hard as a mirror of cast bronze? . . . Now no one can look at the sun, bright as it is in the skies after the wind has swept them clean." In other words, "Job, you don't know enough to understand God's ways."

Then God answered Job (chapters 38 – 41; read it sometime — it's beautiful). God said that he is the one who has created everything the way it is. God sees the sun even when to us it is covered by clouds. Now Job knows he can hear from God. He can understand what God is doing in the world when he learns to consider that God's perspective is so different from ours.

Do you want to hear from God and see his bigger perspective? You can if you will pray with all your heart and ask God to show you his plan and his way.

Dear Lord, I know you made everything, understand everything, yet you want to talk with me. You give me understanding. Amen.

Angel Wars

Then he continued, "Do not be afraid, Daniel. Since the first day that you set your mind to gain understanding and to humble yourself before your God, your words were heard, and I have come in response to them."
Daniel 10:12-13

What would you think if you were standing beside a river one day and looked up to see a man dressed in a white linen robe with a belt of fine gold? That would be shocking enough, but then you see that his body sparkles like a gemstone and his face looks like lightning. His eyes are like flaming torches and his arms and legs are like shiny bronze. What would you do? Would you run away? The Bible describes this man as the angel God sent to Daniel, but Daniel was too shocked to run away. He fell to the ground speechless.

Daniel had prayed for three weeks for God's help but there was no answer from heaven. Then this creature appeared and said that God had heard Daniel the first day he prayed. But the angel had been delayed for twenty-one days in a struggle with a spirit prince — a fallen angel — who was over the land of Persia.

What we learn from this true story is that God hears us every time we pray, but sometimes spiritual forces are at work that we can't see. Even though we can't see those things, God can and is at work to answer our prayers. Don't be discouraged when you pray and don't get an answer right away. God hears you. You can trust him to take care of you.

Dear Lord, You hear when I pray, but sometimes there are circumstances either in your world or in mine that prevent me getting an answer right away. Help me be patient. Amen.

A God Bush

After forty years had passed, an angel appeared to Moses in the flames of a
burning bush in the desert near Mount Sinai.... he heard the Lord's voice: "I am
the God of your fathers, the God of Abraham, Isaac and Jacob ... I have indeed
seen the oppression of my people in Egypt. I have heard their groaning and have
come down to set them free. Now come, I will send you back to Egypt."
Acts 7:30–34

Moses was out in the desert taking care of sheep when a bush
suddenly ignited. There were fires in the desert from time to time,
so a burning bush wasn't so unusual. But this wasn't your typical
burning bush. The bush was on fire but it was not being burned up.
Moses went to investigate this strange phenomenon.

Well, God certainly had Moses' attention. But the burning bush
wasn't the only amazing thing happening with Moses. Moses had
been waiting in the desert for 40 years wondering how God would
rescue his people from Egypt. By this time, Moses was settled into
his life as a shepherd in the desert. But God told Moses that he had
chosen Moses to go back to Egypt where he had once been a prince.
He was to go back to the place where he had lived and lead God's
people out of there.

When God wants to get your attention, he will. But can you
imagine waiting 40 years for God to tell you what your next task
is? Many times God's plan will require a long time of waiting. He is
still working on you. Don't think that the time of waiting is being
wasted. When he's ready to tell you what the next stage of your
journey is, you just have to be ready to listen to what he wants to
say. You probably won't see him in a burning bush as Moses did.
You probably won't meet an angel at the river as Daniel did, but
God will still talk with you.

Dear Lord, I believe that when you are ready to talk with me and lead
me into a new phase of life, you'll find a way. Help me to listen when
you speak. Amen.

No Stress

We do not want you to be uninformed, brothers, about the hardships we suffered in the province of Asia. We were under great pressure, far beyond our ability to endure, so that we despaired even of life ... But this happened that we might not rely on ourselves but on God, who raises the dead.
2 Corinthians 1:8–9

Today we call pressure stress. You hear many people talking about stress. Stress can be bad if all we do is worry. It can be good if it pushes us toward the only One who has answers for our stress — God our Father.

Once a stressful situation has passed, you come out of it with the ability to help other people. Think about the last time you had to study for a hard test. You probably felt pressure until you finished the test. But now when a friend talks about being stressed out about an exam, you know exactly how he or she feels.

Or do you remember a time when your mom got really sick or your dad traveled away for several weeks? Was it stressful for the rest of your family? But when the sickness or travel was over, you were relieved. Now, you can be understanding when others face a similar situation.

The most important thing to remember is that any time you face pressure, turn to God first. If you learn to rely on him, you will experience his peace and the stress won't be as overwhelming. Then you will have a truly helpful answer to offer others — God's strength.

Dear Lord, Everybody talks about being "stressed out." I'm so glad you are the answer to all stressful situations. Amen.

An Ancient Love Story

Before he had finished praying, Rebekah came out with her jar on her shoulder.... Then the man bowed down and worshiped the Lord, saying, "Praise be to the Lord, the God of my master Abraham, who has not abandoned his kindness and faithfulness to my master."
Genesis 24:15, 27

Abraham decided his son Isaac was ready to get married, but he didn't want Isaac to marry any of the girls where they lived as many of them worshiped idols rather than the one true God. So Abraham sent his servant back to the land he came from to find a wife for his son. What a responsibility for the servant! He didn't want to make a mistake. The servant traveled the long distance to Abraham's birthplace. I'm sure as he went he thought, *How am I going to know who the right girl is?* So he prayed.

"Dear Lord, give me success today. I am standing near this spring where the girls come to get water. Let it be that when I say to a girl, 'Please let down your jar into the well so that I may have a drink,' and she says, 'Drink, and I'll give your camels water too' — let her be the one you have chosen for Isaac."

While he was still praying, Rebekah came to get water for her family. The servant asked her to give him a drink and immediately she said, "Drink, my lord ... I'll draw water for your camels too." The servant probably almost fell over. God had answered his prayer before he even finished praying!

Sometimes when we ask God to lead us, he answers right away and what he says to us is very clear. We know exactly what he wants us to do. It's a little harder when we pray and have to wait for him to show us what to do next, but we can believe that he will answer in his own perfect time.

Dear Lord, Thank you for this story of how you sometimes answer prayers right away and with exactly what we asked for from you. Amen.

Sticking Up for Jesus

Jesus commanded Peter, "Put your sword away! Shall I not drink the cup the Father has given me?"
John 18:11

Have you ever been so angry or so scared that you just wanted to hit someone? That's the way Peter felt when soldiers came to take Jesus captive. We don't know why Peter was carrying a sword in the first place, but when the soldiers got close to Jesus, Peter pulled out his sword and whacked off the ear of one of the soldiers. But Jesus didn't need someone to defend him at that point. He knew that what was happening was part of God's plan for him, so he commanded Peter, "Put your sword away! Don't you know that I could ask my Father God and he would send thousands of angels to rescue me?" (Matthew 26:53).

Jesus wasn't afraid of the soldiers—even though they were coming to arrest him. He knew he was going to face a lot of suffering. But he did not try to run away or fight. Jesus' example shows us that God can turn painful situations into lessons or use them to give others a gift. Can you imagine if Jesus decided not to let himself be taken by the guards? What if he hadn't died for us? We would have had to pay for our own sins.

God may ask you some day to do something hard or painful. Will you be open and ready?

Dear Lord, Help me to be ready to face painful situations with courage. I know you will use times like those to spread your good news. Amen.

Night Songs

I remembered my songs in the night. My heart mused and my spirit inquired.
Psalm 77:6

Animals that are active at night rather than during the day are called nocturnal. For example, nightingales are birds that sing at night. That's how they got their name. People aren't like that: we're awake and working while the sun shines, and we go to bed and sleep during the night.

Do you ever have trouble sleeping at night because you are worried about something? David, the man who wrote the psalm above, sometimes couldn't sleep. While he was awake at night, he used the time to pray, sing and think about God. In another place David says, "My eyes stay open through the watches of the night, that I may meditate on your promises" (Psalm 119:148). Instead of worrying about his problems, David took the time to think about God's promises.

The next time you are lying awake, try singing a song from church. Or ask Mom or Dad to pray with you. Perhaps it would help just to remember that God said he would never leave you alone.

Dear Lord, Your promises are just as good in the night as they are in the daytime. Thank you for your love. Amen.

A Great Promise

Commit your way to the Lord; trust in him and he will do this.
Psalm 37:5

What is "this" in the verse above? "This" is whatever we trust God to do. Our job is to work at committing everything about our life to God. Whew! That's a job that lasts a lifetime. We don't like to give up everything to another, do we?

To commit something is to give it over to completely to another's care. It's like carrying a heavy backpack, then giving it to someone else to carry. That's what God wants us to do with the things that trouble us or make us sad. Give your load of concern to God.

Have you committed your life to God? If not, what things are you still trying to take care of yourself? Do you have a problem that you need to turn over to God? When you do this, you can take comfort in knowing that God will take care of the things you commit to him.

Dear Lord, I don't know what to do about the problems in my life. You know how to take care of it, so I'm going to quit worrying about it and give it to you. Amen.

Wit's End

They reeled and staggered like drunken men; they were at their wits' end.
Then they cried out to the Lord in their trouble, and he brought them out of
their distress.
Psalm 107:27-28

Justin crept downstairs one evening when he heard his parents talking. He knew his father had just lost his job and his parents were having a harder time paying all the bills. "I just don't know where we'll find the money," he heard his father say. "I'm at my wit's end." When we talk about our wits' end, it means that we've tried to figure things out and couldn't. We can't think of one more possible solution or see any way out of the difficult situation we're in.

When we get to the end of everything we can figure out, that's where God begins to help us. When we don't have any more resources, money, time, or things, that's when God can begin giving us what we need. So if you've tried to figure out how you are going to make something work out, if you feel like you are at wit's end, look around. God is ready to help you.

Dear God, I know you are very near and ready to help me figure things out. Thank you. Amen.

In God's Time

Sarah ... bore a son to Abraham in his old age, at the very time God had promised him.
Genesis 21:2

Did you ever notice that God doesn't seem to be in a hurry? Often it seems as if he waits until the last moment to answer our prayers. God had promised Abraham that he would make a great nation out of him, but Abraham had no children. How was he to become a great nation if he had no son? It was 30 years from the time God first promised Abraham a son until he held his little boy Isaac. Later, Isaac's son Jacob had twelve sons, and the children started multiplying. After many years they formed a nation—the nation of Israel.

What is your family praying about? Is there something you've waited and waited for? Don't give up. Keep praying, and God will answer in his time, which is always perfect.

When Isaac was finally born there was much happiness in Abraham and Sarah's house. God's promise was worth the wait. And it will be for you too. When Jesus finally answers your prayer, you'll be smiling.

Dear Lord, I'm looking forward to that happy day when you answer my prayer. Amen.

Sticking It Out

Fix this picture firmly in your mind: Jesus, descended from the line of David, raised from the dead. It's what you've heard from me all along. It's what I'm sitting in jail for right now — but God's Word isn't in jail! That's why I stick it out here — so that everyone God calls will get in on the salvation of Christ in all its glory.
2 Timothy 2:8–10, The Message

Paul the apostle started out as a Jewish religious leader who persecuted Christians. Then Jesus appeared to him and first knocked him off his horse, and then knocked some sense into him. After some time out in the desert, training from God, Paul began to preach all over the lands surrounding the Mediterranean Sea. Some of those who heard Paul didn't like what he preached. They beat him and threw him in jail many times, often on made-up charges. But that's when he said, "I might be in jail, but God's Word isn't."

Because of the tough times Paul faced, his preaching spread and many people believed in God. At the time, though, Paul didn't know that he would lead so many to Christ and help start so many churches. Times of struggle or persecution may actually be the most significant moments God asks us to live. You never know how God will use your life and problems to reach others for him.

So we must be faithful to tell others about Jesus so that "everyone God calls will get in on the salvation of Christ in all its glory."

Dear Lord, Thank you for the faithfulness of Paul and all the other apostles who preached even when they got thrown in jail for doing it. Help me to be faithful too. Amen.

Spring Up, O Well!

Then Israel sang this song: "Spring up, O well! Sing about it."
Numbers 21:17

When you are an animal as big as an elephant, you need lots of water. But in Southern Africa, it may not rain for months. So what can an elephant do to find water? Somehow, through some God-given ability, elephants know where the water is hiding under the sand. During the dry season, when water is low, an elephant will dig holes to find underground springs and rivers, drawing up as much as two gallons at a time with its trunk. The water holes also give elephants access to important mineral sources buried deep below the surface. When the elephants finish drinking water, other wildlife will rush in to drink from the holes too. God knows that every living thing has to have water.

When his people were wandering in the desert, God always provided water and food for them. One day God told Moses to call the people together because he was ready to give them water. And when he did, the people sang this song:

Sing the Song of the Well,
the well sunk by princes,
Dug out by the peoples' leaders
digging with their scepters and staffs.

Numbers 21:17 (The Message)

Like the Israelites, praise God for how he cares for you and your needs, often in ways we could never look for or expect.

Dear Lord, Thank you for providing everything we need. Amen.

Full to the Top

"We have here only five loaves of bread and two fish," they answered.
"Bring them here to me," he said.
Matthew 14:17-18

God is not stingy. When he gives, he gives a lot. Think about places where flowers cover a hillside. Are that many flowers really necessary? Think about water spilling over a waterfall. More water than we can use.

There's a wonderful story of God's abundant giving in the New Testament. It happened when Jesus was teaching many people out in the countryside away from any town. He and the people had been out there all day, and the people had grown hungry. The disciples wanted to send them away. But Jesus told the disciples to feed the crowd. They had no food to share except a little boy's lunch of five loaves of bread and two fish. That was enough for God to work with. Jesus took the loaves and fish and broke them up in pieces. Soon they had enough food to feed 5,000 men along with women and children. And here's God's abundance part of the story: twelve baskets of leftovers fed the disciples and their families. God gives abundantly. So whatever you need from him, be sure that he will give it to you, sometimes beyond what you need.

Dear Lord, I know you have enough to meet my needs. I want to trust you to give me what I need and more. Amen.

Would You Wrestle with God?

Then the man said, "Let me go, for it is daybreak." But Jacob replied, "I will not let you go unless you bless me." ... Jacob said, "Please tell me your name." But he replied, "Why do you ask my name?" Then he blessed him there.

Genesis 32:26, 29

Have you ever watched a wrestling match at school or on TV? When two wrestlers are in a competition, they are very close to each other. In fact, they are literally all over each other. It is impossible to wrestle without being in close contact, and the only way wrestlers win their matches is to pin their opponents. Jacob wrestled with a man from God (or angel). Jacob didn't do so well with the wrestling part. The man from God put Jacob's hip out of joint and crippled him because Jacob would not let him go. But then, the man blessed Jacob.

When we are praying for God to do something for us, it can feel as though we are wrestling with God. Just as two wrestlers have to get close to engage each other, so we have to get close to God when we are wrestling in prayer. As we struggle with God about a prayer, we are growing stronger. We are getting closer. And that's a good thing.

Dear Lord, Let me stay close to you, even if I have to wrestle in prayer. Amen.

Friends and Servants

I no longer call you servants, because a servant does not know his master's business. Instead, I have called you friends, for everything that I learned from my Father I have made known to you.
John 15:15

Friendship is wonderful gift that we share with someone else. Here's what makes someone a friend:

- *Someone who will help you.*
- *Someone who will stand up for you when others are being mean.*
- *Someone who says to your face the same things he says behind your back.*
- *Someone who is nearby and will take the time when you want to talk.*
- *Someone who is proud to be your friend and tells others about your friendship.*
- *Someone who will let you do good things for them too.*

Jesus is the friend who stays closer to us than our own family. He is always nearby. He heals us. He defends us when Satan attacks us. He is always available when you want to talk to him in prayer. Jesus told the disciples they were his friends. And that goes for us as well. He invites us to share in his work and be his friends.

Can you think of anything better than being friends with the one who created the universe?

Dear Lord, I know you are right beside me as my friend. Thank you that I can count on you to be always with me. Amen.

The Choir to End All Choirs

And they sang a new song before the throne and before the four living creatures and the elders. No one could learn the song except the 144,000 who had been redeemed from the earth.
Revelation 14:3

Once in a while a writer in the Bible pulls the curtain back and we get to look into heaven. That's what happens in Revelation 14. Wow! What a sight!

Picture this: There are 144,000 believers standing on top of a mountain. Soon there is the sound of harps being played before the throne of God and before the thrones of the 24 elders who are nearby. There are four creatures near the throne that are covered with eyes — even under their six wings. All these creatures constantly give glory, honor, and thanks to God. (See Revelation 4:4 – 11.) Then the 144,000 begin to sing a song about how they had been redeemed (saved) from the earth.

It is a song that only they can sing. It is a song of redemption. The angels cannot sing it. Only those who have experienced God's grace and transforming power can sing this kind of song. What a choir!

Our life on earth, including the hardships, is part of our "training" to sing songs of redemption in heaven. When we accept salvation, we become part of the future choir. God's Spirit says, "Let him who hears say, 'Come!' Whoever is thirsty, let him come; and whoever wishes, let him take the free gift of the water of life" (Revelation 22:17). That's all we have to do to join in the celebration around the throne of God at the end of time.

Dear Lord, I want to be a part of the great choir that sings around your throne in heaven. Amen.

What Will They Say?

You will come to the grave in full vigor, like sheaves gathered in season.
Job 5:26

When someone dies, other people reflect on his life. The idea in the Scripture above is about how living a full life to God's glory is like a good harvest. Try to think of a good harvest like ripe fruit. Have you ever eaten a banana or a tomato before it's ripe? The flavor isn't too tasty; it can actually be bad to eat. But when fruit is ripened just the right amount of time, it's scrumptious.

A life lived for God is like ripe fruit, pleasing and enjoyable to him and to others. But it takes time to develop a life like this — time to make good choices, to follow God and to serve others. Then at the end of your life, others will see God's blessing upon you.

Dear Lord, Help me live the kind of life that will be as pleasing as good fruit. Amen.

It's Not Your Problem

This is the resting place, let the weary rest.
Isaiah 28:12

Do you ever have a difficult time falling asleep at night? You crawl into bed, punch your pillow into a comfortable position, pull the blankets up around your shoulders, close your eyes, and ... nothing. You lie awake thinking of everything that has happened that day and everything that will happen tomorrow. You're lying down in bed, but your mind isn't getting any rest. You're too consumed by worry to relax and get the sleep you need.

But there's good news! You don't need to worry about yesterday or tomorrow. Whatever is going on around you is not your problem: it's God's. God will care for all the problems swirling around in your life, so you can be at peace and rest in him. Before you go to sleep at night, talk to God about your worries and problems and then let it all go. Each problem is safe in God's hands, and you can sleep safely while trusting that the Lord is watching over you and everything important to you.

Dear Lord, Even though I'm just a kid, sometimes I lie awake and worry about stuff. Please help me to put everything in your hands when it's time to go to bed. Amen.

No Money, No Worry

Against all hope, Abraham in hope believed without weakening in his faith.
Romans 4:18–19

More than a hundred years ago in England, there were many orphans with no one to care for them. A man named George Müller and his wife began helping orphans by inviting the children into their own home. Soon he had five orphanages where more than 2,000 children lived. George was a man of great faith and he never asked anyone for money to support his ministry or the orphanage. He never went into debt either. He believed God would give him what he needed, so he decided not to take a salary when he became the pastor of a small church. He trusted God to care for him and his family. God always provided for George's needs and more and that made his faith grow. Many times, there was no food at the orphanage, but George went right on believing God to provide. Food always showed up just in time to feed the children.

By the time he died, Müller had cared for and educated thousands of children. He had given away thousands of Bibles, even more New Testaments, and millions of other religious books. He also supported 150 missionaries. You see, he believed that God could meet all his needs even when there was nothing. He was like Abraham who hoped even when he couldn't see how God would help him

If God took care of George Müller and his orphans, he can take care of you. Is there something your family needs? Pray and believe God will meet your need. You will be surprised at the awesome things God will do for you too.

Dear Lord, Thank you for giving us what we need as we do your work in the world. Amen.

The Perfect Storm

That day when evening came, he said to his disciples, "Let us go over to the other side."
Mark 4:35

Once in a great while, nature puts together some weather events that create "a perfect storm." On Halloween in 1991 in New England, three different weather conditions came together to create a huge storm. Warm air created by a low pressure system came from one direction. Cool, dry air from a high pressure system came from another direction. In addition the air was full of tropical moisture created by a hurricane. All of those weather conditions added up to create the perfect storm — a perfectly horrible storm. Sand washed away from beaches. Buildings were damaged. Fishermen drowned when their boats capsized.

Imagine how scary it would be to be in a boat when that kind of storm hit. That's what happened to Jesus and his disciples. They were in a small open boat on the Sea of Galilee in the middle of a frightening storm. During that awful storm, the disciples learned something about Jesus. He could calm the storm and the waters with just a word — he truly is God's son.

Maybe you have had a bunch of hard things happen at the same time and it felt as if you were in a terrible storm of trouble. When you have to go through a perfect storm, look for Jesus. Call on his name and trust him to calm the storm for you too. He is with you and will show his power.

Dear Lord, When the perfect storm comes to my life, I trust that you will be there with me to help me through it. Amen.

Night Worker

Then Moses stretched out his hand over the sea, and all that night the Lord drove the sea back with a strong east wind and turned it into dry land. The waters were divided.

Exodus 14:21

There is someone who never sleeps. That someone is God, and he worked all the night to drive the Red Sea back so his children could cross to safety. The Bible tells us, "He who watches over you will not slumber; indeed, he who watches over Israel will neither slumber nor sleep. The Lord watches over you ... The Lord will keep you from all harm—he will watch over your life." (Psalm 121:3–7)

When it seems dark around you and you have a hard time seeing God at work, remember that he is there even in the dark times. He works all the time. Often, his activity happens undercover. The children of Israel walked through the Red Sea at night and when morning came, they looked back to see what God had led them through. God had parted the sea for them and swept away their enemies. They were amazed and put their full trust in God.

Take a minute to thank God that he stays awake and takes care of things even in the dark.

Dear Lord, I'm not going to worry because I know you are awake and taking care of everything. Amen.

Pray Big Prayers

Ask the Lord for a sign, whether in the deepest depths or in the highest heights.
Isaiah 7:11

When the circus came to town, Sam wanted more than anything to go. But he never said anything to anyone. He did not ask to go or even hint that he would love to see it. In a few days, the circus moved on and he never got to see it. That's kind of what happens when we don't pray and ask God for what we need. He knows — because God knows everything — but he wants us to ask him for our needs and even for our wants. In the New Testament Jesus said, "Until now you have not asked for anything in my name. Ask and you will receive, and your joy will be complete" (John 16:24).

What do you need? Have you asked God to provide it? Do you believe he can do it? You'll never know until you ask him. What if Sam had asked his parents to take him to the circus and they had said, "Sure Sam. We just didn't know if you were interested. We didn't know if you really wanted to go. We'll get tickets for tomorrow." That would have been pretty exciting.

God wants you to ask for small things and big things from him. He will show you how he can take care of you and your family.

Dear Lord, Help me have the faith to let you take over my needs and wait patiently for your answer. Amen.

All Clear

Be clear-minded and self-controlled so that you can pray.
1 Peter 4:7

"All clear" was a phrase used in war times that meant the danger —whatever it was—had passed and it was safe to move forward. This phrase was often used to let people know an air raid was over.

Prayer is more than getting down on our knees, closing our eyes, and telling God everything we want. Prayer is more like a visit with a good friend. God loves to talk with us when we pray. But sometimes our minds are so full of what we are doing; where we are going next; what tests and reports we have to do, that we couldn't hear God if he were yelling at us. We need to clear our minds before we can hear him.

If we are to be "all clear" when we pray, it means we clear out anything that is concerning us. We remove danger or worry from our minds. We remove clutter from our brains, and for a few minutes we concentrate on God and his love. If we pray with a clear mind, we can listen for his voice.

Dear Lord, Teach me how to clear my mind so I can talk to you in prayer and also hear your voice. Amen.

God's Lullaby

But no one says, "Where is God my Maker, who gives songs in the night?"
Job 35:10

God made the night so that we can sleep. He wants us to go to sleep easily and stay asleep all night, so we can wake up ready for a new day. All his creatures need sleep. Doctors and scientists are learning some important things about sleep:

- *Sleep helps your brain remember information better. People who sleep well do better on tests.*
- *If you do not get enough sleep, you could get into accidents or cause an accident to someone else.*
- *Lack of sleep causes people to be crabby and impatient.*
- *Some people can't concentrate if they are tired. And maybe they don't even have the energy to do things they like.*
- *Part of staying healthy is getting enough sleep. While you sleep, your body restores itself.*

What kinds of things make it hard for you to fall asleep? Sadness? Worry about a grade at school? Anger toward your parents or a friend? Loneliness? Fear of the dark? When you can't sleep, talk to God and ask him to give you a song in your heart that will help you rest.

Dear Lord, Tonight when I go to bed, I'm going to listen for your songs. I know you are nearby and want to relieve me of the things that keep me awake at night. Amen.

A Born Champion

For everyone born of God overcomes the world. This is the victory that has overcome the world, even our faith.

1 John 5:4

One day Kristin awoke with terrible pain in her arms and legs. She couldn't move much at all. Doctors were baffled and couldn't figure out what was wrong with her. For two years, Kristin spent most of her days in bed. Can you imagine how discouraged she must have been? Well, Kristin learned that Jesus was there to help her overcome discouragement. He was still with her; he was still in control. So every day Kristin prayed and asked God to help her be an overcomer even if she couldn't get out of bed.

When we are born of God — become his children by accepting Jesus as our Savior — we become overcomers. This means we can do whatever Jesus gives us to do with his strength and victory.

You can overcome too. By putting your faith in God, you will learn how to overcome any circumstance — even the most trying ones. Sometimes the obstacle may not go away or change, but God will give you his strength to be victorious over it.

Dear Lord, I want to be an overcomer. Help me to face any obstacle with an attitude of victory. Amen.

Do Good!

Trust in the Lord and do good; dwell in the land and enjoy safe pasture.
Psalm 37:3

God reminds us here that even while we are trusting him to take care of us, we should also be doing good. That's a simple idea that would change our lives if we did it day after day. It's not rocket science, it's simple. When someone pushes you out of line, do good and don't push back. When someone says something mean to you, respond in kindness. When you see someone who has a need that you can meet, do it. When you find a lost animal, help it. God is good to you, so show that goodness to others.

We have a great example to follow when trying to learn how to do good. Jesus went about doing good to everyone he met. He healed the sick; he raised the dead; he fed the hungry; he took care of his mother. He loved and cared for everyone. Read the Bible looking for ways Jesus helped others and then try to do the same things he did. God will help you.

Dear Lord, I want to do good. Right now, that means helping out where I can and not complaining about others. Amen.

All Things

And we know that in all things God works for the good of those who love him, who have been called according to his purpose.
Romans 8:28

A-L-L. It's just three-letter word, but what it stands for is enormous. Think about what "all" really includes? How about "all the people in the U.S.A." or "all the world?" We understand what part of the universe might be like, but our minds can't take in all the universe. We know about some places in the world, and if we don't, we can do research online. When the Bible says, "In all things God works for the good of those who love him," it's a little mind boggling. We really don't understand how God could work good in all things.

Think about some of the hard things that have happened in your life. Do you believe that God can use those things for good in your life? Sometimes it's tough to believe that a challenging situation is going to work out for good when you are in the middle of it. But God says it will. Can you believe it? God loves you, and he can take the most awful circumstances and work them out for you.

Dear Lord, Help me trust you when things aren't going so well. Help me believe what the Bible says, that you work all things for the good of those who love you. Amen.

A Hard Lesson

And the Lord's servant must not quarrel; instead, he must be kind.
2 Timothy 2:24

Caleb and Samantha were brother and sister. Like many brothers
and sisters, they quarreled — a lot, especially when they were
riding in the car. They both had to sit in the back seat. As soon as
the doors were closed, they started. Samantha picked at her little
brother, teasing and taunting him. Caleb retaliated by poking,
pinching, or kicking her.

Does this sound familiar? Do you fight with your brother or sister?
When someone irritates you or invades your space, it's probably
easy to yell or do something mean to him or her. But God tells us
not to quarrel. He wants us to be kind and gentle to others, even
when they do not treat us the same way.

Did you know that kindness can quickly change a tense
conversation? "A gentle answer turns away wrath, but a harsh word
stirs up anger." (Proverbs 15:1) The next time you want to yell at
your sibling, try this advice from Proverbs. Respond with gentleness
or nice words. It might be hard, but watch how your feelings change
and calm the situation.

Dear Lord, I quarrel with my family members sometimes. Help me to
think first about being kind even when I get upset. Amen.

What's Your Gift?

For in him you have been enriched in every way—in all your speaking and in all your knowledge.

1 Corinthians 1:5

When we give our hearts to Christ, he makes every area of our lives richer—our actions, our words, our choices, our gifts. We are no longer the same. We now have his eternal perspective. For example, we each have a set of God-given gifts. Some of us will be great athletes. Some will be public speakers. Some will be musicians. Some have minds that work best in science and research. Some of us have great compassion for people who have needs. Without Christ, a person would use these gifts to become famous or be recognized. But as Christians, we can use our gifts for God's purposes instead of keeping them for our own glory.

Even if you don't know yet what gifts God has given you, you can be assured that he will make them richer and show you how to use them. Perhaps you find reading and learning easy. That's a gift. Perhaps you're good at sports or know what to do to help someone who is sad. Those are gifts. It's wonderful to know that you are using the gifts God gave you in the best way you can. You will be growing your gifts throughout your life.

Dear Lord, Help me to appreciate how you enrich each area of my life. Help me not to waste the gifts you have given me. Amen.

Ah, Peace!

Peace I leave with you; my peace I give you. I do not give to you as the world gives. Do not let your hearts be troubled and do not be afraid.
John 14:27

Two paintings hung side by side in an art gallery. Under each painting was the title Peace. The painting on the left showed a wide open prairie with flowers in bloom, a bright sun, and a pretty little stream running through the meadow. That looked very peaceful. The painting on the right was very different. It had a thundering waterfall. Over the waterfall hung a slender branch; on the branch a bird was sitting on a nest. The bird was at rest. It was at peace, even though the thundering water shook the branch. Which painting do you think demonstrated the experience of real peace?

God's peace is not about living without trouble or hard times. Peace is the deep assurance that comes when you know God is in control even when everything seems about to fall down. Only God can give us that kind of peace. When you have problems at school or if your family has money problems or if someone you love is sick — you can have God's peace too. Tell God about your concerns. Tell him you are frightened. Ask him to give you peace.

Dear Lord, Please give me your peace. Amen.

Strong or Weak?

But I have prayed for you ... that your faith may not fail.
Luke 22:32

Here's some exciting news. Jesus is praying for us — right now —
today! And the Bible says that when we are weak God is strong
(1 Corinthians 4:10). Jesus helps us when we are weak and makes
us strong in ways we may not even know. Back in Bible times,
a priest had to pray so the people's sins could be forgiven. Jesus
changed all that when he became the sacrifice for our sins. Then,
when he got to heaven, he sat down at God's right hand to act as
our priest.

He's there right now praying for our faith to stay strong, because
our faith is the connection to God's strength. Without faith, we are
disconnected from all God has for us.

Are you connected to God today? If not, turn to Jesus and ask
him to build your faith. He will.

Dear Lord, Make me strong where I am weak. Thank you for being at
God's right hand. Amen.

Names Have Meaning

The second son he named Ephraim and said, "It is because God has made me fruitful in the land of my suffering."
Genesis 41:52

Names have meaning and most parents spend a lot of time thinking about what to name their baby. Names such as Faith, Joy, or Jonathan, (which means gift of God) tell us what the parents were thinking about when they named their child.

Joseph, the ruler of Egypt, named his son Ephraim, which means, "God has made me fruitful." By the time Ephraim was born, Joseph had been through a lot of suffering. First, he was sold into slavery by his brothers, and then he spent years in an Egyptian prison. But everything changed when he successfully interpreted Pharaoh's dreams and Pharaoh made him a ruler in Egypt. All of a sudden, Joseph had everything anyone could ever want. He had riches and houses and a wife and then two sons. So it makes sense that he named his second son "fruitful" because Joseph's own life had been fruitful even though his early years were very hard.

When you are suffering, remember the name Ephraim. Difficulties, even though they are tough to go through, may be just the elements that God needs to bring forth fruitfulness in your life. Think about difficulties as though they are rain. Rain is needed for flowers to grow. If it never rains, flowers will not bloom and bring beauty to the world. Ask God to use your hardships to bring forth beauty in your life.

Dear God, Thank you for my life, even the difficult parts. Please use the challenges I face to create good and beautiful things down the road. Amen.

Where Do You Find Hope?

Find rest, O my soul, in God alone; my hope comes from him.
Psalm 62:5

Hope is expecting something you do not have or cannot see. When we hope for something, we believe in it even when we can't see how it will happen. What are you hoping for that you have not seen yet? Do you hope to have a great summer with your friends and family? Do you hope to have a good school year when you return in the fall? Do you hope you'll get a new bike for your birthday? Do you hope for peace in the world? All of those things are good to hope for, but there is hope beyond this life and this world.

Paul, an apostle said that Christ Jesus is our hope. When Jesus was born in Bethlehem, hope was born on earth. Jesus is our hope for a home in heaven. He is our hope for healing. He is our hope for protection.

When you tell Jesus about a hope you have for the future, such as becoming a doctor or a ballet dancer, he doesn't think your hopes are silly. He's going to guide you every day. And even if he has a different plan than what you hope for, he will continue to give you hope for his plans and purposes. Jesus loves you so much. He will be there when you need a friend. He will be there when you don't know which way to go or what to do. And he will be waiting for you in heaven when your life is over. Those hopes are greater than any other. What a great and awesome Savior Jesus is to us!

Dear Lord, My hope and trust are in you. Thank you for being an awesome God. Amen.

Hearing God

Then there came a voice from above the expanse over their heads as they stood with lowered wings.

Ezekiel 1:25

A prophet named Ezekiel had a vision from God that even Hollywood filmmakers would have a hard time thinking up. In his vision, Ezekiel saw some amazing creatures. Each creature had four faces, four wings, feet shaped like a calf's, and hands like a man's that were under the wings. These creatures glowed like coals of fire or torches. Lightning flashed around them. When these creatures were in motion, there was a lot of noise from their wings—noise like rushing water. But when they stopped moving and lowered their wings, it became quiet. When it was quiet, a voice from heaven spoke to Ezekiel and said, "Stand up on your feet and I will speak to you." It was the Lord.

When the creatures were making so much noise with their wings, God did not speak. It was only when they folded their wings and became quiet that God spoke. That's a lesson we all need to learn. In order for God to speak to us, we need to be quiet. We must be still—stop talking, stop moving, stop thinking, and listen for his voice. This might take some practice, but hearing from God is worth being quiet and listening.

Dear Lord, I would love to hear your voice telling me what you want me to do and showing me your ways. Teach me to be quiet and listen. Amen.

Getting Stronger

Therefore, strengthen your feeble arms and weak knees.
Hebrews 12:12–13

The only exercise a lot of kids get is their thumbs while they play video games and send text messages. That's great if you want strong thumbs, but what about the rest of your body? To have strong bodies, we have to move and use our muscles. We have to sweat. Our bodies were given to us by God, and each of us only gets one body. We have to take care of it. Just sitting watching TV or at a computer will not strengthen us. We have to get moving and use the muscles God gave us.

Just as we have to use our physical muscles to make our bodies strong, we have to use our spiritual muscles to make our souls strong. We do that by praying, serving others, reading the Bible and learning all we can about God. We also use our faith to believe in and act on what God says. Think about some examples from the Bible: The water of the Jordan River did not part for the people of God to cross on dry ground until the priests put their feet in the river. The walls of Jericho did not fall down until the people walked around it as God commanded. The people of God had to do more than just believe in their hearts. They had to get moving.

What does God want you to do today? He wants you to train yourself to know more about him from the Bible, church, and prayer. He wants you to learn to listen for his voice. He wants you to be ready when he says "Go!"

Dear Lord, Help me to take care of my body and use it how you intended. Help me to get moving with my spiritual life as well. Amen.

Ground Grains

Grain must be ground to make bread.
Isaiah 28:28

Destiny once got an illness that forced her to stay in bed for an entire summer. When Destiny's mom realized that her daughter would be in bed for a long time, she helped her go on the Internet and order free stuff like travel brochures and samples of products and magazines. Through that long summer Destiny got mail almost every day. When she recovered, Destiny remembered how much fun it was to receive mail and how it helped the time pass. So when a friend became sick, Destiny sent mail to her.

Sometimes when God wants to use us, he has to first change us in some way. Today's verse from Isaiah says that before grain can be used for bread, it must be changed from kernels into flour. The idea of grinding kernels teaches us that it is sometimes the hard things we go through that change us into the kind of person God wants so we can help others.

Sometimes an illness teaches us compassion and how to help others who are sick. God uses other hard situations in the same way so that we can offer compassion and kindness to others.

Dear Lord, I want to help others. Please remind me that a hard time may be just the change I need so I can show love and compassion to someone else. Amen.

Left or Right

Whether you turn to the right or to the left, your ears will hear a voice behind you, saying, "This is the way; walk in it."
Isaiah 30:21

Suppose you are blind and you want to go to the grocery store. You can't see anything. A friend says she will go with you to help you find your way. She walks behind you and says, "Go right. Step down one step. Walk straight ahead. Okay, we are at the grocery store. The door is just in front of you." You could get to the grocery store just fine if you trusted the person guiding you.

Today's scripture talks about the way God guides us. It is much like being blind and a voice behind us telling us which way to go. We don't always have to see where we are going as long as we know God is there.

Learning to recognize and trust God's voice may take some time, but it will happen by becoming familiar with the Word of God and who he is. The more you know him, the more you will recognize his voice. Many other voices (your own ideas, the devil, friends who don't know God) will try to pull you away from God's voice. But God is always faithful to guide you. So get to know God, know when he is speaking to you, and learn to be obedient to his voice.

Dear Lord, Guide me every day of my life. I want to know your voice. I know you are leading me here on earth and to a heavenly home. Amen.

Helping a Friend

A few days later, when Jesus again entered Capernaum, the people heard that he had come home. So many gathered that there was no room left, not even outside the door, and he preached the word to them. Some men came, bringing to him a paralytic, carried by four of them.
Mark 2:1–3

One day Jesus went home to Capernaum, a town on the shores of the Sea of Galilee. Soon the people of the town began to gather in front of his door, and a huge crowd formed. Some men arrived carrying a friend on a mat. They wanted Jesus to heal him, but they weren't going to be able to get anywhere near the door of the house because there were so many people. They didn't want to lose the opportunity for their friend to be healed, so they climbed up on the housetop and began tearing away the tiles of the roof. Soon they had a pretty big hole, and they lowered their friend right into the center of the house.

Can you imagine if the man's friends had become discouraged by the size of the crowd? What if they gave up trying to get their friend to Jesus for healing? Sometimes God allows us to face challenges to test our faith and to use us to teach others. The good thing is that the man's friends didn't give up. When Jesus saw him being lowered through the roof, he looked up at the four friends and saw they had much faith. Jesus healed the man and taught the crowd about real faith by the friends' example. The man got off the mat, walked about the door of the house, and went home.

Dear Lord, Help me remember this story and that a challenge doesn't mean I have to give up. Give me the faith to face any obstacle. Amen.

Love Never Fails

Love covers over all wrongs.
Proverbs 10:12

Most things in the world fail eventually. Bridges break and fall down. Buildings wear out and have to be torn down. Cars stop running after a while. Books, toys, and games fall apart. Our clothes have to be replaced; so does our furniture.

The one thing that never fails is the love of God. It doesn't wear out, get lost, or break down. God loves us no matter what! You can never be so sinful that God stops loving you. You can never ignore him so long that he forgets about you. He loves you. He gave his Son so that one day you could be with him in heaven.

Let's see what the Bible says about love:

Love is patient, love is kind. It does not envy, it does not boast, it is not proud. It is not rude, it is not self-seeking, it is not easily angered, it keeps no record of wrongs. Love does not delight in evil but rejoices with the truth. It always protects, always trusts, always hopes, always perseveres. Love never fails. And now these three remain: faith, hope and love. But the greatest of these is love.

1 Corinthians 13:4–8, 13

God wants us to learn to love his way too. When we love others — even if they are mean to us, hurt us, or do something wrong — we show the strength of God's love. And it is powerful enough to change someone's life.

Dear Lord, Thank you that we can depend on your love. I want to do what is right because you love me. Will you help me to love others so they can know you too? Amen.

Walking on Water

"Come," he said. Then Peter got down out of the boat, walked on the water and came toward Jesus. But when he saw the wind, he was afraid and, beginning to sink, cried out, "Lord, save me!"
Matthew 14:29–30

Poor old Peter. At first he believed and climbed out of the boat and walked on the water. You have to admire him for his courage. Then he started looking around and probably thought, *What am I doing? This is water. No one can walk on water! Yikes!* Down he went. He was about to drown when Jesus rescued him. Can you imagine the two of them strolling on the water back to the boat and climbing in? What do you think the rest of the disciples said? Or were they speechless?

Don't try walking on water at home! It isn't possible. It can't be done—unless you are the Son of God. He is the ruler over all the elements such as wind, water, storms, and hail. He is the ruler over everything.

Though Jesus probably won't ask you to walk on water, he will ask you to do other things. When he asks for something hard, keep your focus on him. Don't worry about whether the task is tough or others think you'll fail. Jesus will be right there. He'll help you do it. Set your mind and heart on him alone.

Dear Lord, I don't need to walk on water, but I need you in my life so I can do what you ask of me. Amen.

Questioning God

This is what the Lord says — the Holy One of Israel, and its Maker:
Concerning things to come, do you question me about my children, or give
me orders about the work of my hands?
Isaiah 45:11

Did you know it's okay to ask God questions? King David did it
many times. In fact, he even gave God a command. He said,
"Answer me when I call to you, O my righteous God." He demanded
that God answer him (Psalm 4:1). In another Psalm he said, "Why,
O Lord, do you stand far off? Why do you hide yourself in times
of trouble? (Psalm 10:1). It's all right to talk to God like that. He
doesn't want us to be scared or tentative. He wants us to pray in
ways that urge him, based on who he is. For example, God has told
us that he will save us if we ask. So we can pray, "God save my
[uncle, brother, mom, or anyone.]" He is delighted when we talk to
him that way.

You see, God is our Father in heaven. Just as our earthly fathers
love us and want to answer our questions so that we can learn and
grow, God wants to do the same. He is not threatened when we
doubt. He does not get angry when we ask again and again why
something is the way it is. He does not get upset if we pray boldly.

If you have questions about why God allows some things to
happen, talk to him about it. If you need God's help with a problem,
tell him. If you see a situation that needs supernatural intervention,
urge God to step in and take over.

Dear Lord, Sometimes I'm not sure how to pray or I've been a little
afraid to really talk to you about my questions. From now on, I'm going
to let it all out. I know only you have answers to many of life's
problems. Amen.

Move On

Then the Lord said to Moses, "Why are you crying out to me?
Tell the Israelites to move on."
Exodus 14:15

Moses and the people of God stood on the shore of the Red Sea.
They had been waiting 400 years for this moment, the moment
when they would finally leave Egypt and slavery behind forever, but
it looked as if all their hopes had been for nothing. There was water
ahead, and Pharaoh and his armies behind. It looked like there was
no place to go, but God said, "Move on." So Moses raised his staff
and God parted the waters, giving the Israelites a way to escape
from the soldiers and into the land he had promised them.

Maybe you feel as if there is no place for you to go, but God is
telling you to move on, just like he told the Israelites. When you run
into a problem as big to you as the Red Sea was to Israel, be assured
that God will help you, just as he helped his children thousands of
years ago.

Dear Lord, I want to remember that you will be with me through every
trial. Help me to move on when you tell me. Amen.

God Won't Fail

What if some did not have faith? Will their lack of faith
nullify God's faithfulness?
Romans 3:3

As you continue to grow up to be an adult, you will learn that there are people who do not believe in God at all. These people can be very loud in speaking about what they believe and do not believe. Sometimes these people are teachers. Sometimes they are politicians. Other times they are actors. Just because these people don't believe doesn't change who God is and what he can do. But these people would have a very hard time seeing God even if he were standing right in front of them on the street.

Faith opens your eyes to see God. It also connects you to his power. When you pray without faith, it's like you're blind to what God can do. Without it, your requests are like empty words to God. Sure, he can answer your prayers. But he knows that if you don't have faith, you'll have a hard time recognizing his answer. With faith, you will see God's power in each of his answers. Then your faith will grow even more.

Grow strong now, and get to know God very well. Believe that he is faithful.

Dear Lord, Make my belief and faith strong, so I can receive your answers. I don't want to be blind to what you're doing. Amen.

Bring on the Power

Summon your power, O God; show us your strength, O God, as you have done before.
Psalm 68:28

How many sources of power can you name? Let's see ... gas, coal, wind, solar, dynamite ... Wow! There are a lot and probably many we don't even know. But the greatest source of power in the universe is the awesome power of God. God has the power to do anything and everything.

Here are a few examples: God stopped the sun in its tracks so Joshua could win a battle in the daylight. God cleared a path in the Red Sea and the Jordan River so his people could cross on dry ground. God used a tiny army under Gideon's leadership to defeat a power enemy that vastly outnumbered Gideon's troops. God sent thunderclaps from heaven to scare away an enemy. God helped a shepherd boy knock down and kill a giant. And God, by the power of his Holy Spirit, sent his own Son to be our Savior.

His power goes on and on, even today when you need it. Those examples from the Bible probably help you see how God can take care of you with no problem. Suppose kids at school are picking on you. God's power can help you stay strong and not be hurt by what they are saying. Suppose your family doesn't have much money. God's power can miraculously provide you with food and clothes. God is alive and powerful.

Dear Lord, I really don't understand the greatness of your power, but I'm glad it is there for me when I need help. You truly are an awesome God. Amen.

The Open Door

After this I looked, and there before me was a door standing open in heaven.

Revelation 4:1

An open door means, "Come on in." When you come running home from school and find the door open (and maybe even the smell of warm cookies), you know that you are welcomed home. On the other hand, if a door to a building or room is bolted and chained, you know no one wants you inside. Have you ever gone to an amusement park or restaurant and arrived to find the door chained because the place has gone out of business? What a disappointment that is.

The door to heaven will never be closed to those who have chosen to Jesus as their savior. An angel said, "See, I have placed before you an open door that no one can shut" (Revelation 3:8). Jesus said, "Here I am! I stand at the door and knock. If anyone hears my voice and opens the door, I will come in and eat with him, and he with me (Revelation 3:20).

Won't it be wonderful when it is time to go to heaven to find the door open? Jesus will be there to meet us, and we will be with him forever. Maybe your family has had to move around a lot and you don't feel like any place is home. When you get to heaven, you will be and feel at home. You will never have to leave.

Dear Lord, Heaven must be a wonderful place. While I want to live my full life here on earth, I'm really glad to know that the door to heaven is open and you will be there to welcome me home some day. Amen.

Mighty Bugs

We saw the Nephilim there (the descendants of Anak come from the Nephilim). We seemed like grasshoppers in our own eyes, and we looked the same to them.
Numbers 13:33

There were people who lived on earth in the early days of Bible history who were giants. They were also great warriors. When Moses sent spies to see what the Promised Land was like, they came back telling stories of these giants. The spies said they felt like small bugs compared to those giants. Ten of the spies were terrified of the giants and loudly told their fearful story to the people. But two of the spies, Joshua and Caleb, were not afraid. They knew that "bugs" with God on their side would become mighty bugs.

The people were very upset by the report of the ten spies. They began to think that Moses had brought them into the desert to die. Joshua was upset too, but for a different reason. He said, "The land ... is exceedingly good ... the Lord will lead us into that land ... and will give it to us ... do not be afraid of the people of the land because we will swallow them up" (Numbers 13:6–9). Caleb agreed and said, "We should go up and take possession of the land, for we can certainly do it." You see, a small weak person plus God equals victory. It doesn't matter how big the problems are.

We all face big things that seem overwhelming. Perhaps you struggle with math or reading or have a physical problem that slows you down. These problems are like giants, but God can help you overcome your giants and achieve great things in spite of them.

Dear Lord, Help me believe that no matter how small or weak I feel, if I join with you, we can overcome anything. Amen.

Clear Out the Noise

A form stood before my eyes, and I heard a hushed voice.
Job 4:16

God often speaks quietly. To hear him, like Job did, we have to become still enough. Here's an experiment. Get down on your knees to pray. Try to think of nothing but what you want to say to God and to hear from him. You will probably find that no sooner do you kneel down and try to think about God than a ton of thoughts come into your head. Did you know that your mind is often a busy, noisy place? It is difficult to quiet our minds so that we can hear what God wants to say to us.

To help slow and clear your mind, write down all your thoughts that come to mind as you pray. Take them out of your head, and put them on paper to deal with later. The first few times you do this you will spend more time writing down thoughts than praying. But this exercise will train your mind to focus on God.

Here are some other ideas to help you quiet your mind:

- *Read one or two verses, and recite them a few times.*
- *Tell God everything on your mind, then sit in silence.*
- *Practice sitting completely still for a few minutes each day.*
- *The main thing is to get quiet enough so God can talk to you.*

Dear Lord, I want to learn how to listen for your voice. Teach me how to do that. Amen.

Believe It, It's True

Blessed is she who has believed ... what the Lord has said.
Luke 1:45

The Bible is full of the promises of God. Here are just a few of them:

- *"Never will I leave you; never will I forsake you."*
  Deuteronomy 31:6

- *"The Lord replied, 'My Presence will go with you, and I will give you rest.'"*
  Exodus 33:14

- *"Before they call I will answer; while they are still speaking I will hear."*
  Isaiah 65:24

- *"Call to me and I will answer you and tell you great and unsearchable things you do not know."*
  Jeremiah 33:3

- *"If you remain in me and my words remain in you, ask whatever you wish, and it will be given you."*
  John 15:7

God's promises. They are for you. They are for today. The only way we can know a promise of God is true is to try it out. So if you believe that God will always be with you no matter where you go, you will have the courage to do difficult things in your life. God has promised. We believe. What happens next is up to God. He keeps his word. You can count on it.

Dear Lord, Thank you for your promises to me. Help me to believe. Amen.

You Won't Fall Down

When you walk, your steps will not be hampered; when you run, you will not stumble.

Proverbs 4:12

In places like Minnesota and Montana where there is a lot of snow in the winter, it gets very muddy when the ground begins to thaw in the spring. In fact, there are places where it gets so muddy you can't walk because the mud sucks shoes or boots right down into it. Wouldn't it be something to try to run a race on a track that was that soft and muddy? You would stumble and fall down. It would not be possible to walk, much less to run. Your feet would be "hampered" as the verse today says.

Do you ever feel like you're being hampered by a problem? Like mud is stuck to your boots? God knows you will face difficulties that could drag you down. But if you have faith in him, he'll help you trudge through. When he comes alongside you, it's like he builds a bridge over the muck. You still have to cross it, but God is there to help you.

Dear Lord, Please help me to put my faith in you when I face "muddy" situations. I know you are there to help me through. Amen.

Everything at the Right Time

When a farmer plows for planting, does he plow continually? Does he keep on breaking up and harrowing the soil?
Isaiah 28:24

In the valleys of California, farmers grow one crop after another on the same piece of land. It is interesting to see the process. First, the rich black soil is plowed, often leaving big clods of dirt. Second, a harrow passes over the field breaking up the clods and smoothing the field for planting. Nutrients are then added to the soil, which is important because the continual use of the soil depletes the nutrients. Workers put in the sprinkler systems that will water the crops. Next, small plants that have been started in greenhouses are planted outside in rows at precise distances from each other. Then the farmer steps back and lets God do his part to make the crop grow.

In a couple of months, the crop is ready for harvest. Workers descend on the field to harvest the crop and pack it into boxes. The boxes are put on trucks and hauled to a warehouse for distribution all over the country. It takes less than a week to harvest one field. Within two or three days after the harvest is complete, the farmers are back out in the field plowing and the whole process starts over.

Just like the right timing is important for every step in farming, there is a right time for everything in our lives. There is a time to learn a time to grow, a time to do. Moses, Jesus, and the apostle Paul all spent years learning, waiting, and getting ready for certain tasks God wanted them to do. Just as there is a time when fruits and vegetables are perfect for harvest, there will be a time for God to pick you to do something for him. When the time is right, God will lead you to the next step. For now, be content in the place where God has you. Focus on your purpose now, whether it is learning, waiting, or growing.

Dear Lord, Sometimes I wonder what I should do with my life. Will you put my mind at rest and help me trust your timing? Amen.

The Waiting Game

*For the revelation awaits an appointed time ... Though it linger, wait for it;
it will certainly come and will not delay.*
Habakkuk 2:3

Has there ever been a birthday when you knew you would be
receiving an exciting gift? Was it hard to wait for your actual birthday
to get the gift? Has there ever been a movie you really wanted to
see but your parents told you you'd have to wait to see it on DVD?
Waiting doesn't change the fact that you will get the gift or see the
movie, right?

Prayer can be the same way. We ask God for a change, a gift, an
answer, but he tells us to wait. Or he may not tell us anything for
a while. God knows just the right time to respond to each prayer. If
you have to wait, it doesn't mean he's not answering you but that
he's waiting for an appointed time.

Dear Lord, I know you care about me and hear my prayers. Help me to
be patient for your answers. Amen.

A Door of Hope

I will lead her into the desert and speak tenderly to her.... and will make the Valley of Achor a door of hope.
Hosea 2:14–15

If you learn only one thing from reading this book, this is it: No matter how desperate your situation might be, there is always a door of hope that God will open for you. Perhaps your parents are divorced and there is no hope of them getting back together. God sees that and he wants you to hope in him for your future. He will help you get through it. Or maybe someone you love is terribly sick. There is hope. Miracles, both medical and supernatural, do happen. Pray, hope, and wait for God to work.

People can survive almost anything if they have hope. People who have been prisoners of war often have very little but hope that some day they will be rescued. People put their hope in many things: friends, money, good grades, etc. The ultimate hope is knowing that God is there for us no matter what happens. Hang onto that hope. God sees and cares, and he is the one who can finally open the door for you.

Dear Lord, Whenever I face something tough, please remind me that I must put my hope in you, not in the things around me. Amen.

The Battle Is Not Yours

O our God, will you not judge them? For we have no power to face this vast army that is attacking us. We do not know what to do, but our eyes are upon you.
2 Chronicles 20:12

King Jehoshaphat had a big problem. An army was marching upon his nation. He called all the people together to pray. Jehoshaphat was scared, but he believed God would help them. He prayed, "We do not know what to do, but our eyes are upon you."

Then God answered through a man who was also there to pray. He said, "This is what the Lord says to you: 'Do not be afraid or discouraged . . . for the battle is not yours, but God's.'" He gave the king specific instructions that God wanted the people to know, then he said, "Go out to face them tomorrow, and the Lord will be with you."

Every time we need help from God, he will be there to answer us. When we pray, what God most wants is for us to let him fight our battles. He can do so much more than we can.

Dear Lord, What a great thing to know you are fighting our battles. Help me remember that no battle is mine to face alone, but yours to win. Amen.

A Polished Arrow

He made me into a polished arrow and concealed me in his quiver.
Isaiah 49:2

Hundreds of years ago, Native Americans used bows and arrows for hunting. They couldn't run down to the arrow store and buy arrows, so they had to make their own. They made the arrowheads by taking a piece of flint (a hard stone) and chipping away at it to form a sharp triangle. Then the arrowheads were polished and attached to a rod to make an arrow. The finished arrows were put into the hunter's quiver, or case, for the next hunt. Hunting for the Native Americans was much more than sport; the animals they caught fed and clothed their families.

Do you think they could have just attached a piece of raw flint to the shaft without the chipping and polishing? Would it have been a good weapon? The chipping and polishing turned a plain stone into an effective tool for hunting.

Do you ever feel as if everything is against you, or that your problems are chipping away at you? Perhaps God is using the hard things in your life to shape you into a tool he can use. The tough things we go through teach us about life, about what others are going through, and make us ready to serve God. Without his polishing, our lives will not be sharp enough for God to use.

Dear Lord, I don't really like for you to put me through tough times, but I understand that you are preparing me to serve you. So I accept what you are doing in my life. Amen.

Soaring on Eagle's Wings

Those who hope in the Lord will renew their strength. They will soar on wings like eagles; they will run and not grow weary, they will walk and not be faint.

Isaiah 40:31

Eagles are amazing birds with a wingspan of five to seven feet. Those wings carry them high where they catch thermal currents rising from the earth. They can stop flapping their wings and ride the currents, sailing effortlessly to wherever they want to go. They soar above the landscape looking for prey. When they spot something they want to eat, they drop silently out of the sky and grab the unsuspecting animal. They are amazing birds who do not worry about their next meal or where to fly. They just ride the currents and wait for the opportunity for food.

Today's Bible verse is a promise from God that will last you all your life. When you are discouraged or tired, if you hope in the Lord you will find new strength. You will rise above the problems like eagles soaring on the thermal currents. If you feel like giving up, ask for God's help.

Dear Lord, Thank you for the promise that if we hope in you, our strength will be made new like that of the soaring eagle. Please give me your strength. Amen.

This Is a Test

*See, I have refined you, though not as silver; I have tested you in the
furnace of affliction.*
Isaiah 48:10

Not too long ago, many toys made in China were recalled. Tests
discovered that there was lead in the paint, which can be very
dangerous to kids. What went wrong? Somebody didn't originally
test to make sure the toys were safe. Or if they did test, they didn't
test carefully enough. Testing is important for many things. Scientists
with a new idea have to test and test and test it to make certain
their results are accurate. Cooks have to test recipes to make sure
food tastes good.

We get tested too—by God. Testing by God doesn't mean we sit
down at a desk with a piece of paper and a pencil to take a test. It
means we are given choices that might be hard to make. If you are
told to do something that you don't want to do but it is the right
thing to do, that is a test. The same thing is true when you are told
not to do something and you have to keep yourself from doing it.
When we make the right choice, we pass the test. When we make
the wrong choice, we often have to go through the test again

Because we are human and still learning and growing, we will
go through some tests from God more than once. That's okay. God's
tests show whether we are ready for his next assignment.

Dear Lord, I don't like being tested, but I can see that it is important.
So go ahead and test me. I want to grow up to be a person who has
learned to make good choices. Amen.

Never Too Late

I called him but he did not answer.
Song of Solomon 5:6

Someone said that God is never too late when we pray to him, but he sure can scare us to death. It does seem that sometimes when we ask God for something, it's as if he hasn't heard us and we will never get our answer. Never fear, God heard and he has planned a time when he will answer. We just can't see it.

Suppose you asked God to give you a new bike. You prayed and prayed, but no bike landed on your porch. Instead, the neighbor called and asked you to rake her leaves for pay, and another neighbor asked you to walk her dog, and another asked you to help clean the garage. Before long, you have enough money to buy a bike. Did God give you the bike or not? Well, he didn't park a new bike on your porch, but he certainly provided the jobs so you could buy the bike yourself. In the process, you would learn so much about working and trusting him. He answered your prayer, but not in the way you thought he would. He had a better idea — one that taught you while he was giving you the answer. God answers our prayers, just not always the way we expect.

Dear Lord, Help me to trust that when I pray to you, you go to work to answer my prayer in the way that is best for me. Amen.

Just Waiting

Some time later the brook dried up because there had been no rain in the land.
1 Kings 17:7

Have you ever felt yourself in a panic situation? Most of us have.
That's what Elijah felt when he was beside the brook — his only
source of water — and it began to dry up. He didn't know what
to do. If he'd run around looking for water, he'd have wasted his
energy and become thirsty. He couldn't run somewhere else because
all the brooks were drying up. There wasn't any place to go. Then
Elijah heard God's voice, "Get up and go to Zarephath." It was God,
and God had a plan to take care of Elijah.

Elijah's story is a good reminder of stay focused on God rather
than on bad circumstances. The troubles around you often lead to
panic. Panic often leads to frantically trying to fix a problem beyond
your control. Panic won't solve anything. Talking to God about the
situation, listening for the ideas he gives you, and acting when he
says is the best course of action.

Dear Lord, When I see a big problem ahead of me — one I can't get
out of — I don't want to panic. Help me to talk with you, listen for your
voice, and do what you tell me to do. Amen.

Shining Like Gold

But he knows the way that I take; when he has tested me,
I will come forth as gold.
Job 23:10

That beautiful, shiny stuff we call gold doesn't start out all that beautiful. Most gold comes from deep in the earth, and the gold itself is embedded in solid rock. In order to get the gold out of the rock, refiners use a variety of methods. One method used is called cupellation. In this process, heat is used to separate the gold from other elements. After the mixture has been melted and cooled, the pure gold remains at the bottom of the heating vessel. The value of gold is determined by its karat weight. The higher the karat weight, the more valuable the gold and the softer it is. Twenty-four karat gold, the most precious, can be bent with your fingers.

In today's Scripture, Job expresses his faith in God's testing and refining process. He knows that if he yields to God's process, he will come out like pure gold. This same principle is true for us. When we go through hard times that test our character, God can use those times to change us from the inside out. God wants us to be like twenty-four-karat gold, the softest gold of the highest quality, so he can form us with only the slightest pressure from his hands.

If you feel that troubles and problems are coming at you from every side, be patient. Ask God to show you how he will use those situations to soften you for his plans. God is at work making you into a 24-karat Christian who shines for him.

Dear Lord, Refine my life so that I can be useful and shine for you. Amen.

What Is Not, Is

God ... gives life to the dead and calls things that are not as though they were.
Romans 4:17

What is not, is. What does that mean? It means that no matter how impossible something may seem, no matter how big the promise God has given, he has the power to make it happen. God promised Abraham and Sarah a son when they were too old to have children. Their age didn't matter to God. He gave them a baby anyway. When Jesus promised he would be raised from the dead in three days, it didn't seem possible. But God doesn't know impossible. So on the third day, Jesus rose just as he had promised. The Bible is full of God's promises. Some of those promises are that he will take care of us, lead us, guide us, and provide our needs. It doesn't make any difference to him how impossible things look. He can take care of it just fine.

What do you think God has promised you? Have you prayed and asked God to make your faith strong? God can keep any promise, and he wants to do much more than we can even imagine. What do you want from God? Is it something God has promised? Is it in line with what the Bible teaches? If so, go ahead and ask and believe.

Dear Lord, I believe in your promises. I will believe even when things look impossible. Nothing is too hard for you. Amen.

It's a Celebration!

The Lord is God, and he has made his light shine upon us. With boughs in hand, join in the festal procession up to the horns of the altar.
Psalm 118:27

Do you like celebrations? Who doesn't? We love celebrations that have fireworks and ice cream and cake and presents and all kinds of wonderful things.

Did you know God planned celebrations into the life of the people of Israel? Every 50 years there was a year of jubilee. At that time, nothing was planted and the land rested. Debts were forgiven, and people got to start over. It was a wonderful time of great joy. Other celebrations marked victories and times to remember what God had done for them in past years. With many of these parties, the people took time to renew their commitment to God. They would vow to continue to serve him.

If you've had a victory in your life, celebrate. If you've overcome some difficult things like an illness or a hard test or a broken bone, celebrate. Celebrate when you pass your grade. Celebrate when you see an answer to prayer. Every time you celebrate, remember how God is part of each of those moments in your life. Thank him and recommit your heart to him.

Dear Lord, I'm so glad you include celebration as part of your plan for our lives. Amen.

Faith Equals Victory

Everyone born of God overcomes the world. This is the victory that has overcome the world, even our faith.
1 John 5:4

Sometimes it's easy to trust God. That's when life is going smoothly, we're getting good grades, our friends are being nice to us, our parents are happy, and we're looking forward to things staying easy. At times like that, it isn't hard to see that God loves us and wants only the best for us. He loves us so he's made life easy for us, right?

It gets a little more difficult to understand God's love when times are tough and everything seems to be going wrong. Our teachers have expectations we can't meet, our friends are spreading rumors about us, our parents are fighting about bills, and we can't see when all of this trouble will come to an end. It's hard to believe that God is still watching out for you in those situations.

That's when reading the Bible to remember how God has always cared for his people is a good thing to do. It is God's plan that we overcome — defeat — any trouble that comes our way, and soon the times will be good again.

Dear Lord, I know that you and I together can beat any tough thing that comes my way. Amen.

Big Sacrifices

"I swear by myself," declares the Lord, "that because you have done this and have not withheld your son, your only son, I will surely bless you and make your descendants as numerous as the stars in the sky and as the sand on the seashore. Your descendants will take possession of the cities of their enemies, and through your offspring all nations on earth will be blessed, because you have obeyed me."
Genesis 22:16–18

When Abraham became willing to obey God and offer his only son—the son who was a promise from God in the first place—he might have doubted God. But Abraham went right ahead and believed that God knew what he was doing. Abraham obeyed and prepared to sacrifice his son. Because he did that, God said, "Through your offspring, all nations on earth will be blessed because you have obeyed me." God saved Abraham's son and brought amazing blessings to both of them.

So what does that have to do with you? There will be times when God asks you to sacrifice something very dear to you. When you obey him, God has greater things in store. When you sacrifice, he will bless you. His blessing may be like Abraham's—when he asks you to give up something you love but then gives back even more to you. God doesn't typically tell us what our blessing will be, but it is always good.

Dear Lord, I want to be ready to sacrifice anything for you even when you ask me to give up something I love. Serving you is better than keeping anything I own. Amen.

From a Distance

This is what the Lord says to me: "I will remain quiet and will look on from my dwelling place, like shimmering heat in the sunshine, like a cloud of dew in the heat of harvest."
Isaiah 18:4

A few years ago there was a song that talked about what you can see "from a distance." When you are flying in an airplane, you get an entirely different view of the earth. If you are at the top of a tall building, you see things you can't see from the street. Astronauts who've flown around Earth tell us how beautiful and how fragile our planet is and how it moves around the sun at exactly the right distance.

Have you ever thought about what God's perspective must be like? Today's Bible verse says that God is watching. He may appear to be quiet, but he is watching from his home in heaven and he has a bigger perspective on our circumstances than we do. God promises that he is watching over us in love. Nothing ever happens to us that God does not see. He knows about absolutely everything, even things that haven't happened yet. What a wonderful and amazing and awesome God! And he cares for you.

Dear Lord, Thank you for never taking your eyes off me. Amen.

The Eyes of God

For the eyes of the Lord range throughout the earth to strengthen those whose hearts are fully committed to him.
2 Chronicles 16:9

Today's Scripture says that God looks throughout the earth to make strong all those who are his people. What does it mean that he will strengthen you? It means that he gives his Holy Spirit to help you live for him and make good choices. Once you've committed your life to him, he will never leave you on your own. He will make you strong for whatever comes in your life.

The Bible also says that he we are "as the apple of his eye" (see Deuteronomy 32:10). The apple means the pupil of the eye. The Bible also says that anyone who touches God's people touches the apple of his eye (see Zechariah 2:8). The pupil is a very sensitive place. What the Scripture means is that we are very precious to God, and he will protect us. He looks out for those who are loyal and committed to him.

Dear Lord, I am very thankful that you are watching over me. Help me to give myself completely to you every day. Amen.

Radical for Jesus

*Jesus commanded Peter, "Put your sword away! Shall I not drink the cup
the Father has given me?"*
John 18:11

Peter was a radical disciple. He was the one who jumped out of the
boat to walk on water. He was the one who pulled out his sword
and whacked off the ear of the servant who was trying to take Jesus
into captivity in the Garden of Gethsemane. It was all right to be a
radical for Jesus, except Peter didn't have the big picture of what
God wanted to do. Peter wanted to save Jesus from death, but Jesus
knew he had to die to save people from their sins. Jesus had to
suffer; it was part of God's bigger plan.

Suffering is not fun. Our first response — just like Peter — is to try
to stop a tough situation. We don't want to suffer or hurt. But God
can use suffering to help others and grow our faith.

There have been many radicals for Jesus. There are missionaries
who have gone to remote places where they faced illness or
persecution. But they were able to teach people about Jesus. They
are radicals like Peter. But they understood that sometimes being
radical means going through tough times. Maybe God wants you
to be a radical for him too. Who knows, maybe someday we will be
reading about all the great, radical things you did for God in
this life.

Dear Lord, I'd like to be a radical Christian for you, but I don't want to
be afraid of suffering. Will you teach me what to do? Amen.

Someone Who Cares

Therefore, since we have a great high priest who has gone through the heavens, Jesus the Son of God, let us hold firmly to the faith we profess. Let us then approach the throne of grace with confidence, so that we may receive mercy and find grace to help us in our time of need.
Hebrews 4:14, 16

We have a friend in heaven who is there to help us. His name is Jesus. Jesus acts as our high priest. In the Old Testament, people could not go directly to God and ask forgiveness for their sins. The high priest did that for them. Once a year the high priest went behind the heavy veil of the tabernacle or temple into the Holy of Holies — a place where God's presence lived. This was serious business. God's power was nothing to take for granted or to mess with. Behind the curtain, the priest offered a sacrifice for the people's sins.

That's the way it was until Jesus became the perfect sacrifice when he died on the cross. People would no longer need the help of an earthly high priest. Now they could go directly to Jesus. He is our personal advocate. He talks to God on our behalf. So whenever you pray, Jesus goes right to God with your request. Isn't that great?

Dear Lord, Thank you for becoming our high priest who goes to God the Father for us. Amen.

Putting Out a Fleece

Then Gideon said to God, "Do not be angry with me. Let me make just one more request. Allow me one more test with the fleece. This time make the fleece dry and the ground covered with dew."
Judges 6:39

There's a wonderful story in the Old Testament about someone who was a lot like us. His name was Gideon, and he struggled to believe God's words. He was a farm boy who was minding his own business when an angel visited him. "The Lord is with you mighty warrior," the angel said. Gideon probably looked around to see who the angel was talking to because he didn't consider himself a "mighty warrior." The angel told Gideon to go defeat the Midianites, an enemy people who were ruining Israel. Gideon thought the angel had the wrong person. He asked the Lord to give him a sign. Gideon put out a sheep's fleece on the ground, and if in the morning the fleece was wet and the ground all around it was dry, he would accept it as God's sign.

When Gideon woke up the next day, the fleece was wet and the ground was dry—a miracle! But Gideon still wasn't sure. Next he asked God to do the opposite—make the fleece dry and the ground wet so he could be sure it was God speaking to him. God did that too.

Sometimes we are like Gideon; we don't have much faith. We want a special sign from God to help us believe. God doesn't get upset with us when we do this. He loves us, and he understands that sometimes we have a tough time believing. But as we grow in our faith we learn to trust God's words even without signs. Some day our faith may grow so strong that nothing will shake it. We will trust God with every aspect of our lives even when we can't see him working. We can ask him for whatever we need, and he will help us believe.

Dear Lord, I wish I could believe your word instantly, but sometimes I struggle. The story of Gideon helps me know that I can ask you for help in believing. Will you help my faith grow as I grow up? Amen.

A Good God

Yet the Lord longs to be gracious to you; he rises to show you compassion.
For the Lord is a God of justice. Blessed are all who wait for him!
Isaiah 30:18

There are lots of things are not ready until a certain time. For example, if you pick an apple too soon, it won't taste good. It will be sour and could give you a stomachache. But when you bite into an apple that is ripe, it is good and juicy and nutritious. If you eat raw bread dough, it isn't good either. Bread needs time to rise and bake before you can eat it. But freshly baked bread is a wonderful treat.

Today's Scripture says that God wants to be gracious to us. That means he wants to do good things for us. However, we have to wait until he is ready. God's timing for giving us things is perfect. If you are waiting for God to do something, he will when the time is right. The Bible says those who wait for him will be blessed.

What do you wish would happen right now? What are you praying about that seems as if it will never happen? Perhaps it is not the right time for your prayer to be answered. Perhaps you are not ready yet. Be patient, and keep praying and listening for God.

Dear Lord, I'm going to be patient for you to send good things to me. And I'm going to be content while waiting. Amen.

Thanks for Everything

Always giving thanks to God the Father for everything, in the name of our Lord Jesus Christ.
Ephesians 5:20

Have you ever seen someone play the piano or played one yourself? If so, you know that the keyboard is made up of short black keys and long white keys. Would it be possible to make music playing only the white keys or only the black keys on the keyboard? Yes, it's possible, but it would severely limit the kinds of music you could play. Now think about what kind of music you could make if you used all the keys and used them well. You could make beautiful music.

You can think about life as though it's a piano. The white keys represent the good stuff. The black keys represent the tough times. God uses both. He wants you to learn to appreciate each kind of key. Though it may sound strange to thank God for the black times, he will use them to make beautiful music in your life.

Dear Lord, I like the happy times in my life when everything is going my way. But I know I have to go through tough times too. Please help me to be thankful for everything in my life and how you will use it. Amen.

Believing Is Seeing

Then they believed his promises and sang his praise. But they soon forgot what he had done and did not wait for his counsel. In the desert they gave in to their craving; in the wasteland they put God to the test. So he gave them what they asked for, but sent a wasting disease upon them.
Psalm 106:12–15

The people of Israel were wandering around in the desert because they kept forgetting God. God kept them out there until they could believe in him long-term. These people were the biggest whiners ever. They whined when they didn't have food. Then God miraculously provided, but they still whined. Next, they whined for meat. When God gave it, they weren't happy with that either. Finally, God had enough.

Remember Thomas in the New Testament? He didn't complain like the Israelites, but he is sometimes called Doubting Thomas because he couldn't believe that Jesus had risen from the dead until he saw him. And truthfully, if we had been there, we might have needed to see Jesus in the flesh before we could believe too. Once he saw Jesus with his own eyes, though, he did believe.

God wants us to get to a place in our faith where no matter what we see or don't see, we will believe him and accept his answers. We can trust that God will take us safely through whatever is ahead of us.

Dear Lord, It is much easier to believe when we can see what will happen. But I know it doesn't always work that way. Please teach me to believe, even when I can't see. Amen.

What Are You Making?

Jesus replied, "You do not realize now what I am doing,
but later you will understand"
John 13:7

John and his sister Linda were spending summer vacation with
their grandparents on the farm. When they arrived, they saw that
their favorite climbing tree had been cut down. They used to climb
it every day in past summers, using the tree as a fort, a home base,
and a reading spot. John and Linda headed to the woodshed where
Grandpa was cutting up the tree. Inside the shed was a big mess.
Sawdust, piles of boards, and tools were everywhere.

"What are you doing, Grandpa?" John asked.

"Why did you cut down our favorite tree?" Linda chimed in.

"You'll see," Grandpa told them.

The children went back to the house still sad. A few days later,
they were curious when Grandpa hauled all those boards out to a
different tree. He got a ladder and soon he was hammering away.
Then they knew. Grandpa was building a tree house. They kids were
so excited they could hardly wait for him to finish. The treehouse
was ten times better than their climbing tree.

Sometimes God does things like this. He changes something in
your life, and it doesn't make sense at first. Don't get upset right
away. If you are patient, soon you'll know what he is up to, and it
will be something good.

Dear Lord, When changes don't make sense, will you show me what
you are doing in my life? Amen.

Hurry Up and Wait

*But by faith we eagerly await through the Spirit the righteousness
for which we hope.*

Galatians 5:5

Probably more than anyone else, kids understand the phrase,
"Hurry up and wait."

"Hurry up and get ready for school." "Wait until I'm ready to leave."

"Hurry up and get ready for the soccer game." "Sit on the bench,
and wait for the coach to put you in."

"You'll have to wait until tomorrow to get your allowance."

On and on it goes. Wait for Dad to finish his phone call before
he can play ball. Wait for Mom to get her shopping list ready before
you go to the mall.

You get the picture because you've had lots of practice in waiting.
So when the Bible says we are to eagerly wait, you can understand
the idea. Patience will get you what you need in the end. You know
God is good and loves you, so you can believe that he will give you
what you need even if you have to wait for it.

Dear Lord, Teach me patience as I wait for many things in my life.
Amen.

Give and Take

"Bring the whole tithe into the storehouse, that there may be food in my house. Test me in this," says the Lord Almighty, "and see if I will not throw open the floodgates of heaven and pour out so much blessing that you will not have room enough for it."
Malachi 3:10

A tithe is a tenth, so a tithe of our earnings is one-tenth of what we get. If you get a dollar, one-tenth of it — a dime — belongs to God. That's pretty easy, but if you earn $100,000, the tithe is $10,000. That seems like a lot of money to give up. Many people have never learned to give a tenth of their money. However, if you train yourself when you only have a dollar, it will be much easier for you when you have thousands of dollars.

In the verse above, God asks for a tenth, but he also reminds us that he can give us more than we could ever think to ask of him. He has thousands of ways to meet your needs. You can't out-give God. He has more resources than you can imagine.

Dear Lord, I'm going to begin giving a tenth of all the money I receive. I will trust you to provide everything I need and more. Amen.

In a Whirlwind

His way is in the whirlwind and the storm, and clouds are the dust of his feet.
Nahum 1:3

A young boy sat on a hillside and watched as below him a storm swept across the valley. The heavens turned black. Lightning flashed and thunder rolled. It seemed like the pretty little valley was suddenly a different place. Its beauty seemed to disappear.

Soon the storm swept on and left the valley. If the boy had gone back to the valley the next day and asked, "Where is that terrible storm, with all its terrible blackness?" the grass might have said, "Part of it is in me." The daisy would have said, "Part of it is in me." The fruits and flowers would have said, "Part of the storm is now in me."

When your life seems stormy, know that God's blessing is in the storm. Once it passes, you will see how God used the storm to make you grow.

Dear Lord, Just as flowers live and grow stronger because of storms and rain, let me grow stronger because of the stormy times in my life. Amen.

Scraggly Packages

Have you entered the storehouses of the snow or seen the storehouses of the hail, which I reserve for times of trouble, for days of war and battle?
Job 38: 22–23

Suppose a delivery man rang your doorbell and handed you a scraggly looking package. The paper is dirty and torn, and the tape is coming off. Would you be excited about opening the package? Problems can be like those packages. They look rough, and you don't really want to know more about them. But problems are really great opportunities in disguise. When you solve a problem, you learn something you didn't know before. Problems don't have to be obstacles to us. They can become stepping stones to something better. If we could think about our lives and our problems this way, we would begin to see rainbows instead of storm clouds.

Many of us will find that when we look back a little way in our life, we can see that our heavenly Father often gives us the best gifts when we've gone through a tough time. God's jewels are often sent to us in scraggly packages. They don't look nice from the outside, but inside are treasures of great value. In other words, when a problem comes your way, try to see beyond the problem to the wonderful thing God will do through that problem.

Dear Lord, Thank you for all your gifts—even problems. Help me to see them as stepping stones. Amen.

Give What You Have

And if anyone gives even a cup of cold water to one of these little ones because he is my disciple, I tell you the truth, he will certainly not lose his reward.

Matthew 10:42

The poet Henry Wadsworth Longfellow wrote, "Give what you have to someone, it may be better than you dare to think."

It doesn't take a lot to encourage someone who is discouraged — maybe just a smile. It doesn't take much money to help a child in a foreign country go to school — maybe just a few dollars a week. You can help others even though you just are a kid. Jesus said that if we give a cup of cold water to someone who is thirsty, he sees us do it and he will reward that action. On the other hand, if we don't help others when they need it, we are the losers.

Think of three things you might do to encourage someone else. Could you take cookies to a neighbor? Could you make a get-well card for someone who is sick? What could you do to encourage someone else?

Dear Lord, I want to remember every day that I can do something for someone else. I want to be a helper rather than someone who ignores the needs of others. Amen.

A Light at the End of the Tunnel

David shepherded them with integrity of heart;
with skillful hands he led them.
Psalm 78:72

There is a neat ride in Disneyland called Mr. Toad's Wild Ride. If you have ever read *Wind in the Willows*, you know that Mr. Toad could get himself into some awful problems. Well, in the Disneyland ride, you see many of the events he experienced. Then, at the end, you hear a train that sounds like it's coming straight at you. But you can see a light at the end of the tunnel. At the last second, a door flies opens and you are out in the open air! It's a lot of fun.

Grownups often talk about "the light at the end of the tunnel." It means that when a person has gone through a number of problems but they see a good change coming soon, it's as though a light has come into the darkness. He can see a way out of the problems. In the darkness of difficult times, God is there with us. He is guiding us just as David cared for his sheep. God will show us his light in the darkness.

Dear Lord, Be with me in the dark times of my life. Show me light at the end of the tunnel, and lead me out into your light. Amen.

The Right Hands

Offer yourselves to God, as those who have been brought from death to life.
Romans 6:13

Do you enjoy going to the dentist? Even though it can make you nervous, you can let the dentist do his work because he knows what he is doing. He went to college and learned how to clean and fix your teeth. He knows what instruments or tools to use as well. But he can't take care of your teeth unless you open your mouth and sit still. You have to let him do his job.

The Bible says in the verse above that we are to offer ourselves to God. We are to put ourselves in God's hands. Just like the dentist knows which tools to use to make our teeth healthy, God knows how to bring out the best in us and use our lives to bring him the greatest glory. We can give ourselves to God without worry because he knows all about us. In his hands, we will be cared for and used for his purposes.

Dear God, I want to surrender to you, so that you can do your work in my life. I offer myself into your hands. Amen.

The Train Under the Sea

I will turn all my mountains into roads, and my highways will be raised up.
Isaiah 49:11

Along the usually quiet coastline of England in 1987, a strange sound could be heard. Not the sound of waves or sea gulls, but the sound of a gigantic motor digging its way into the sand. Workers had just started up the Tunnel Boring Machine (TBM). Their mission: dig a tunnel 150 feet deep underneath the English Channel all the way to the other side—31 miles away.

Meanwhile, another team was doing the same job from France toward England. Two TBMs, tunneling from different directions, met in the middle on May 22, 1991. As they broke through the last wall of dirt, the two tunnels became one. Now that the tunnel is finished, several high-speed trains pick up passengers at a station in England and zip off underneath the sea, arriving just 35 minutes later at a French station.

Tunnels and mountain passes are constructed so that we can go through something that cannot be moved. In the Bible, God tells us that he will make a path where there is no path. He will do the things for us that we are not powerful enough to do for ourselves. We simply need to ask him for his help.

Dear God, Right now in my life there are problems that seem too hard to change. Please make a way through these situations when I can't see any way to fix them. Thank you for taking care of me. Amen.

Losers Becoming Strong

Be on your guard; stand firm in the faith; be men of courage; be strong.
1 Corinthians 16:13

When you hear the words *guard, stand firm, courage,* or *strong,* what kind of person do you think of? A wrestler flexing his muscles? An Olympic gold medal swimmer? Or perhaps even your mom or dad? When the apostle Paul uses these words in his letter to the church at Corinth, he isn't talking about the outside of a person; he's talking about what goes on inside of a person.

Paul knew all about becoming strong on the inside. He faced some terrible situations while trying to spread the gospel to other countries. He was shipwrecked, faced persecution, had to flee from people trying to kill him, and was thrown into jail more than once. Yet in each situation, he turned to God. He knew God would give him the strength to handle each hardship and survive.

God is there for you too, to give you the strength to face any situation. When you start to feel afraid or weak, turn to God. Ask him for his strength to be yours.

Dear Lord, No matter what happens in my life, please help me to be strong and to have courage. Help me see the good that you are bringing about in my hard situation. Amen.

The Mummy Lives

So they took away the stone. Then Jesus looked up and said, "Father, I thank you that you have heard me."
John 11:41

Jesus had a good friend named Lazarus. Jesus loved to go to Lazarus' house to spend time with him and his two sisters, Mary and Martha. One day when Jesus was busy in another town, he found out that his friend was very sick. By the time Jesus got to his friend's house, Lazarus was dead. Jesus was very sad. What he did next, though, didn't seem to make sense.

Jesus asked some of the people gathered there to move the heavy gravestone away from the tomb where Lazarus' dead body lay. What a gross thing to do! Even Martha said it wasn't a good idea, because the body had been in there for four days and was really going to stink. Still, Jesus had them move the stone. Then he did something else that seemed odd. He began to thank God joyfully for hearing his prayer even before he had an answer.

Jesus said, "Lazarus, come out!" Lazarus, wrapped like a mummy, came shuffling out of the grave. What would you have done? Run away quickly? Hid behind a bush? Jesus asked the people watching to unwrap Lazarus. Lazarus was alive!

Sometimes it's hard to understand what God is doing. You pray for something and wait and wait and wait. This can make you feel as if he doesn't hear you. But he does! After telling him what you need, thank him for hearing you and for doing what needs to be done for you — even if you don't understand or know what he's doing.

Dear Lord, I come to you now and lay these things that I have been worried about before of you. Please take care of them. I am letting go of them and putting them into your hands. Amen.

The King's Favor

My grace is sufficient for you, for my power is made perfect in weakness.
2 Corinthians 12:9

Have you ever been in a situation where you know what God is calling you to do ... and you do the opposite instead? Maybe your mom asked you to babysit your baby brother for the evening, but you wanted to hang out with your friends instead. Maybe the dog needed to be taken for a walk or the dishes needed to be washed, but you were busy playing games on the computer. Maybe there was a kid at school being bullied, and instead of being a friend to him you joined in the teasing. God is always calling us to be strong Christians, but humans can be weak creatures. We don't have the strength to do the things God calls to do.

When we need to be strong but are weak, that is the time that God steps in with his grace and becomes our strength. When we are too shy to make a new friend, God gives us his courage to try. When we are having a hard time doing the right thing, we can ask God to help us. He will make us strong on the inside and help us to make the right choice. He can be our strength in every area of our lives, if we will just ask him. Why don't you ask him right now?

Dear Lord, I am not strong enough to take care of all the problems facing me. Please be my strength. Amen.

Do You Smell Good?

Awake, north wind, and come, south wind! Blow on my garden, that its fragrance may spread abroad.
Song of Solomon 4:16

If you are in a car at night and riding through farmland, you might smell something that you would never expect: the beautiful sweet smell of night flowers in bloom. Most flowers have a unique scent that attracts certain kinds of insects to pollinate them. A flower's main job is not to bloom and look pretty in a vase on your dining room table, but to create seeds. A seed, when planted, will make another flower. The way flowers draw the insects to come for the pollen is to send out a powerful scent that brings a bee or fly to them.

Did you know that your life has a scent? When Jesus comes into your life and changes you, other kids know that you are different. When they see Jesus working in your life, they might want to know the reason why. When you go through tough times with a sweet attitude, other kids will be drawn to you to find out how you can be so strong in a tough time. When you tell them the reason, some of them will want to know Jesus too.

Dear God, Please come into my life and change me. Make my life so sweet that when others look at me, they will see you in my life. Amen.

The Power of an Engine

After they prayed, the place where they were meeting was shaken. And they were all filled with the Holy Spirit and spoke the word of God boldly. With great power the apostles continued to testify to the resurrection of the Lord Jesus, and much grace was upon them all.

Acts 4:31, 33

Riddle: How do you pull ten tons of iron and seventy men if you just have a big heap of coal and some water? You can only do this if you have a steam engine. The first steam engine tramway locomotive was invented by a man named Richard Trevithick. On February 22, 1804, he set off down the rails, pulling a huge load of iron and men.

Here is how steam engines worked. A man would shovel coal into the firebox. He was also in charge of watching the steam gauge and adding water. The combination of heat from the burning coal with the water made steam—similar to when a teakettle boils. The steam traveled down pipes where it was forced into cylinders, and eventually the pressure caused the wheels to turn. Coal, water, and even steam don't seem very powerful on their own. Yet when an expert puts them together, they can do mighty things.

There may be things in your life that are too hard for you. That is when you need to ask God for help. You will be like that steam engine, and God will be the expert. Just as today's Bible verse says, God will send the Holy Spirit to help you. When he comes to help you, you will have his strength, courage, and the power to do mighty things.

Dear Lord, I need your help. Please send your Holy Spirit to help me be strong, brave, and to do mighty things that I can't do by myself. Amen.

You Are on the Winning Side!

You are my King and my God, who decrees victories.
Psalm 44:4

God is always victorious. Whenever he is on your side, you will win over evil. Can you recall some of the characters in the Bible who won battles because God was on their side?

How about Samson? As long as he obeyed God, he had enough strength to defeat the Philistines, no matter how many came against him or his people. What about King David? Many times, God miraculously turned David's enemies over. Gideon, who didn't even think he was worthy of being a soldier, overtook the huge army of the Midianites — and Gideon only had 300 men with him.

These Bible stories show us how powerful God is. We are in a war too. But in our war against evil, we know we are on the winning side. Jesus is our leader, and he will save us! He doesn't need our power or strength, just our willingness to be used. Then he will bring us into victory.

Dear Lord, I feel so happy that I get that I'm on the winning side. You set me free and give me victory. Amen.

Lemonade?

Blessed are those whose strength is in you, who have set their hearts on pilgrimage. As they pass through the Valley of Baca, they make it a place of springs; the autumn rains also cover it with pools.
Psalm 84:5, 6

Have you ever heard someone say, "When life gives you lemons, make lemonade?" Do you know what it means? Well, most people don't enjoy eating plain lemons because they are too sour. However, if you squeeze out the juice and add sugar and water, you end up with a tasty drink.

Life is sometimes sour. There are days when everything seems to go wrong. Guess what? God makes great lemonade. He takes all the things that go wrong and changes them into something good. Sometimes it is hard to see the good things right away, but they will come.

Today's verse talks about a place called the Valley of Baca. Baca means weeping. In this verse, God says that when you go through that place of weeping or sadness, God will turn your tears into a well full of fresh cold water to drink. In other words, he can take the sadness and give you his comfort.

Dear Lord, There are some things that are making me very sad (or mad). Thank you for caring about my tears. Please take these things and turn them around. Please give me your comfort. Amen.

Jesus Waits

Yet when he heard that Lazarus was sick, he stayed where he was two more days.
John 11:6

The Bible verse for today is a hard one to understand. Lazarus, one of Jesus' good friends, was sick and about to die. Instead of running to heal his friend, Jesus stayed where he was for two more days.

When Jesus arrived at Lazarus' home, everyone was crying, because they had loved Lazarus and now he was dead. When Jesus saw them weeping, he was filled with emotion and wept too. Those watching Jesus that day said, "See how he loved him [Lazarus]!" (John 11:36). Jesus truly loved and cared about his best friend.

So why did Jesus wait two days and let Lazarus die? Many of the dead man's family and friends asked the same question. Jesus did it so everyone could see the glory of God. On approaching the tomb Jesus speaks to his heavenly Father and says, "Father, I thank you that you have heard me I knew that you always hear me but I said this for the benefit of the people standing here, that they may believe that you sent me" (John 11:41 – 42). Now, in front of the gathered crowd, he raised Lazarus from the dead so that all who were there would believe that Jesus was sent by God.

Jesus not only cares about our bodies, but also about our hearts. He is always looking for ways to show us who he really is and how much he cares about us.

Dear Lord, when I ask you for help, please give me patience. Help me to be able to wait for your answer and trust that you are going to do the best thing for both me and my family and friends. Help me not to get discouraged as I wait. Amen.

What to Do on a Very Bad, Really Rotten Day

Though the fig tree does not bud and there are no grapes on the vines, though the olive crop fails and the fields produce no food, though there are no sheep in the pen and no cattle in the stalls, yet I will rejoice in the Lord, I will be joyful in God my Savior.
Habakkuk 3:17, 18

Have you ever listened to country-western music? Many of the songs are famous for letting you know how hard life is for the person singing it. Musicians sing about how someone stole their horse, their family left them because they smelled bad, even their dog decided to live at the neighbor's house, oh, and now it's raining outside...

Today's verse sounds a lot like a country-western song. There are no figs on the fig tree. There are no grapes on the vine. There aren't even any olives. There are no sheep in the pen. There are no cows in the stall. Everything is going wrong.

Our verse today, though, has a happy ending. Even though the prophet Habakkuk is going through so many bad things, he rejoices in the Lord. When we have hard days, we need to look at God and say, "I don't like what is happening today, but I love you, God. I trust you and I want your joy in my heart." It takes a lot of courage to be joyful when everything is going wrong. Having joy even when everything is rotten pleases God because it's like saying, "God, I don't know what's going on, but I trust you."

Dear Lord, When everything in my life seems to be going wrong, even on really rotten days, I will choose to praise you. Amen.

Be Firefighter Ready

Through these he has given us his very great and precious promises.
2 Peter 1:4

Firefighters must be ready when they are called to a fire. They wear special clothing that keeps them safe and have many pieces of equipment that help them put out the fire. They have axes, pike poles, and saws that allow them to check for fires above the ceiling or to break through a wall where a fire might be blazing. They have huge hoses that can spray water or foam to put out fires.

When they hear the alarm at the fire station, they have to be ready to leave immediately. So before an alarm ever goes off, the firefighters put a great deal of time and effort into knowing how to use their equipment. If they weren't familiar with their tools, they wouldn't be ready when the alarm goes off at the station.

Your tools are God's promises. He promises to give you joy, strength, faith, peace, goodness, salvation and more so you can live your life for his glory. But to use those, you need to be prepared. You need to spend time with him reading your Bible and praying. Then, when you go out into the world, to school, or to any place, you will be ready to do the right thing and put his promises to work.

Dear Lord, Please give me every piece of equipment that I need to make the right decisions. Help me to learn your promises by reading my Bible and talking to you. Make me ready, Lord! Amen.

The Apple Falls

If clouds are full of water, they pour rain upon the earth.
Ecclesiastes 11:3

One day a scientist named Sir Isaac Newton saw an apple fall from a tree. Instead of picking the apple up and eating it, he began to think about that apple. Why did the apple fall down to the ground and not up to the sky? The more he thought, the more questions he had. What kept the ocean in its place? What kept a human or an animal on the ground instead of floating in the air? He realized that there was some force that kept things from floating away. He named that force gravity. Gravity is one of the laws of science.

The laws of science, like gravity, have always been and will always be. Today's verse is a perfect example. If a cloud is full of water what happens? It pours rain upon the earth. When someone cuts a tree, what does it do? It falls. The laws of science show us that someone with great intelligence put this universe together. God is that someone. He created everything and then set laws in place so that we could live on earth. The laws of science, like gravity, apply to our lives in many ways. Today's verse is a perfect example. If a cloud is full of water, what happens? It pours rain upon the earth. What does that mean for your life? Well, when it feels like storm clouds hit you, it's time to expect rain. But those hard times aren't for nothing. God uses them to bring blessings — just like the real rain brings forth flowers and prevents drought.

God wants us to know that we cannot only trust these laws, but we can also trust him and his laws. He will always be there. He will never leave us. He will always love us.

Dear Lord, Thank you for creating the universe. Thank you for bringing blessings even from the rainy times. You will always be there to protect, love, and care for me. Help me to trust you. Amen.

He's Got the Whole World in His Hands

Jesus answered, "You would have no power over me if it were not given to you from above."
John 19:11

In the 1940s Obie Philpot was getting his things together. He would soon be leaving for another country with other World War II soldiers. He had many worries. So he took out a piece of paper and read the words that he had written about his feelings. Here is what he read:

He's got the whole world in his hands.
He's got the wind and rain in His hands.
He's got the sun and moon in His hands.
He's got the little bitty baby in His hands.
He's got you and me brother in His hands.
He's got everybody here in His Hands.
He's got the whole world in His hands.

Obie worried about being away from his wife and newborn son. He wanted to get through the war safely. So he said these words as a prayer. He gave all of his worries to God.

God heard his prayer. Obie came home safely from the war. He is a very old man now with many brothers, sisters, children, grandchildren, and even great-grandchildren. Years later, someone found Obie's note and read it on the radio so that everyone could hear. Even later, the words were made into a song that became famous. You probably know it.

God is in control of everything, even when it seems like nothing is going right. Sometimes you cannot see God's help until you need it. So don't give up!

Dear Lord, I know you are powerful. You are in control. I know you care about me. Please keep me in your hands. Amen.

The Queen

"We must go through many hardships to enter the kingdom of God."
Acts 14:22

How does a boy or girl learn to be a prince or princess? In the case of a ten-year-old girl named Elizabeth, it meant many years of special studying and training. Elizabeth was a child just like you, who liked to play and eat ice cream. Then her father became the king of England. Her normal life changed. She became a princess. She also became the next person in line to rule England.

Along with learning how to spell and do math problems like you do in school, Elizabeth also had to study the history and laws of her country. She took special classes with leaders of her country and her church. She even spent time with her father to learn what he did as a king. As Elizabeth grew older, she had to study even more. She learned to speak French. She studied art and music. She learned to ride horses. Every year brought new and harder challenges.

When Elizabeth was a teenager, she began to work with her parents. She also started performing some of their duties. She joined a lot of clubs. She met a lot of people. She was appointed to a lot of positions. When she was fourteen, she had to speak on the radio to all of England. She learned that her life did not only belong to herself, but also to the people of England. When Elizabeth was crowned Queen of England on June 2, 1952, she was ready. All the years of learning and training had taught her how to be a good ruler.

Did you know that you are a prince or princess in training? When you have a hard day, ask God to teach you what to do. God uses everything that happens in your life to help you learn and grow as his royal child.

Dear Lord, Sometimes I don't feel very special. Please help me to always remember that I belong to your royal family. I am a child being trained every day by you, my Father. Amen.

The Ant's Voice

I waited patiently for the Lord; he turned to me and heard my cry.
Psalm 40:1

Can an ant make noise? Yes. Ants do make sounds by rubbing their legs together. These sounds are so high-pitched that human ears cannot hear them. If you want to hear an ant, you will have to use a microphone to amplify its sound.

Sometimes you might feel like an ant when you talk to God. You may feel that he is so big that he can't hear you. Today's verse tells us the opposite. The psalmist waited for God to help him. He said that when he did, God turned to him and heard him asking for help.

Another version of the Bible uses the word "inclined" instead of "turned" — "he inclined to me and heard my cry." To incline in this case means "to bend down." When you talk to God, you are so important and precious to him, he bends down to hear you. He wants to know what you have to say. But sometimes you have to be patient. Even though God always hears you, he may not reply instantly. His timing may not be right yet. He may want to know how serious or committed you are to your request. As you wait for his answer, your patience and faith will grow.

Dear Lord, You say in your Word that you want to hear what I have to say. Help me to be patient for your reply. Amen.

747 Faith

I have faith in God that it will happen just as he told me.
Acts 27:25

An airplane is a marvelous invention. Large 747 airplanes that can weigh up to 870,000 pounds are able to carry up to 600 people. Have you ever wondered how a gigantic heavy metal container can easily lift off the ground, zoom up into the air, and fly for thousands of miles without stopping?

You probably know that in order for an airplane to get into the air, it must have powerful engines and strong wings. You also know that many people fly on airplanes because they are very safe. Passengers may not know the parts of the engine or how the radar is used, but they trust the pilot and crew to keep them safe. They sit in their seats trusting the plane will lift off the ground and take them where they need to go.

Faith is kind of like an airplane. You know that God is good. You know that you have salvation. You know that he will take care of you. The Bible, God's very words, tells you these things. Faith then means that you trust what you know. You let God take control of your life, your problems, and your choices.

That is faith. In what part of your life do you need faith right now? Take that to the Lord. He promised that when you lack faith, he will help you.

Dear Lord, I am so glad I can trust you. I believe that what you say is true. I believe that you love me and are watching over me. Amen.

Idol Worship

The Lord alone led him.
Deuteronomy 32:12

There are stories in the Bible about times when people had nothing to rely on except God. Some had no place to call home — like Moses after he fled Egypt. Some had no friends or family around to help — like King David while he was hiding from Saul. Others had no food or water — like the Israelites who were hungry and thirsty in the desert. But God was there. He provided work and a home for Moses. He showed David where to hide. He provided food and water to the Israelites.

In your life, there may be times where you have nothing to rely on but God. He will be more than enough for you. He will give you guidance, answers and provide for your needs. Trust him to care for you. Nothing is too hard for him.

Dear Lord, Please help me to come to you for help first. I know you can take care of all my needs. Keep me close to you. Amen.

Poor = Rich?

Sorrowful, yet always rejoicing; poor, yet making many rich; having
nothing, and yet possessing everything.

2 Corinthians 6:10

Today's verse talks about some pretty amazing people. These are people who think about the good things, even when sad things are happening. They remember that they are royal children of God, even when they don't feel important. They know that God owns everything and that they belong to God.

God never tells us that it's supposed to be easy to act like that. It isn't easy to rejoice when there's been a death in the family, or when you've left all your friends behind as you moved to a new city. It isn't easy to feel rich when your shoes are a size too small and your parents can't afford a new winter jacket for you. It isn't easy to feel like you have everything when you're sitting alone at lunch. But the Apostle Paul tells us in this passage that through Christ's strength, we can feel like royalty in the kingdom of God.

Dear Lord, Please help me not to focus on the bad things going on around me. Help me instead to think about you and how good you are to me. Amen.

Big-Time Wrestling

So Jacob was left alone, and a man wrestled with him till daybreak.
Genesis 32:24

Jacob had a brother named Esau. When they were younger, they had a horrible argument that was so bad that Jacob had to run away to his uncle's house. There he worked for his uncle, got married, and had many children. The years passed and Jacob became a wealthy man. He also became homesick. One day he packed up his family, his animals, and everything he owned, and headed for home. Jacob was afraid though. He thought his brother would still be angry, so he sent some servants ahead with presents for Esau. The servants returned and told Jacob that Esau was on his way to meet him. Yikes! Now Jacob was even more afraid. He prayed and reminded God that God had promised everything would work out. God told Jacob that he would be with him.

That night, an angel appeared. He and Jacob started to wrestle. The angel was very strong, but Jacob really wanted to make sure God would bless him, so he wouldn't let the angel go. They wrestled until the sun came up. Finally, the angel had enough. He popped Jacob's hip out of joint, but Jacob held on. Jacob told the angel that he would not let him go until he promised to protect and help Jacob. The angel promised, and Jacob limped away a happy man. Soon he met his brother, and Esau was happy to see him. God had blessed Jacob after all.

Dear Lord, Please help me to always come to you when I am facing someone or something that is too strong for me. Be my strength. Be my protection. Help me not to give up! Amen.

What Does God Think About You?

He rescued me because he delighted in me.
Psalm 18:19

What does God think about you? Is he proud of you? Does he think that you are his friend? You may be wondering some of these things. How can you find the answers? The Bible is one way that God talks to us and tells us how he feels about us.

Today's verse gives us a clue. God says that he rescues us or sets us free because he delights in us. The word delight means to bring extreme joy and happiness to someone. The Bible says that you bring extreme joy and happiness to God.

How much does God love you? Romans 5:8 says, "But God demonstrates his own love for us in this: While we were still sinners, Christ died for us." God has always loved you. God loves you now. God will always love you. Even when you make bad choices. Even when you fail. Even when you don't love him back. God loves you. He loves you so much that he took all your bad choices and gave them to his son Jesus to carry. He did all of this before you could even love him back.

So, what else does God think of you? If you want to know more, read your Bible. You will find out just how wonderful and special you really are to God.

Dear Lord, Thank you for loving me. Thank you for telling me how you feel about me in the Bible. Amen.

Shipwrecked!

*The rest were to get there on planks or on pieces of the ship. In this way
everyone reached land in safety.*
Acts 27:44

After Paul gave his life to Jesus, he traveled around telling everyone
about how God had changed him. On one of his journeys, he went
aboard a ship bound for Rome. The ship was caught in a horrible
storm and started to sink. The men began to throw cargo into the
sea to make it lighter. Finally, they got ready to abandon the ship.
Paul told them that an angel of God had told him that if everyone
stayed on the ship, they would be safe. The sailors were probably
looking for a different answer, but they listened to Paul and stayed.
Eventually, they made it to shore.

Sometimes when we pray, we want a certain answer, maybe even
a miracle — and it doesn't come. God's answer may be ordinary —
like the way Paul's shipmates stayed safe by remaining on the ship.
The crew was ready to do something drastic, but God provided a
simple, easy answer. When you are listening for God, be open to
whatever he wants to do in your situation. He may tell you
something you don't expect.

Dear Lord, I want to listen to your directions and to be able to
understand them. Please teach me when I am reading the Bible about
all the wonderful things you did for those that listened to you. Amen.

We're Taking a Surprise Trip

By faith Abraham, when called to go to a place he would later receive as his inheritance, obeyed and went, even though he did not know where he was going.
Hebrews 11:8

Family road trips can be a lot of fun. On the day of the trip, everyone gets into a car packed with luggage. Then you're off on an adventure. Your parents seem to know which roads to take even though you are in a new city. They also know where to stop for lunch or for the night. Long before the trip ever started, they used a map to plan where your family would go. If they say they are taking you to Disneyland, you know you will end up there. But how do you know? Have you seen the map or their plan? You believe what they say because you trust them.

Today's verse tells us that God told Abraham to pack up his family and things and go on a road trip. One problem: God didn't tell Abraham where he was supposed to go. He didn't give him a map or a plan. It wasn't a problem for Abraham though. He did exactly what God told him to do each day. He trusted God and the Bible describes him as a man who had great faith.

So the next time you are facing the unknown, remember that God is the one who leads us. He has the map for your life. You can put your trust in him just like you trust your parents on a road trip.

Dear Lord, I want to see my life as an amazing adventure that you have planned and mapped out. I know you have good things for me. Thank you for guiding me. Amen.

God's Favorite Perfume

I am amply supplied, now that I have received from Epaphroditus the gifts you sent. They are a fragrant offering, an acceptable sacrifice, pleasing to God.
Philippians 4:18

Perfume is made of plant oils, a secret fragrance, and other ingredients. The secret fragrance can be taken from bark, flowers, fruit, roots, seeds, woods, or pitch. The recipe is kept secret by the perfumer, so no one else can copy it.

Perfume has had many uses throughout history. Some perfume was so expensive that it was given as a gift. In the Bible, the wise men brought baby Jesus gold, frankincense, and myrrh. Frankincense and myrrh were perfumes that only the very rich could afford to buy.

The first perfume ever made was incense — a good-smelling material that had to be burned in order to give off the fragrance. Incense was used in the God's house. Today's verse is about a different kind of incense or perfume.

The Apostle Paul wrote a letter to a church in Philippi. The people there had given Paul money, food, and a place to stay when he didn't have much. They even sent him the things he needed after he had left Philippi. He told them in the letter that they made him very happy. More important, they made God happy. God saw how willing they were to help people who were poor and homeless. Paul said that their generous giving was like a wonderful perfume that God could smell, and God loved it. When we help others, it is like creating a beautiful fragrance that God loves.

Dear Lord, I want to make you happy. I want the things that I do each day to help others to be as a wonderful perfume. Show me ways that I can do that. Amen.

The Lion Is Free

Before this faith came, we were held prisoners by the law, locked up until faith should be revealed.

Galatians 3:23

There once was a lion cub named Elsa. When Elsa's mother died, she had no one to take care of her until George and Joy Adamson found her. The Adamsons lived in Kenya. One of their jobs as game wardens was to watch over the wild animals in their area. When they found Elsa, she was only a few weeks old. They took her to their home. While she was small, she acted like any housecat. Joy and Elsa became friends.

When Elsa got bigger, Joy realized that Elsa needed to learn to be a free lion, not a kitty cat. So she began to teach Elsa how to hunt for food. The day came when it was time to set Elsa free. This was hard for Joy to do. She loved Elsa and was sad to see her leave, but she knew it was right. At first Elsa wasn't sure what to do. She didn't really know what freedom was. Then she started to explore. Soon she was gone.

The word *law* in today's verse is kind of like the nice house that Elsa lived in when she was a cub. It was a good place while she was little. But when she grew up, it became more like a prison. While she was treated well by the Adamsons, she needed to be out in the wild, not in their living room.

Faith is like Joy setting Elsa free. Elsa is like you and me. When we trust in Jesus, he releases us from the law and sets us free to be what he created us to be. The laws in the Old Testament were there to protect God's people, kind of like the Adamsons protected Elsa. The laws helped the people know how to live and make sacrifices for their sins. But then Jesus came to earth. He came to free us. We don't have to make sacrifices for our sins any more. Jesus took care of that. We are free to live forgiven and be what he created us to be.

Dear Lord, Thank you for the freedom you brought through your death on the cross. Help me to live the way you created me to live. Amen.

Cave Wisdom

The deep says, "It is not in me;" the sea says, "It is not with me."
Job 28:14

Currently, the world's deepest known cave is Krubera, located in the West Caucasus near the Black Sea. On October 19, 2004, a team of cave climbers reached the lowest point that anyone had ever been—6,824 feet below the earth's surface. That's the equivalent of four Empire State buildings stacked on top of each other. The climber's journey took them through narrow tube-like rooms where they had to lay on their stomachs to squeeze through. Much of the cave was underwater. They had to wear special suits and masks to help them breathe and to keep them warm from the icy water. Many scientists believe that soon they will be able to find a way to go even deeper into this cave.

If you have ever been in a cave, you know that caves are good for exploring, but about all you will find in the cave is darkness. Today's verse is about looking for wisdom. Wisdom is being able to know what is true or right. Many people like to explore in other ways. Some look high and low for wisdom. They think that if they can go where no one else has ever been, they will find wisdom. They dig deep down, not in caves, but in ideas and religions. But when they get to the bottom of the religion or idea, they find it is as empty and dark as a cave. What they have not yet learned is that God is the source of wisdom. Only he can give wisdom to you. In the book of James it says, "If any of you lacks wisdom, he should ask God...." If you want to be wise, ask God to give you wisdom. The deeper you know God, the more wisdom you will find.

Dear Lord, I want to know what is true and what is right. Please give me your wisdom. Amen.

God's Plan vs. Our Plan

After he took him aside, away from the crowd, Jesus put his fingers into the man's ears. Then he spit and touched the man's tongue.
Mark 7:33

Today's verse might seem kind of silly to you. Why did Jesus put his fingers in the man's ears? Why did he spit and touch the man's tongue? Jesus, many times, did things that seemed silly to the rest of the world. The religious leaders that met Jesus were always trying to get him to do things their way. They would get angry with him when he wouldn't. Jesus talked to God everyday. He knew what God's plan for his life was. He followed God's plan everyday, and sometimes that didn't include what the religious leaders had planned.

The man in our verse today was deaf and could hardly speak. The crowd of people who were watching begged Jesus to lay his hands on the man and heal him. Instead, Jesus took the man away from the crowd. He healed the man when they were finally alone.

God uses quiet times to accomplish great things. You don't have to be busy or be noticed by others for God to move in your life. He may ask you to come away with him for some solitude. You never know what he'll do during those quiet moments. He may heal you or change you.

Dear Lord, Give me the courage to do what you want me to do even if it doesn't make sense to me. Help me to learn to enjoy times of quiet with you too. Amen.

Pure Water

Then Moses cried out to the Lord, and the Lord showed him a piece of wood. He threw it into the water, and the water became sweet.
Exodus 15:25

When hikers go for an overnight expedition, they must remember many safety tips. One thing is never to drink water out of a stream, river, or lake, without purifying it first. Water found on a trail could have tiny bacteria that would make them very sick. Hikers can boil water, run it through a filter, or mix it with special chlorine tablets to kill the bacteria.

In the Bible, Moses was leading all of the Israelites through the desert. They had been without water for three days. Finally, they saw a lake up ahead. One problem — the water was bad. What a tough spot they were in! But God loves to show his power when we are tight situations. The Israelites were dying of thirst. Moses talked to God it. God showed Moses a piece of wood and told him to throw it into the water. Moses obeyed, and the water was instantly purified. The thirsty Israelites were able to drink until they were satisfied.

There was nothing special about the wood. What was special was God. He is the one who made that water drinkable, so the Israelites could see how mighty he is.

Dear Lord, When I have a problem that I cannot fix, please help me come to you. Tough spots aren't too tough for you. Thank you for always having the answer. Amen.

Your Cross

Carrying his own cross, he went out to the place of the Skull (which in Aramaic is called Golgotha).
John 19:17

Have you ever looked at a friend's life and thought he or she had it easy? Or maybe you have a friend who is handicapped or constantly sick? You probably think that your life is so much better. Each of us has different burdens and blessings.

God has given you certain things to face in your life, and they will be different from those around you. He may ask you to do something hard, like break off a friendship with someone who is a bad influence. But he may ask someone else to stay friends with that same person. It's best not to compare your life or your problems to anyone else.

Grownups often use the phrase "my cross to bear." Jesus had his own cross to bear, too; no one else could die in his place. God knows which cross you can handle. When you yield yourself to him, he'll equip you to handle the unique challenges that come to you.

Dear Lord, Prepare me to face any burdens that come my way. Help me to be careful not to envy others who seem to have an easier life. Remind me to pray for those who have more challenges than I do.

Wonders in the Oceans

Others went out on the sea in ships; they were merchants on the mighty waters. They saw the works of the Lord, his wonderful deeds in the deep.
Psalm 107:23, 24

Several ships out on the ocean today have a mission to find all sea life and record it. The mission is called the Census of Marine Life. They have made many discoveries of new creatures.

One of the discoveries was near an underwater volcano. When they took the temperature of the water, it was 765 degrees Fahrenheit. This was the hottest part of the ocean ever discovered. Sitting on the side of the opening to the volcano were mussels and shrimp that didn't even seem to notice the temperature. Another discovery was made off the coast of New Jersey. The ship's sound-based technology detected a school of eight million fish. That grouping of fish would be the size of Manhattan Island in New York.

As the mission takes ships through the waters of the world, they are finding creatures so amazing that it shows us someone great must have created all of this. That someone is God. The more we learn about the world and everything in it, the more we are surprised every day by how creative and wonderful God is.

Dear Lord, All the wonders that you have made on this earth are amazing. Thank you that you have made me too. Amen.

So Small, So Brave!

Then Jesus told him, "Because you have seen me, you have believed;
blessed are those who have not seen and yet have believed."
John 20:29

There once was a young man named David who had several older
brothers. They went to war while David stayed home and took care
of his father's sheep. One day David's father asked him to go visit
his brothers to take them some food and find out how the battle
was going.

When David arrived at the soldiers' camp, he was shocked by
what he saw. As his brothers were getting ready to fight against the
Philistines, suddenly a giant named Goliath walked out from the
Philistine army. He yelled and cursed God and the Israelites. He
dared any man to come out and fight him and promised to kill any
man who tried. The Israelite army, including David's brothers, ran
back to safety. David was angry. He knew that Goliath didn't have
any right to be saying bad things about God. He didn't like the fact
that the Israelite army was so afraid they didn't trust God. So he
told everyone he would go fight Goliath.

David took only his shepherd's stick, sling, and five smooth
stones. Goliath saw David coming and made fun of him. When he
began to curse God again, David said that God was on his side.
Everyone in the land would know how great God was because
he had used a boy and some rocks to kill a giant. Before Goliath
could say another word, David started swinging his sling ... and ...
THUD! Down went Goliath.

With God on your side, you can have the courage to do anything
he asks of you. He will take care of you even when you feel like
you're facing a giant. When you are afraid, talk to him. He wants
to give you courage. He wants you to know that he is very strong.
He will win your battles for you, if you will only come to him and
believe that he can.

Dear Lord, I am afraid of all the problems that seem too big for me to
face. I believe that you can give me the strength and courage to face
them in your name! Amen.

Hidden Beauty

O afflicted city, lashed by storms and not comforted, I will build you with stones of turquoise ... All your sons will be taught by the Lord, and great will be your children's peace.
Isaiah 54:11

Turquoise, a beautiful blue-green stone, has been mined in the Sinai Peninsula for 5,000 years. The Egyptians used it for decoration in their buildings and even in the death masks made for their pharaohs. The Persians often used turquoise to decorate their buildings. The prophet Isaiah would have known about the beauty of turquoise since it was also mined in Israel.

These precious stones don't look pretty when they are first brought from the earth. They are encased in drab-looking rock. Unless you know what you are looking for, you might miss the turquoise. Miners dig the stones from the soil mostly by hand; the stone is brittle and could break if machines were used. Then the stones are cut and polished to be sold for jewelry or decorations.

In the verse above Isaiah compares God's people to a city that has had a hard time. The city has been lashed by storms. But now, the Lord is going to rebuild the city with beautiful stones of turquoise. He's going to make something beautiful in the place of hardship and suffering. That's what God wants to do for us. He wants to take all the ugly things that have happened to us and rebuild our lives into something beautiful.

Dear Lord, Even though I'm still a kid, I know how awful life can be sometimes. I'm so glad your word promises to turn the hard times into something beautiful. Amen.

Going Through the Fire

For it has been granted to you on behalf of Christ not only to believe on him, but also to suffer for him.

Philemon 1:29

Gifted potters know how to turn sticky clay into beautiful vases and dishes that have great value. How do they do it? By putting their clay creations into super-hot kilns, not once, but several times. That's what makes the vases and dishes both strong and beautiful.

Now imagine that God is the gifted potter and we are the clay. God creates us in his image. Then we become strong and resilient as we go through "fires," times that are hard and challenging. Our faith grows and becomes more beautiful every time we go through a hard time. Some of those hard suffering times may be because you are a Christian. It might be about being teased about going to church and Sunday school. It might be about being excluded from a party or event because you chose to live morally.

When we suffer for Jesus and our faith, God sees that and he will reward us either later in our life, in heaven, or both. We will become stronger Christians. Don't be afraid to stand strong for Jesus.

Dear Jesus, I don't like the idea of suffering, but I want to do what is right and I want to stay true to you. Please help me. Amen.

Coming About

He saw the disciples straining at the oars, because the wind was against them.
Mark 6:48

It is very difficult to sail into the wind, but sometimes the only way to get where you want to go is to do that. Sailors use a maneuver called a tack or coming about. The sails are adjusted to catch the wind and drive the boat forward. By going as far as they can one direction then shifting the sails to the other side and using a zigzag course, the boat can actually sail against the wind. It takes a lot of skill and a lot of patience.

Jesus looked out across the lake and saw his disciples in a boat that was trying to move against the wind. They were rowing the boat but not making much progress. He walked by on the water. When they saw him, they were nearly frightened to death. Who would have expected Jesus to show up walking on the water? He called out to them, "Take courage! It is I. Don't be afraid." Then he climbed into the boat with them, and the wind stopped instantly.

When you feel like you are sailing into the wind of life, and it is tough and scary, look around, you may see Jesus coming toward you to help you in your tough time. Jesus loves you and will never leave you. He'll show you how to make the adjustments in your life that will help you sail right into the problems and still keep going.

Dear Lord, You are never going to be far away from me even if I feel like I am sailing into the wind. Help me to call to you for rescue. Amen.

A Done Deal

When you hear them sound a long blast on the trumpets, have all the people give a loud shout; then the wall of the city will collapse and the people will go up, every man straight in.
Joshua 6:5

The city of Jericho was an ancient, double-walled city that sat on a mound of earth. There was a spring inside the walls, and the people stored large jars of grain there. Archaeologists discovered that the people of Jericho had plenty to eat and enough water. They could have lived inside the city for many months while God's people walked around outside. However, God told his people that they were to march around the city for six days. On the seventh day, they were to go around seven times, then blow the trumpets and shout. Then the walls would collapse. Archaeologists have discovered that this really happened. The red bricks from inside the walls fell outward and landed near the outside wall, making a ramp. All the soldiers needed to do was climb up the ramp and go into the city and take it for God. And there was one more thing: God had promised that Rahab's house would not fall down. A section of the wall was found that had not fallen down. Perhaps that is where Rahab's house stood.

The whole event happened just as God said it would. You see, when God says something is a done deal, it is! You can count on it. What are you praying about that God has already promised you? It's a done deal.

Dear Lord, I'm so glad we can depend on you for everything we need. Thank you for your promises that we know will come true in your time. Amen.

Not Ready

Yet the Lord longs to be gracious to you; he rises to show you compassion.
For the Lord is a God of justice. Blessed are all who wait for him!
Isaiah 30:18

There's a very interesting story in the Bible about a young man who wanted to do something he wasn't ready to do. It happened like this.

A young man named Ahimaaz said to Joab, captain of the army, "Let me run and take the news to the king that God has delivered him from his enemies." Joab told him no and sent someone else. Pretty soon, Ahimaaz said again, "Please let me run behind the other messenger." Joab asked, "My son, why do you want to go? You don't have any news that will bring you a reward." But the young man was determined, so Joab let him go. The young man took a shortcut and beat the regular messenger to the city.

When Ahimaaz arrived and the king started asking questions about the battle, Ahimaaz didn't have enough information. He wasn't ready to bring the final news to the king. He should have waited. Finally, the other messenger came and gave the king the good news that God's people had won the battle and the bad news that the king's son, Absalom, was dead.

We have to learn and experience some things so that what we say is wise. If we just talk and haven't learned what we are talking about, we will be like Ahimaaz who didn't know everything he was supposed to say at the king's palace. It's important to wait until God is ready for us to go out and do his work. We have to be ready for what he asks us to do.

Dear Lord, Help me to wait for you and listen for your voice before I leap into important decisions. Your time is perfect! Amen.

You Remain

They will perish, but you remain.
Hebrews 1:11

Most of us have more clothing than we can keep track of. We wear things for a while, get tired of them, and throw them out. Then we buy more. But that's not the way it was in the past. In biblical times, people had to clip wool from sheep, wash the fleece, spin it into yarn, dye the yarn if they wanted color, and weave the threads into fabric. Clothes were treasured, and most people didn't worry about style as long as they had something to wear. If you wanted something new to wear, you had to make it from scratch. Eventually, the clothing did wear out and had to be replaced.

Everything on this earth wears out.. There is just one thing that does not wear out — get any older — and that is God. He was around before anything existed, and he will be there forever. He is eternal — like a circle that has no beginning and no end. It's important to remember that God is always around, especially when you feel lonely or sad. He will be with you forever. One day, he will bring you to heaven with him.

Dear Lord, Thank you for being with me when I feel alone. I am so glad that you never change. Amen.

A Promise to Count on

God is our refuge and strength, an ever-present help in trouble.
Psalm 46:1

What's a refuge? It's a place of shelter or protection from danger —
a place to hide until something that could harm you is past. In
the Old Testament, God hid Elijah in a cave when King Ahab and
Queen Jezebel were after him. God protected him until the trouble
passed. When Daniel was in the lions' den, God was his refuge and
strength. God didn't hide him away from the lions; he kept Daniel
safe as he stood right before the beasts. Those lions couldn't open
their mouths to bite him.

God is our refuge. He will always provide a safe place for us
when we need it. He is also our strength — he is a mighty God who
can be our champion. He is always available to help when we are in
trouble. This is a promise from God you can count on. God will help
you when you are in a desperate place. Run to him, and tell him all
your troubles. You can lean on Jesus, because he loves you and has
promised never to leave you.

Dear Lord, What an awesome promise — that you will be there for us
no matter what happens! Thank you for being my refuge. Amen.

Can You Hear Me Now?

Answer me when I call to you, O my righteous God. Give me relief from my distress; be merciful to me and hear my prayer.
Psalm 4:1

When you ask God, "Can you hear me now?" the answer is yes. We don't know how God hears every prayer, but he does. And he remembers them as well. In the last book of the Bible, the writer describes an amazing vision where he saw our prayers:

I saw a Lamb, looking as if it had been slain, standing in the center of the throne, encircled by the four living creatures and the elders.... He came and took the scroll from the right hand of him who sat on the throne. And when he had taken it, the four living creatures and the twenty-four elders fell down before the Lamb. Each one had a harp and they were holding golden bowls full of incense, which are the prayers of the saints.

   Revelation 5:6–8

What an amazing vision! Did you catch that last line? It describes the prayers of God's people as incense kept in golden bowls. That's a beautiful picture of how God feels about our prayers. To him, our prayers are like a wonderful fragrance. Our prayers are so valuable to him that he keeps them in golden bowls. Isn't that wonderful and amazing?

Is there something you've been praying about but feel like maybe God hasn't heard your prayer? God not only hears your prayers, he treasures them. He loves to hear from you, and he wants you to tell him everything that's on your heart. Never doubt how precious and valuable your prayers are to God.

Dear Lord, You are an awesome God. Thank you for not only hearing my prayers, but also for keeping them. Amen.

How Does Your Garden Grow?

Some fell on rocky places, where it did not have much soil. It sprang up quickly, because the soil was shallow.
Matthew 13:5

Have you ever tried to plant seeds on a rock? They won't grow without soil. What if you added an inch of dirt over the rock? What would happen then? Your seeds would probably come up right away, but then the plants would start to look weak. Eventually, they would bend over and lay on the ground because there is not enough soil to put down strong roots. To put down strong roots, a seed needs rich, deep soil.

Today's Jesus told a story comparing God's Word to a seed that is planted in our hearts. Some people have such hard, rocky hearts that God's life cannot grow in them for long. We need to keep our hearts soft toward God. We need to take care of our hearts so that his seed can grow in us. We can cultivate a heart full of rich, deep soil when we follow Jesus' commandment to love God and love others (Matthew 22:37 – 39). And we can nurture the seeds God plants in our lives when we read the Bible, pray, and learn about God from those who know God better than we do.

Dear Lord, Make the soil of my heart soft and ready for your Word. I want your life to grow in it. Amen.

No Way to Fail

The Lord will fulfill his purpose for me.
Psalm 138:8

God has a plan for your life, and if you'll let him, he will fulfill that plan. When we are trying to follow God's plan for our lives, we will make mistakes. We get hung up on all kinds of problems. We feel like failures. Here's some good news: Everyone fails at some point. What matters most is not that you fail but what happens after you fail. Do you give up, or do you try again?

Carpenters use a saying to prevent mistakes in their work: "Measure twice, cut once." That means that when a carpenter needs to cut a piece of wood to a certain length, he will measure the wood more than once to be sure he is accurate before he starts cutting with a saw. Even then mistakes can happen. Once he cuts, he can't go back and fix a mistake. So if he messes up, what does he do? Does he use a piece of wood that is the wrong size? No, he says, "I made a mistake. I'll have to get a new piece of wood." He goes right on with his project. He gets back on track.

Sometimes in life you will make mistakes trying to follow God's plan for your life. Don't give up when you make a mistake! Failure isn't final. When you fail, ask God to give you the strength to get up and try again. God will help you get back on the plan—the purpose—he has for your life. He cares more than you do that you are successful in living his way.

Dear Lord, I do make mistakes in trying to live a good, clean Christian life. Help me not to become discouraged, but to get up and continue following you. Amen.

Never Give Up

And so after waiting patiently, Abraham received what was promised.
Hebrews 6:15

Many years ago, a missionary went to Tibet before cell phones,
text messaging, and satellite phones. When missionaries went out
in those days, they seemed to disappear. Only an occasional letter
would come from them. Tibet was a hard place to preach the good
news about Jesus. The people didn't want to hear. This missionary
worked for 16 years before he had one person come to Christ. That's
patience — not to give up even when it seems so long before you
God do a work.

Our verse today says that Abraham knew patience too. God had
promised him so many descendants that they would be almost
uncountable. Yet at that time, Abraham didn't even have one child.
When he was old, he finally received the child God had promised.

The missionary in Tibet didn't get to see what happened in Tibet
long after he died. The church where he had served eventually
reopened. And someday that missionary will receive a great reward
from Jesus himself.

Dear God, Help me learn how to be patient, especially when it seems I
have to wait so long for something to happen. Amen.

Sometimes
Leaning Is Good

Who is this coming up from the desert leaning on her lover?
Song of Solomon 8:5

Have you ever hurt yourself on the playground? Did someone come support you so you could hobble to get help? Weren't you glad you had help? Did you know you can lean on God when you need help? The Bible tells us, "There is a friend who sticks closer than a brother" (Proverbs 18:24). When you need someone to lean on, God is right there — closer than your own brother. Wow! That's great to know!

There is an old song that talks about leaning on God:

> What a fellowship, what a joy divine,
> Leaning on the everlasting arms;
> What a blessedness, what a peace is mine,
> Leaning on the everlasting arms.
> Leaning, leaning,
> Safe and secure from all alarms;
> Leaning, leaning,
> Leaning on the everlasting arms.
>
> —Elisha A. Hoffman

So when we are sad, tired or even angry, we can lean on Jesus. The way we lean on Jesus is to pray and tell him about the problem and ask him to change our attitude. We remember that he said he would always be there to help us.

Dear Lord, I'm leaning on you to help me when I face problems. Amen.

Good Morning

Be ready in the morning, and then come up on Mount Sinai. Present yourself to me there on top of the mountain.
Exodus 34:2

Morning is a special time of day. Most mornings are quiet. The air is fresh and warm when the sun is shining. Fall mornings are especially nice when the trees have changed into many colors. Saying good morning to God is a great way to start the day — to talk with him before you talk to anyone else. It doesn't need to be anything more than opening your eyes and saying, "Good morning, God!"

God called Moses to the top of a mountain early in the morning to give him the Ten Commandments. God told Moses to come alone. Meeting with God was serious business. Do you know what happened on the mountain on that morning? God came down in a cloud and met with Moses. We cannot even begin to imagine what that would be like, but one thing we know for sure: it would be awesome — the most awesome thing that could ever happen to someone.

If you want to know God a little better, try talking to him the first thing every day. Thank him for the night's rest. Ask him to be with you all day long to help you in your work.

Dear Lord, I think I'll try to start meeting with you first thing in the morning. I want to feel you close to me all day long. Amen.

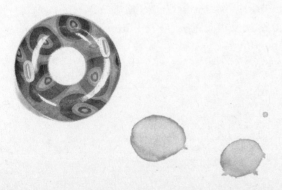

Follow the Leader

If anyone would come after me, he must deny himself and take up his cross and follow me.
Mark 8:34

Follow the leader is a fun game to play, especially if the leader is daring and creative and leads you up, over, through, and around challenging places. Following our leader, Jesus, is a wonderful life adventure. You have no idea where he might lead you. You can know that he will go with you wherever he leads. Let's think about some places he might take you and the adventures you might have in life.

You might become a doctor who makes a break-through discovery that saves lots of lives. Or you might become a senator or representative of the people of your state. If that happened, you could make important decisions to help people. Girls might become mothers; guys might be dads. Parenting is one of the most important and toughest jobs. Perhaps God will lead you to become a preacher or a missionary who goes to far places on earth.

As you grow into the person God wants you to be, part of your adventure will take you through challenges. You can't become a doctor without going through lots of school. You'd also see some very sick and hurt people, which would be hard. Even moms and dads face hard decisions about their children.

In today's verse, picking up your cross means accepting the challenges that come your way. When you follow God through each one, he'll use it to teach you. He'll bless you for following him.

Dear Lord, If you will lead me, I will follow—even through challenges. Make your way plain to me. Amen.

Something Smells Good

Awake, north wind, and come, south wind! Blow on my garden, that its fragrance may spread abroad.
Song of Solomon 4:16

There are some wonderful public gardens in the United States. One is Longwood Gardens in Pennsylvania. This is a huge garden with beautiful fountains, trees that have been trimmed into wonderful shapes, statues everywhere, and lily pads that are twelve feet wide. In the middle of the garden is a huge glass house called a conservatory. Inside that conservatory are gorgeous displays of flowers, even in winter. Inside the building, it is always warm and the air is filled with the fragrance of thousands of flowers.

Our lives are like gardens. The good, sweet things we do are like a perfume that drifts out of our lives and blesses all the people we meet. Now if we do mean things and are horrid to other people, it would be like us stomping through a field of onions. That wouldn't be such a great smell, would it? What kind of a life do you want to have—one that is good, kind, and sweet or one that is stinky, mean, and bitter? You get to make the choice.

Dear Lord, I want to be good and kind. I want the fragrance from my life to be sweet and lovely. Amen.

Sometimes You Have to Get Away

Hide in the Kerith Ravine, east of the Jordan.
1 Kings 17:3

The Prophet Elijah had just been through a very hard time. He had just stood up to the King of Israel and said, "As the Lord, the God of Israel, lives, whom I serve, there will be neither dew nor rain in the next few years except at my word." In other words, "It ain't gonna rain until I say so." Well, that didn't go over too well with the king, so Elijah had to hide. God sent him east of the Jordan River and took care of Elijah until the drought and famine were over.

Sometimes when we are confused and we can't figure things out, we need to get away to a safe place where we can be alone with God and pray about what to do next. Even Jesus had to get away from people sometimes. He would go off by himself where he could talk to God his Father. He'd go to a place where he could rest, think, and pray. So if Jesus needed to do that, we probably need time alone to pray and think too.

Dear Lord, Sometimes I feel like I need a quiet place to think. I'm going to try to take time to talk to you. Amen.

Looking for God

He is the Lord; let him do what is good in his eyes.
1 Samuel 3:18

Did you know God called out to Samuel in the middle of the night when Samuel was still a little boy? God had work for Samuel to do, and that was to give Eli the priest a message. It wasn't a happy message. God called Samuel three times before he recognized it was God talking. It isn't always easy to recognize God's voice or his work. But once you know his voice and his deeds, you'll be able to hear and see him better — just like Samuel did for his entire life.

Have you ever gone on a God hunt? Try one. First, think about what happened in your life today. What happened at school that was good? You should be able to think of one or two things easily. Now, what happened at school or home that was bad? How could God be working in that thing? What good might he bring out of it? Once you've thought of something good, you've found God's mark. Throughout the next week, search for God's work in different situations in your life. Soon you'll begin to see him more than you ever have before. You'll see that everything he touches shows his goodness.

Dear Lord, I would like to be a person who recognizes your voice and sees your work in everything in my life. Show me where you are and what you are doing. Amen.

Can You See?

Where there is no vision, the people perish.
Proverbs 29:18, KJV

Long ago in the kingdom of Swaziland, Africa, King Somhlolo had a dream. In his vision, a heavenly being came to him and showed him some people who had light-colored skin. It was different from the skin of his people. These people had pointed noses and straight hair like cow tails. In one hand they held a book, and in the other a round piece of metal. The heavenly visitor told the king to ignore the round metal object — which was a coin — and to eat the book because it would bring life to his people. The book was the Bible.

Of course, he was not really to eat the pages of the Bible, but he was to study it and take it into his life as though it were as important as food. When the king awakened, he knew he was to bring the Bible to his people. He sent for missionaries to come to his land. They came and taught the people of Swaziland about God's love. Through the vision, the king could see that God wanted to do something in his land. Because he obeyed God, today many people in Swaziland know Jesus Christ.

God wants to talk to us. One way he does that is through the Bible. God has a plan and a vision for all of us. He wants to lead you every day. A good habit is to have a quiet time each day to read the Bible, pray and listen to God. This will help you tune into God. You may not see a heavenly being in a dream, but God can show you through the Bible what he wants you to do.

Dear Lord, As I read your Word and listen for your voice, show me what your plan for my life is. Amen.

Bunches of Fruit

I am the true vine, and my Father is the gardener.
John 15:1

Gardeners know that the way to get fruit trees to bear lots of fruit is to prune them, which means to cut off or cut back parts of the tree. Trees that have not been pruned can become a tangled mass of shoots and branches that don't produce fruit and home to lots of insects and diseases.

Jesus said that our lives are like vines or fruit trees. He also taught that God is the gardener. He cuts off every branch in us that doesn't bear fruit. All the branches that do bear fruit get pruned so that they will be even more fruitful. That means that if God sees things in your life that are not good, he's going to take them out. And if he sees things that are good, he works on them some more so that they will be even better. God knows exactly what needs to go and what can stay. He won't take away more than is needed to help you become more like Jesus. Just as expert gardeners know what the results of their pruning will be even before they start cutting, God knows the kind of growth and fruit that will result before he goes to work on us. If we let him do what he wants to do, he'll make something beautiful out of us.

Dear Lord, Work on my life to help me become more like Jesus. Please prune what is needed. Amen.

Believing is Seeing

Then Jesus said, "Did I not tell you that if you believed, you would see the glory of God?"
John 11:40

What if you went to a funeral and one of the guests told the dead person to get up out of the casket? Would that freak you out? Most people would be freaked out by a dead person coming back to life. That's what Jesus did one day. His friend Lazarus had died. Mary and Martha, Lazarus' sisters, sent for Jesus, but he didn't come right away. Jesus wasn't troubled by the news because he knew something they didn't know. He knew he could bring the dead back to life. Jesus said to Lazarus's sisters, "Didn't I tell you that if you believed, you would see the glory of God?"

Just as Mary and Martha didn't understand why Jesus let Lazarus die, we sometimes wonder why difficult things happen to us. We don't understand why people we love get sick or move away, why families break up or why we don't have enough money to buy the things we need. Rather than focusing on all of the "whys," the things we don't understand, Jesus wants us to trust him. He wants us to have faith that he knows things we don't know. What do you need Jesus to do for you? Start today by asking him for what you need.

Dear Lord, I believe you are able to do anything, and I believe that I will see the glory of God through your answer. Amen.

A Rotten Deal

What is more, I consider everything a loss compared to the surpassing
greatness of knowing Christ Jesus my Lord, for whose sake I have lost all
things. I consider them rubbish, that I may gain Christ.
Philemon 3:8

There's an old, old story about a man named Faust who wants to
know everything. He studies for years, learning about law, science,
philosophy, literature — every field of study that exists. But he's
never satisfied, because there will always be some bit of knowledge
that eludes him.

One day, the devil appears and offers Faust all the knowledge
under heaven in exchange for his soul. Faust agrees and is able to
enjoy his new knowledge for a few years, but in the end his soul
belongs to the devil.

That was a rotten deal that Faust got himself into. He was so
focused on having a better life on earth that he couldn't see the
trouble he was bringing. We too can get ourselves into some real
messes. Some people get themselves into similar trouble by
focusing too much on the all the good things they have. They love
their money or their possessions more than anything else. If they
lose any of it, they are devastated.

The Bible says, "What good will it be for a man if he gains the
whole world, yet forfeits his soul? Or what can a man give in
exchange for his soul?" (Matthew 16:26). Making God our first love
will keep us on the right path. We'll be able to accept blessings and
hardships with the same good attitude. And if we lose something
precious, we won't be shaken up because we still have God. We
can do what the Scripture verse above says and consider everything
in our lives as nothing — rubbish — compared to finding God's love
through Jesus Christ. The most important thing of all — the best
deal — is to love and serve Jesus Christ even if it means giving up
everything else.

Dear Lord, I want to make the best deal, and that is to follow Jesus all
the days of my life. Amen.

Jesus Prays for Us

"Simon, Satan has asked to sift you as wheat. But I have prayed for you, Simon, that your faith may not fail. And when you have turned back, strengthen your brothers."
Luke 22:31, 32

Jesus was talking to Simon Peter in this verse. Jesus knew that the devil was going to try to get Peter to fail and turn against Jesus. Even though we don't usually see it, a spiritual war is going on around us. Satan wants to make us sin and fail, but God, Jesus, and his angels are there to help us. We can be so glad that God's power is stronger than Satan's. With God's help, we can win over Satan.

In this verse, Jesus says he is praying for Peter. Before he went back to heaven, Jesus prayed for his followers like this: "My prayer is not that you take them out of the world but that you protect them from the evil one" (John 17:15). Now that Jesus is in heaven, does he still pray for us? Yes. Part of his job is praying for us. Jesus sits next to God and tells him what we need. Jesus cares for us. He sympathizes with our weaknesses because he was tempted too. He knows how hard it is not to give in to temptation.

Dear Lord, I'm so glad I don't have to struggle to do right all by myself. I'm so glad you are praying for me. Amen.

A River of
Living Water

Whoever believes in me, as the Scripture has said, streams of living water will flow from within him.

John 7:38

Have you ever been thirsty? So thirsty that your tongue stuck to the roof of your mouth? It's an awful feeling. Dehydration (being thirsty to the point of illness) is serious business. Mild dehydration can be fixed by drinking a lot of water. Some people have become so dehydrated, though, that they've had to go to a hospital and have fluids put into their body through their veins. Once they have enough fluids inside them, everything in their body starts working again the way it should.

The same thing happens in our souls. We can get dehydrated if we don't "drink" the spiritual water we get by spending time with Jesus. We can get sick in our spirits. We don't love others the way we should. We give in to temptation. We don't have anything good to tell others about what Jesus means to us. That's when we need to go to the River of Living Water, Jesus, and spend time drinking up his presence and reading his Word. Then we will be full of his Spirit and have the strength we need to love God and others.

Dear Lord, I want to be thirsty for more of you. Help me to drink in your Word so I can live my life the right way. Amen.

Don't Go There

When they came to the border of Mysia, they tried to enter Bithynia, but the Spirit of Jesus would not allow them to.
Acts 16:7

Paul and his friends were on a missionary journey. They thought they knew where they were supposed to go next: to a country named Bithynia. But they were wrong. Wham! God shut the door. The Bible doesn't say what stopped them other than to say the Spirit of Jesus would not let them go there. Maybe they all looked at each other and said, "Now what?" During the night Paul had a vision in which a man from the country of Macedonia said, "Come over and help us." That was a clear direction from God. Paul didn't fool around. He and his friends got up and went as fast as they could to Macedonia.

One of the ways God guides us is to block our path. We may even be headed in a direction that is good, but it's not for us. God may want us to rest for a bit and wait on him. You may not see a vision like Paul did, but God has ways of letting you know what you are to do. His guidance might come when you are reading the Bible. It might come when you are praying. It might come when some wise person gives you advice. It might come when your plan is blocked. God will find a way to lead you if you are listening. So pay attention to which doors he opens.

Dear Lord, If you shut a door in my face, help me to know what you want me to do instead. Amen.

God Can Never Forget You

Say to God my Rock, "Why have you forgotten me? Why must I go about mourning, oppressed by the enemy?"
Psalm 42:9

Have you ever lost something and forgotten all about it until a long time later when you discovered it again? It was like finding something new. Or maybe you said, "Oh that's where I put that. I had forgotten I even had it."

The poor man who wrote this psalm was very depressed. He felt that God had forgotten him. But it is impossible for God to forget us — his children. There is no way. And the writer knew that because in another part of this psalm he says: "By day the Lord directs his love, at night his song is with me — a prayer to the God of my life" (verse 8).

Hope is powerful. No matter what we are going through, if we have hope, we will make it. The best hope to hold onto is that God loves us and is watching over us. He is never far away. He will provide everything we need in our life. We serve an awesome God, and if you think about that — especially when times are tough — you'll have hope.

Dear Lord, I want to understand who you are and what you can do for me so that I never lose hope. Amen.

Going Where You Cannot See

We live by faith, not by sight.
2 Corinthians 5:7

In 1934, an explorer William Beebe and an engineer named Otis Barton created a steel chamber called a bathysphere so that they could go to great depths in the ocean. They went down about 3,200 feet to look around. They were hooked to a ship on the surface by a long cable and they had a telephone. Beebe looked out the window and reported what he saw to a person on the surface. In 1948 Swiss physicist Auguste Piccard created a diving vessel he called the bathyscaphe. He went down 4,600 feet. In the 1950s Jacques Piccard joined his father, and they built a vessel that went down to 10,300 feet. In 1958 the U.S. Navy had a ship called the Trieste, and it went to the deepest point known on earth: 35,810 feet. That is deep!

Explorers like Beebe and Piccard led risky lives because they went where no one else had been. They didn't know exactly what would happen when they descended into the ocean. It took a lot of faith to do what they did — especially the first time. They had to have faith in their idea and faith in the people who helped them build their vessels.

As children of God, we also lead lives that require faith. We don't know what tomorrow may bring. It could be exciting and fun. Or it could be scary and sad. It's important to have faith in God. Whatever happens, he is going there with you.

Dear Lord, I know you are with me wherever I go. Amen.

Ransomed

I have found a ransom for him.
Job 33:24

A ransom is the price paid to get someone back. People have been taking others captive and asking for ransoms for thousands of years. In 78 BC some pirates captured the Roman Emperor Julius Caesar and demanded a ransom. They got it, too.

During the Middle Ages, knights fighting in wars were worth more alive than dead because those who captured them could ask for a ransom. In order to stay alive and be ransomed rather than be killed in battle, the knights developed a shield that they flew from a flagpole or that they wore on their clothing. That shield told the captors the family to which the knight belonged. Someone in that family would pay to get the knight back alive. They would buy back the knight.

In the Bible when the word ransom is used, it means to buy back. That is what Jesus did for us. He bought us back from the sin and death that all humans were captured by when Adam sinned. So now we belong to God through the price Jesus paid to save us. It's a good thing to be ransomed, and the family of God is a good place to be. He will always rescue you.

Dear Lord, Thank you for ransoming me and making me part of your forever family. Amen.

Promised Peace

I have told you these things, so that in me you may have peace. In this world you will have trouble. But take heart! I have overcome the world.
John 16:33

Once a great violinist named Paganini walked onto the stage to play a concert. All at once he realized something was wrong with his violin. He stood looking at it then realized he had the wrong violin. It was not his best, most valuable one. He went backstage to get his best violin and discovered someone had stolen it. What could he do? The audience was waiting for the concert. Quickly, he made a decision and walked out with the inferior violin. He explained to the audience what had happened. Then he said, "I will show you that the music is not in the instrument, but in the soul." He played as he had never played before. Beautiful music poured out of the instrument. The audience was thrilled, and they clapped so hard the sound almost raised the roof of the concert hall.

There is a spiritual lesson in this story. The violinist is like us, and the inferior violin is like the problems in our lives. Just as the violinist took that inferior violin in his hands and made beautiful music, we can look at our problems and say, "No matter what the circumstances are, the music is still in my soul. I still have peace and joy, and I'm not going to let circumstances make me sad and miserable." No matter what goes wrong in your life, you can have peace. Only God can give us the kind of peace. His peace helps us face any circumstance with confidence that we can survive it.

Dear Lord, Please give me your peace so that nothing hard shakes me. Amen.

Why Is Prayer Important?

I am a man of prayer.
Psalm 109:4

Hezekiah was a good king. He trusted in God. He held onto God in good times and bad and God was with him. But as time went on, his enemy to the north, King Sennacherib of Assyria, began to invade and trouble his land. Hezekiah had spent his life dedicated to God, so he knew he must pray. Soon Hezekiah had his answer. God sent Isaiah the prophet with a message: God was going to rescue Hezekiah and his people.

This story might make you wonder: if God loved the Israelites and wanted to save them from the Assyrians, couldn't he have done it without Hezekiah's prayers? If God knows everything and can do everything, why do we need to pray? Couldn't he just fix problems without our requests? Yes, he could, but he has chosen to involve us in his work through prayer.

God is unchangeable, always the same, always wanting the best for his children. We cannot know the mind of God, but we know that our prayers change us. Prayer brings us closer to God and helps us understand his purpose for us. It is through prayer that we participate in a conversation with God. Hezekiah was a man of prayer and God heard his prayers. God wants you to be a boy or girl of prayer too. Start now to develop a life of prayer that will keep you close to God.

Dear Lord, Through my prayers, show me your will for my life. Lead me into a closer walk with you. Amen.

Fly Like an Eagle

He shielded him and cared for him; he guarded him as the apple of his eye,
like an eagle that stirs up its nest and hovers over its young, that spreads its
wings to catch them and carries them on its pinions.
Deuteronomy 32:10–11

Eagles must teach their young to fly. When the young birds are
ready to fly, the parents stir up the nest so that there is no
comfortable place for the chick to rest. Then they encourage the
young birds to the edge of the nest where they totter and cry. The
nests are very high in trees and on rocky cliffs. It is a long way to
the ground, and the little birds don't yet know they can fly. The
parents stop bringing food to them and try to coax them out of
the nest.

It takes a while for the young birds to get up the courage to leave
the nest. Usually their first flight is straight down to the ground.
The parents then feed them and coax them to fly back to the nest.
Eventually, the eaglets learn how to fly on their own and can go
everywhere just as their parents do.

Sometimes we are like those young eagles standing on the edge
of the nest wondering what to do next. God may be asking you to
do things that you are unsure you can do. When those times come,
remember God is right there beside you. He will even carry you if he
needs to so you can accomplish the task he has given you. You can
do more than you ever thought when God is with you.

Dear Lord, I've already had to do some things I was sure I could not do.
Help me, Lord, to trust and follow you. Amen.

Going Through Hard Times

It was good for me to be afflicted so that I might learn your decrees.
Psalm 119:71

Here's a word we wish we could do without — "affliction." To be afflicted is to experience great mental or physical distress. It involves pain and suffering. Now why would the person who wrote Psalm 119 say it was good to be afflicted? One reason is that being afflicted, going through hard times, makes us strong. God can use our problems to teach us lots of things we might not learn any other way.

What hard things are happening in your life? Is school is a hard place where kids tease you? Do you want to live for Jesus but find it difficult because one or both of your parents don't believe in God? Do your friends lie or do things you know are not good for them? Do they try to get you to do those things? These are some examples of what it means to be afflicted.

It isn't easy to be a strong when you are afflicted, but if you will stand with Jesus, he will help you. He can take the hard things that happen in our life and use them to help us be more patient, kind, wise, and peaceful. That's what all of us want to be.

Dear Lord, I don't want to be afflicted but I trust that you are with me when I go through hard times. I believe you can use my problems to teach me things and to create something beautiful in my heart. Amen.

Quiet Town

Then he took them with him and they withdrew by themselves to a town called Bethsaida.

Luke 9:10

Sometimes Jesus sent his disciples out to help people. After some time they would come back to him. Jesus was very smart. He knew that when he and his disciples got tired because they had been helping many people, they needed to get away by themselves to rest. So he took them to Bethsaida, a little town near the Sea of Galilee. There they could rest and talk and get ready for the next time they would meet many people.

What do you suppose it was like when all the disciples got back together after traveling and helping people? It must have been wonderful to be alone again with Jesus. The disciples probably told stories about sick people being made well when they prayed for them. They probably told about the times they preached and the people listened and believed in Jesus. Rest time was important and so was their time with Jesus.

Time spent alone with Jesus is good for us too. Without the noise from the TV, the phone, or an iPod, consider what he means to you. Resting in him helps you remember that God is big enough to help with all of life's problems. Try it sometime.

Dear Lord, Sometimes it's hard for me to settle down and rest. But I know it's good, and it's even better if I rest in Jesus and his love. Amen.

A Quiet Whisper

After the earthquake came a fire, but the Lord was not in the fire. And after the fire came a gentle whisper.
1 Kings 19:12

Elijah was a devoted prophet of God who lived courageously in the face of death and opposition. He witnessed God's amazing power in a dramatic ways, like heavenly chariots and supernatural showdowns with false prophets. But Elijah knew that God was more than just strength and power. Because they had a deep, loving relationship, Elijah knew the voice of God, even when it came in a quiet whisper.

"What are you doing here, Elijah?" God once gently whispered. The care, concern, and closeness God showed Elijah, he gives to us. He whispers to our hearts that he is nearby and he sees us and knows what's going on. And like the prophet, we too can lean on our fellowship with the living God, listen for his leading and respond with confident obedience.

Wouldn't it be wonderful if the next time you felt really sad you could hear God's voice calling you by name and asking, "Are you all right?" Remember Elijah who went to be alone with God and waited for his care. Even when you are troubled or under pressure, you never have to wonder if God is close. Sometimes you just have to wait.

Dear Lord, Since you assure me that you care for me, help me focus more on hearing your voice than on worrying about the circumstances. Amen.

Better than Ever

The Lord blessed the latter part of Job's life more than the first. He had fourteen thousand sheep, six thousand camels, a thousand yoke of oxen and a thousand donkeys.
Job 42:12

Have you ever listed all of your blessings? Maybe you'd start with your family or the roof over your head or your great brain? Would your difficulties or heartaches make the list? If you believe the dictionary that describes "blessed" as "bringing comfort or joy," how can the Bible count suffering as a blessing?

Because blessings often come in packages we don't expect.

Consider the itchy, ugly, restless illness of chicken pox. You see the sores. You feel the itch. You suffer through the sickness. What you don't see is that through the illness, your body becomes stronger, building a protection against chicken pox that stays with you the rest of your life.

Job suffered from more than chicken pox, physically and emotionally. Through the pain he clung to the Lord and realized hope that only God can give. The blessings from the struggles he endured — strength of character, depth of faith, breadth of patience — would never be taken away.

Dear Lord, In all the difficult things I face, help me trust you. Give me lasting blessings from my struggles — peace in Christ and hope that can't be shaken. Amen.

No Water

Some time later the brook dried up because there had been no rain in the land.
1 Kings 17:7

Do you remember the story of how God sent Elijah out to the desert when King Ahab and Queen Jezebel threatened to kill him? They were angry because Elijah had said there would be no more rain on the land until he said so. Without rain, the crops wouldn't grow. Without crops people would go hungry. It would be a terrible time. God told Elijah he would take care of him and sent him out in the desert to a brook. Birds came and fed him. Well, that was then, but now the brook was drying up. Do you think maybe Elijah said to God, "What gives? I came here like you told me to and now I'm not going to have any water?"

What Elijah didn't know was that it was time for him to move on to another place. It wasn't long until God said, "Go at once to Zarephath of Sidon and stay there. I have commanded a widow in that place to supply you with food." God was about to perform a wonderful miracle that not only saved Elijah's life, but the life of the widow and her son. God multiplied her flour and oil so that it lasted throughout the entire time there was no rain or crops. She baked bread from the flour and oil and kept all three of them alive.

We need to be listening in case God gives us a new set of instructions that take us in a different direction. He loves us and will guide us. Our job is to listen for his voice.

Dear Lord, I know you want to guide me. Help me listen for your voice. Amen.

Times to be Wise

As a sheep before her shearers is silent, so he did not open his mouth.
Isaiah 53:7

When Amy heard that her friend Charlie had lied about beating her in tennis, she was angry. Now she had a choice to make. Should she —

- *March right up to Charlie and give him a piece of her mind until he admits to everyone that he lied.*
  A fool gives full vent to his anger but a wise man keeps himself under control.
  Proverb 29:11

- *Make up something to get back at him, since he lied first.*
  Do not answer a fool according to his folly, or you will be like him yourself.
  Proverb 26:4

- *Slow down. Pray about forgiveness or handling things in private. After all, he is a friend.*
  Whoever gives heed to instruction prospers, and blessed is he who trusts in the Lord.
  Proverb 16:20

Throughout his life, Jesus was misunderstood, lied about, betrayed and plotted against. Sometimes he exposed corrupt officials with profound wisdom. Sometimes he displayed fierce, righteous indignation at immorality. Sometimes he spoke hard truth with loving gentleness. Sometimes he said nothing at all. Withdrawing to pray all the time, Jesus' insight and discernment came directly from his fellowship with the Father.

Take a lesson from the one who handled conflict and injustice the best. Like Jesus, spend time talking to your heavenly Father — who loves you, knows the truth and holds ultimate wisdom. Then you will be ready to act wisely when difficult things come up.

Dear Lord, Please help me know what to do and when to do it. I trust you. Amen.

Walking in Darkness

Who among you fears the Lord and obeys the word of his servant? Let him who walks in the dark, who has no light, trust in the name of the Lord and rely on his God.

Isaiah 50:10

Nobody likes to walk in darkness. That's a good way to stub your toe. But sometimes in our life, we can't see what's going to happen next and it is a little frightening. That's a little like walking in the dark. Often in life we have a choice between doing something safe and familiar — something that won't challenge us — and going on an adventure for God. There will be some risks involved, but trusting God and his plan for you means that you will be challenged and changed in ways you could never have anticipated.

You have been invited into a relationship with the One who shines light in darkness and who knows your future. If worry, doubt or confusion are interrupting your peace, go to the Word and remind yourself who is in control and how much he loves you.

Dear Lord, I'm so glad I can put my hand in yours and know you will be with me. Help me replace my worries with trust in you. Amen.

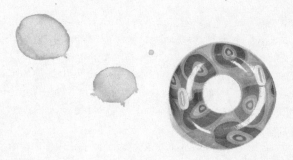

Lay Down Your Cares

Do not be anxious about anything, but in everything, by prayer and petition, with thanksgiving, present your requests to God.
Philemon 4:6

Worry has been compared to sitting in a rocking chair—it keeps you busy, but it doesn't go anywhere. Instead of spending your energy with anxiety and worrying about things you won't be able to change, go to the One who is in control of your situation and can comfort you.

Talking to God helps us trust him. And when we give our burdens and concerns to him we can rest.

Just as the camel gives up its load at the end of day to rest, so you can give up your concerns. Take your worry to the One who can nurture you, give you courage, ease your anxiety, and give you rest.

Dear Lord, Tonight I'll give my cares and burdens to you to take care of while I sleep. Amen.

Summer Will Come Again

Yet the Lord longs to be gracious to you; he rises to show you compassion.... Blessed are all who wait for him!
Isaiah 30:18

When the seasons turn cold, long, V-shaped lines of geese start heading south for warmer weather. Winter will be dark and tough—just like some times in our life are dark and tough. It can be easy to lose hope that anything will ever change. But just as the seasons come and go, so do tough times. God planned it that way.

> Oh, every year has its winter,
> And every year has its rain—
> But a day is always coming
> When the birds go north again.
> When new leaves swell in the forest,
> And grass springs green on the plain,
> And alders' veins turn crimson—
> And the birds go north again.
> Oh, every heart has its sorrow,
> And every heart has its pain—
> But a day is always coming
> When the birds go north again.
> 'Tis the sweetest thing to remember,
> If courage is on the wane,
> When the cold, dark days are over—
> Why, the birds go north again.
>
> —Anonymous

If your heart is heavy with sad time, hang on to hope. God is at work and good times will come again.

Dear Lord, I know that you are watching over Earth, and you are watching over me. Let me hang on to you. Amen.

No Fretting Allowed

Do not fret.
Psalm 37:1

"Fret." What an interesting word. We think of someone who frets as a worrier. The dictionary says the word means to eat away at or gnaw into. A dog chewing at a bone could be said to be fretting the bone. Fretting is something that rubs at us like an itchy sweater. It makes us irritable. Some people fret when the wind blows. When babies are fretting, we say they are fussy. You get the idea.

Now, if God is our heavenly Father, and if he loves us so much he sent his only Son to die for our sins, and if he is preparing a home in heaven for us, and if we are going to live with him forever, what have we got to worry or fret about? Not a lot. Then why do we do it? Could it be because we really don't know God very well? Could it be because we don't really know what God has promised us as is written in the Bible? The answer to both those questions is probably "yes."

If you open your Bible and find the verse above and then read on a bit, you would read this, "Trust in the Lord and do good ... delight yourself in the Lord and he will give you the desires of your heart" (Psalm 37:3–4). That's about as good as it gets when it comes to God's promises.

Dear God, I want to know you better so that I can trust you more and so that I can stop fretting. Amen.

From Seeds Come Oaks

Dying, and yet we live on.
2 Corinthians 6:9

If you live where there are oak trees, you've probably seen the ground beneath the tree littered with acorns. You probably have plenty of squirrels too, as squirrels love to eat and hide acorns. When you hold an acorn in your hand, it is really hard to believe a huge oak tree could grow from such a small seed — for the acorn is a seed. And all those squirrels hiding the acorns by burying them in the ground are helping plant new trees. They bury so many acorns they could never remember where they put them all, and soon new seedling oak trees are popping up.

When the squirrel puts the acorn into the ground, the seed begins to deteriorate. The hard shell softens so that roots can begin to work their way out of the seed. If you looked at a deteriorating acorn, you would think it was dead. Yet out of that old dying shell, new life comes. Jesus told his disciples, "Truly I tell you, unless a kernel of wheat falls to the ground and dies, it remains only a single seed. But if it dies, it produces many seeds (John 12:24). For us that means learning to consider what God wants before we consider what we want. And like the decaying acorn seed, it might not be pretty at first. Maybe we do something we know is right but our attitude is reluctant and grudging. But each time we practice, a new root of selflessness grows. Gradually God nurtures you into someone with a broader, richer, more generous life than you ever considered before.

Dear God, I understand you have bigger, more exciting plans for me than I imagine. Help me embrace you and "die to myself" so I can live an abundant life. Amen.

Whatever You Do

While Joseph was there in the prison, the Lord was with him; he showed him kindness and granted him favor in the eyes of the prison warden . . . the Lord was with Joseph and gave him success in whatever he did.
Genesis 39:20–23

During World War II when the Jews were under attack by the Nazis, some Christians set out to help them. Corrie ten Boom and her family courageously followed God and virtuously protected Jews — and it landed them in jail. Even while conditions were difficult and scary, she saw signs — both miraculous and mundane — that God was with them. And so when fleas made them even more miserable and uncomfortable, she learned to thank God for his goodness, even with the fleas. Later they learned that the biting insects kept the cruel jailers away, leaving Corrie and her group of prisoners alone to study God's Word and praise God.

God's plans don't stop at prison doors. He uses every corner of life for good — even prison, even sickness, failure, and disappointment. You may feel your life has been interrupted by bad circumstances but don't give in to self-pity or discouragement. God is not surprised or stumped by what's going on. He's with you. So praise him anyway. Trust him anyway.

Dear Lord, I want to be in your will. Help me to not be discouraged if it doesn't look like what I expected. Thank you for never leaving me. Amen.

Tell Jesus

Do not be anxious about anything, but in everything, by prayer and petition, with thanksgiving, present your requests to God.
Philippians 4:6

When we are anxious we feel jumpy, scared, worried, and uneasy. Just talking about those feelings makes us feel anxious. When we are anxious, we are living our life as if we were waiting for someone to jump out and scare us. It's an awful way to live. It causes us to pump a hormone called adrenalin. Adrenalin makes our heart beat faster and it makes our body ready to react to what it thinks is danger. And all that can make you very tired.

God says we don't need to live that way. Instead, we can tell Jesus everything in prayer. And oh, yes, we are to have thankful hearts as we ask Jesus for what we need. That's all there is to it: ask it and forget it. Then whatever happens is up to God. It's pretty simple. When God is in control, you can study and play and sleep and do everything you love to do without worry. God knows what you need and he is going to take care of everything. You can lie down and go to sleep and not worry about a thing.

Dear Lord, Sometimes I worry about things, but it doesn't do any good. I'm going to give everything to you in prayer and stop worrying. Amen.

What Would You Do If?

About midnight Paul and Silas were praying and singing hymns to God, and the other prisoners were listening to them.
Acts 16:25, 26

Imagine that you had spent all day long telling people about Jesus and then were accused of something you didn't do. Then you were stripped, beaten, thrown into the deepest, darkest part of the jail, and left to spend the night sitting up and bleeding? What would you do?

That's the situation Paul and Silas found themselves in. So what did they do? Whine and complain? Not at all. One of them probably looked at the other and said, "Well, what do we do now?" The other one probably answered, "Trust the Lord. Let's sing and pray." That's what they did, and that's when the real excitement began. Suddenly there was a violent earthquake. Stuff began to rattle, dirt fell out of the ceiling,the stocks on their feet began to shake and then popped open. In fact, all the doors flew open and the chains fell off everyone in the entire jail.

The jailer was terrified because if the prisoners escaped, he would be severely punished. He might even lose his life. He was ready to kill himself when Paul said, "Don't hurt yourself. We are all here." The jailer and his family believed in Jesus that night and were saved. They put medicine on Paul's and Silas' wounds and gave them dinner. They did not put them back into chains.

It's encouraging to see bad things turn into good and helps us to remember that God is in control. Your strength in difficult times may give hope to your friends. Your courage in the face of failure may help others strive to succeed. Your unwavering faith in God's goodness may bless others. Never forget that sometimes the worst things that happen turn out for good.

Dear Lord, Help me to learn to praise you in whatever situation I'm in — even if I'm going through a hard time and feel like I'm in chains. Thank you for all the wonders you can work! Amen.

Broken and Restored

By reason of breakings they purify themselves.
Job 41:25, KJV

There once were three boys locked in a room. They all wanted to get out, but none of them had the key. So the strongest said, "I'm going to bust my way out of here," and he had the muscles to do it. He kicked and pounded and threw himself against the door until he fell to the floor exhausted.

The second boy, the smartest of the group, thought he had a better chance to get out of the room. He analyzed the door, studied alternate angles, and considered complicated theories. "From my calculations," he finally said, "I figure it's completely impossible to get out of this room." And he sat down.

So the third boy got up. He was small and weak, slow and simple. Certainly, they all thought, he doesn't stand a chance to get out of the room. The boy walked to the door, knocked quietly and said, "Excuse me, will you let us out?" And the one with the key heard the knock and happily opened the door.

When you think you are strong, you depend on your strength. When you think you are smart, you depend on your brain. When you think you are clever, you depend on your wits. But when you are broken, you depend on someone who can help. You depend on a Savior — which is exactly the way God likes it.

What a blessing to know when you're broken, because you are already on the path to finding wholeness and hope.

Dear Lord, I am broken. I can't do things on my own. Thank you that I can depend on you for strength and hope and life. Amen.

Run Free!

Therefore, since we are surrounded by such a great cloud of witnesses, let us throw off everything that hinders and the sin that so easily entangles, and let us run with perseverance the race marked out for us.
Hebrews 12:1

An athlete who is training for a race uses special equipment. A swimmer wears a special suit (called a "drag suit") while he practices. This suit gives him more resistance as he slides through the water, making him work harder to go the same speed. A runner wears heavy training shoes that protect her feet and add extra weight. When race day comes, the swimmer wears a sleeker suit that helps him zip through the water as quickly as possible. The runner wears light shoes that protect her feet without weighing her down. Since the athletes have practiced with heavy clothing, they are able to go faster than before for the big races.

When we are running the race of life, we have to get rid of stuff that drags us down—stuff like lying, stealing, being lazy, being disrespectful, sadness, anger, and many more things that slow us up in being what God's wants us to be. This would be a good time to ask God to help you get rid of those problems in your life so you can be freed up to become more like Jesus.

Dear Lord, Help me overcome the weights that will keep me from running fast for your kingdom. Amen.

Eating Humble Pie

May I never boast except in the cross of our Lord Jesus Christ, through which the world has been crucified to me, and I to the world.
Galatians 6:14

Hundreds of years ago, in England, the very best food—the best meats, the best pastries, the best cheeses, and the best fruits—were reserved for the lords and ladies. The servants had to eat something called "humble pie." This was a pie made with an animal's innards, like the heart and the liver. Today, when someone has to admit that they made a mistake or bragged about something that was not true, we say that they have to eat humble pie. It means they need to admit their mistake and apologize.

No one likes someone who brags all the time. In today's scripture verse, the Apostle Paul is reminding us that as Christians, we know that we have nothing to brag about. Every ability we have or good thing we do is done through Christ. We can't take any credit for ourselves. If we do, we have to eat humble pie. The next time you are tempted to think that you are better than someone else, remember that we don't have a right to brag about anything except what Jesus has done for us.

Dear Lord, It is so easy to brag. It makes me feel important—for a minute. I don't want to have to eat humble pie, so help me not to brag except about you. Amen.

Do God's Promises Really Come True?

As the sun was setting, Abram fell into a deep sleep, and a thick and dreadful darkness came over him. Then the Lord said to him, "Know for certain that your descendants will be strangers in a country not their own, and they will be enslaved and mistreated four hundred years. But I will punish the nation they serve as slaves, and afterward they will come out with great possessions."
Genesis 15:12–14

Long before Abram — later called Abraham — had a son or any grandchildren, God said that his descendents would be strangers in a country that was not their own. God said that they would be slaves, but when they left Egypt they would be very rich. Did that come true? You bet! There was a famine in Israel but there was food in Egypt. Abraham's grandson, Jacob, moved his entire family to Egypt so they would not starve. At first it was great for them, but after a while a new pharaoh began to rule and he turned all those people into his slaves. God's people were in Egypt for 400 years, most of the time as slaves. Then came Moses and the ten plagues, and suddenly the people were free. As they left Egypt, the Egyptian people gave God's people all kinds of jewels and coins and wealth of every kind just to get rid of them. So what God said would happen, happened exactly as he said.

There are many promises of God in the Bible that have already come true — like the promises of Jesus being born, living as a man, dying on a cross, being resurrected on the third day. There are many more promises that have not yet come true. But they will. One of them is that Jesus will come back and take his own people to heaven to be with him forever. Just like God's people in Egypt didn't know when it would happen, and the people who were looking for a savior didn't know when it would happen, we don't know when Jesus will return. We just know he promised it and it will happen.

Dear Lord, Thank you for your promises. Help me be faithful while I wait on your plans. Amen.

Following the Leader

So they set out from the mountain of the Lord and traveled for three days. The ark of the covenant of the Lord went before them during those three days to find them a place to rest.
Numbers 10:33

In the story of the Pied Piper, a musician comes into town and plays a magical tune that attracts children. Without thinking, they follow him wherever he goes, even into danger. Now you are old enough and smart enough to know better than to follow a flute-playing stranger. But every day you make choices about whom you will follow. Would you follow a friend who didn't listen to his teacher? What would you do if your older sister asked you to lie to your parents?

The Israelites followed God (although not always very well.) They were told to follow his directions, his commandments, and his spokesmen as they followed him out of Egypt, across a parted sea, into the desert, into battle, and into the Promised Land.

God wants us to follow him too — by knowing what is in his word and listening to people who can help steer you right. Exodus 23:2 says, "Do not follow the crowd in doing wrong." Choose your friends wisely. It's always easier to have a friend who follows Jesus too. Together you can remember John 10:4 – 5: "[Jesus] goes on ahead of them, and his sheep follow him because they know his voice. But they will never follow a stranger; in fact, they will run away from him because they do not recognize a stranger's voice." If you know Jesus and follow his voice, you are exactly where you are supposed to be.

Dear Lord, You are the leader I want to follow. Surround me with people who love you who can help me too. Amen.

How Big Is God?

And the peace of God, which transcends all understanding, will guard your hearts and your minds in Christ Jesus.

Philippians 4:7

Suppose you got a new puppy and it had to go outside. Would you just stick it outside the door and leave it to roam on its own? No, never. You would either put the puppy on a leash and take it out, or you would put it inside a fenced yard where it would be safe. If you put it inside a fenced area, the puppy could run and play and maybe even go to sleep and still be perfectly safe. That's something like the kind of peace God promises us.

When God wraps you up in his peace, it's as if he puts a fence around you. You can see what's happening outside the fence, but what's out there can't get to you. You are safe. Nothing can get through that fence. God is protecting you. You don't have to worry about it. In today's verse we are promised the "peace of God which transcends all understanding." In the verse, the word transcends means that God's peace is bigger and stronger than anything we might face in the material world.

If you tend to worry a lot, you can let those worries go. Jesus can help you. Pray and ask him to help you not to worry and to give you his peace.

Dear Lord, Help me not to worry. Help me lay down and sleep in peace. I know you are right there watching over me. Amen.

How About a Mansion?

Now we know that if the earthly tent we live in is destroyed, we have a building from God, an eternal house in heaven, not built by human hands.
2 Corinthians 5:1

Here is great news. Jesus went back to heaven to prepare a place for us. He said: "There is plenty of room for you in my Father's home. If that weren't so, would I have told you that I'm on my way to get a room ready for you? And if I'm on my way to get your room ready, I'll come back and get you so you can live where I live" (John 14:2, The Message). How exciting is that? What kind of house do you think God has? It has to be something more wonderful than anything you have ever seen or ever will see on earth.

God wants us to live long happy lives while we are here on earth. He wants us to learn about him and serve others and have families and go to church and love him and others. But someday, a long way down the road, it will be time to leave this life. No worry. He'll be there to meet us when the time comes and he will take us home to that place he is preparing for us. It doesn't matter what kind of house you have here on earth, you have a better home waiting for you. It doesn't matter if you are rich or poor: if you live for Jesus, one day you will have a wonderful home in heaven. And that's exciting news.

Dear Lord, I want to live my whole life here on earth for you. Then, when I am old and tired, will you come get me and take me to your mansion in heaven? Amen.

While You Are Doing Your Job

Now Moses was tending the flock of Jethro his father-in-law, the priest of Midian, and he led the flock to the far side of the desert and came to Horeb, the mountain of God. There the angel of the Lord appeared to him in flames of fire from within a bush. Moses saw that though the bush was on fire it did not burn up.

Exodus 3:1, 2

Lots of people would like to see a miracle, and it would be exciting. But if you go looking for miracles, you probably won't find them. Usually God comes and does miraculous things when we least expect them. That's what happened to Moses. He was out on the desert, working by taking care of his father-in-law's cattle when he saw something strange. He didn't know it yet, but that burning bush had an angel in it — an angel with a message for him. How exciting!

God wants us to be faithful in our work, whether it's tending sheep as Moses was doing, or completing our chores and homework as we must often do. If he wants to speak to us, he can while we are doing our jobs.

Saint Francis of Assisi was hoeing his garden. Someone asked him what he would do if he learned he would die before the day ended. He said, "I would finish hoeing my garden." He knew God could minister to him right there in the garden — even if it wasn't with a miraculous burning bush. So he wanted to go right on doing what God had given him to do and not worry about the future.

It takes discipline to not fuss about the work you have to do. It takes discipline to just keep working at a task until it is finished. In it God will fashion you into the person he wants you to be for his purposes.

Dear Lord, I know you have purpose for all things. Help me do work and ordinary things with the same attitude I do exciting things. Amen.

Praise Be to the Lord

Not one word has failed of all the good promises
he gave through his servant Moses.
1 Kings 8:56

When the Israelites had been delivered from Egypt, they sang and
celebrated all the way out of town ... until they entered the desert.
Thirsty, hungry and worried, they looked around in confusion.
Where was the Promised Land, flowing with milk and honey? "You
should have just left us in Egypt," they whined to Moses. "At least
we had food."

God's plan didn't look like what they expected. Hadn't he heard
their prayers? Of course he had, but he was answering them in a far
richer way. They were willing to return to slavery, while God was
showing them freedom. Sadly in the desert, their confusion and
worry was drowning out their faith.

As the creator of the universe, author of life, ruler of heavens and
earth, God is bigger than we can imagine and understand. But he
has assured us with trustworthy promises that he is all-good and
all-powerful. So even if we feel confused or lost, we can call upon
him in faith. We remember what we do know — God loves us.

Dear Lord, Today instead of worry, I choose to trust. Thank you for
loving me enough to hear my prayers and answer them in the best
way. Amen.

Becoming Valuable

I will make you into a threshing sledge, new and sharp, with many teeth.
You will thresh the mountains and crush them, and reduce the hills to chaff.
Isaiah 41:15

A threshing sledge was a tool that was used in ancient times to separate the grain from the chaff on stalks of wheat. It was a valuable tool that started as a simple bar of steel. In order to be useful, the steel had to be pounded, molded and sharpened into a device designed to help gather grain.

Followers of Christ are like these bars of steel where training, trials and hard lessons serve to mold them into useful tools for God. During difficult times, we are being sharpened for his work and purposes. And through it all, he encourages us: "For I am the Lord, your God, who takes hold of your right hand and says to you, Do not fear; I will help you" (Isaiah 41:13).

Dear Lord, Thank you for being with me as you use me in your plans. Amen.

A Rule We Can Love

Until now you have not asked for anything in my name. Ask and you will receive, and your joy will be complete.
John 16:24

Most of us have lots of rules in our lives. The rule might be to get up or go to bed at a certain time. It might be to do homework in a certain place and before doing other more fun things. It might be to practice music or a sport—even when you don't feel like it. Grownups have lots of rules too. There are traffic rules and tax rules and paying bills on time rules. Sometimes we all get tired of rules. But here is a rule—really, a command—that Jesus gave his disciples. It's one we can love. He said they should ask for anything in his name and he would give it to them. And what he told those disciples goes for us as well. He has commanded us to ask for the things we need.

At some point in their lives, most people have prayed prayers that have not yet been answered. So what about that? Perhaps what they prayed for will come later on. Or perhaps what the person asked for would be harmful and cause sorrow rather than joy. Our job is to ask for what we need and leave it with God. His job is to answer in a way that brings us joy. Some of the things we foolishly ask for would hurt us. Because God loves us, he won't give us those things. So keep on asking and see what God will do for you.

Dear Lord, I believe you hear me when I pray and you will answer in a way that is good for me. Amen.

Quiet Time

After he had dismissed them, he went up on a mountainside by himself to pray. When evening came, he was there alone.
Matthew 14:23

In a home in Africa where orphan children are loved and cared for, every day is filled with study, chores, eating, play, and a quiet time. Even the big kids have a quiet time. Why? Well, the people who care for the children have found that they get along better and are happier when they have a quiet time in the middle of the day. After lunch, everyone goes to his or her room to lie down for a time. Some of the kids sleep. Some of them read. Some of them just think.

A rest time is a good thing for everyone — grownups as well as kids! We live in a very busy, noisy world. There are lots of things to do every day — so much to do that sometimes we can't keep it all straight. We need a quiet time. Jesus was God's Son and he needed time away from all the people who wanted him to heal them and teach them. He would often sneak off by himself and go to a mountain to talk to his Father. If Jesus needed a quiet time, don't you think we might too? And as part of your quiet time, perhaps you can talk to God too.

Dear Lord, I'm so glad I can talk to you and depend on you. When it's quiet, I want to get close to you. Amen.

Riding the Waves

Deep calls to deep in the roar of your waterfalls; all your waves and breakers have swept over me.
Psalm 42:7

This verse sounds like the person who wrote it might know what a wipeout is. A "wipeout" is a word surfers use to describe what happens when a wave comes crashing down and knocks them off their boards. Surfers try to avoid wipeouts because they can be dangerous.

Even if you've never been on a surf board, you might have had a wipeout experience — it's when something big happens to you and you feel like you can't do anything about it. If your parents have gotten a divorce, you know what a wipeout feels like. If someone you love gets very ill and maybe even dies, that feels like a wipeout too. Wipeouts are the things that happen in life that leave you feeling hurt and helpless. But guess what? God isn't helpless. He sees your situation and he will help you. He can use your wipeout experience to make you strong inside and to help you become more like Jesus. He promises to love you all day long and he can put a song in your heart. He can help you rest in his peace despite the chaos in your life.

Dear Lord, I didn't ask for the stuff that has wiped me out to happen in my life. Will you help me get through it? Amen.

Sitting with Jesus

But because of his great love for us, God, who is rich in mercy, made us
alive with Christ.... And God raised us up with Christ and seated us with
him in the heavenly realms in Christ Jesus.

Ephesians 2:4–6

What do you think of the idea of sitting beside a king? Wouldn't
that be wonderful? What would it be like to sit beside Jesus in
heaven? We can only imagine just how wonderful that would be.
The Bible says that we will sit with Jesus in heaven. Because we are
part of God's family, we are already princes and princesses in his
kingdom on earth. Jesus told a couple of his disciples who asked to
sit beside him in heaven, "To sit at my right or left is not for me to
grant. These places belong to those for whom they have been
prepared" (Matthew 10:40). God is preparing a place for us to sit
near Jesus in heaven.

Now, we can't apply to sit on a throne near Jesus. We can't buy
a place in heaven. There is only one way to get that seat near Jesus,
and that is to let Jesus come into your heart and life. Then we have
to live for him every day of our life. We have to learn to listen to
him and obey him completely. It's easy to do what God asks when
we remember that he only wants what's best for us. That doesn't
mean life will be a piece of cake, but it does mean that whatever we
go through, Jesus will be there to help us and guide us and bring us
out of our troubled time with victory. Then we will be a little more
ready to sit near Jesus in heaven.

Dear Lord, As I go through hard times help me to learn from my
experience and understand how to trust you more.

Making Gold

He will sit as a refiner and purifier of silver.
Malachi 3:3

Here is a poem about becoming like pure gold. Gold is made pure and beautiful when it is refined — heated — with fire until all the impurities come out. Our lives become pure when we let God take away the stuff that keeps us from looking like him. In the poem below, God is the refiner and we are the gold being refined.

He sat by a fire of super-hot heat,
As He watched by the precious ore,
And closer He bent with a searching gaze
As He heated it more and more.
He knew He had ore that could stand the test,
And He wanted the finest gold
To mold as a crown for the King to wear,
Set with gems with a price untold.
And the gold grew brighter and even more bright,
But our eyes were dim with tears,
We saw only the fire — not the Master's hand,
And we questioned with anxious fears.
Yet our gold shone out with a richer glow,
As it mirrored a Form above,
That bent over the fire, though unseen by us,
With a look of wonderful love.
So he waited there with a watchful eye,
With a love that is strong and sure,
And His gold did not suffer a bit more heat,
Than was needed to make it pure.

When we are distressed, it's easy to be wrapped up in the heat of the moment. But remember that God's strong hands and loving eyes are on us.

Dear Lord, I want to be as bright as gold, so bring into my life exactly what I need to be the best I can be. I know you will be with me. Amen.
Let us run with perseverance the race marked out for us.
Hebrews 12:1

Going the Distance

As Jane lined up for the marathon, she concentrated on the finish line. In the back of her mind, she knew the hilly course was long, but she had been practicing for months. She had built up her endurance and she was ready.

The fog had rolled in that morning, and it was hard to see the road ahead. But she watched her steps and kept going. When her sore knee started to swell, she slowed to a walk but kept going. As the sun finally broke through, Jane felt exhausted. She had run farther than she ever had before, but in this race there was still a long way to go. She kept going — through the unexpected weather, through the pain, through the fatigue.

Life is a marathon that takes endurance, perseverance, and patience. Some days we feel strong and courageous. Other times we feel tired and discouraged. It's all part of a long journey. With prayer and experience, we are training to cross the finish line in victory. If your heart is weighed down, keep going. If you're weary with despair, don't give up. With your eyes on the goal and your mind on God, you can face hardship and keep on. You won't be alone.

Dear Lord, I don't want to run this race of life without you. Lead me on. Amen.

God Understands

In the same way, the Spirit helps us in our weakness. We do not know what we ought to pray for, but the Spirit himself intercedes for us with groans that words cannot express.
Romans 8:26, 27

Sometimes mommies know what a baby wants just by the way it acts. But not always. Sometimes when babies start to talk it is very hard for the mother and father to understand what the baby is saying. Often brothers and sisters who are just a little older understand what the baby wants and can tell their parents. They are something like translators.

Translators are people who can listen to one language and explain what was said in another language. For example, if someone is speaking in Spanish, a translator would be able to tell us in English what that person is saying.

Translating is something like what the Holy Spirit does for us when we pray. Sometimes when we pray, we just don't know what to ask for. We might not know what would be best for us or what God wants for us. That's when the Holy Spirit translates our prayers for us. Even if we can't put our prayer into words, God understands us because the Holy Spirit helps us communicate with him. We can't see the Holy Spirit, but he is with us all the time helping us in every way he can.

So when you pray, ask the Holy Spirit to help you. Ask the Holy Spirit to give you the words to say. And even if you can't think of anything to say, believe that the Holy Spirit can take your thoughts and turn them into prayer to God.

Dear Lord, Even though I can't see your Spirit, I know it is here to help me. Thank you for giving us the Holy Spirit. Amen.

The Go-Ahead Signal

When the cloud remained over the tabernacle a long time, the Israelites obeyed the Lord's order and did not set out.
Numbers 9:19

Which would you rather do: charge off into the unknown and face whatever is out there on your own, or wait for God to give you the go ahead signal to move out and he will go with you? The answer to that question may seem obvious, but many people can't wait for God to work something out. Off they go and they really don't know where they are going. In Psalm 40:1 the writer said, "I waited patiently for the Lord; he turned to me and heard my cry." God is listening even when you don't know what to do next — which way to go. If you pray and are patient, he'll show you what comes next.

Here's something you might keep in mind when it seems you'll never get what you are praying for:

W-onderful answers
A-re waiting for you
I-n God's perfect
T-ime

If we truly believe that God has the answers, then we can relax and trust that he will provide what we need when the time is right.

Dear Lord, I don't want to get ahead of you, but waiting is so hard. Help me to be patient and wait for your direction. Amen.

Walking-Out Prayer

So Peter was kept in prison, but the church was
earnestly praying to God for him.
Acts 12:5

Peter was in prison. He hadn't done anything to cause him to be thrown in jail, but there he was, locked up by King Herod. He wasn't just in prison. He had four squads of four soldiers each — 16 soldiers guarding him. Herod was going to put him on trial as soon as Passover celebration was over. The night before the trial, Peter was sleeping between two soldiers. He was bound with chains and there were guards at the entrance to his cell. Suddenly an angel appeared and lit up the cell. The angel had to shake Peter to get him awake. "Quick, get up!" the angel said. And as he said that, the chains fell off Peter's wrists. Evidently, the soldiers didn't see the angel. They didn't try to stop Peter.

"Put on your clothes and sandals and follow me," said the angel. Peter thought he was seeing a vision. But he didn't risk that it was only a vision. He was out of the cell in a flash. Then he and the angel walked past all the guards and came to a huge iron gate. It popped open by itself and they walked out. Then the angel vanished. What do you think Peter was thinking at that moment? He must have been shaking his head and trying to wake up, even though he was already awake. He headed straight for his friends' house to let them know he was free and then he left town and went to a place where he would be safe.

God can do anything. He can do more than we can even imagine. When you ask for something, don't try to figure out how God is going to answer your prayer. He has ideas and answers to our prayers that we haven't even considered. So don't limit him by trying to guide him or suggest what to do. Pray and then expect him to give you the very best answer to your prayer.

Dear Lord, I'm so glad that you're all-knowing, all-powerful, and my friend. Thank you for listening to me and loving me and knowing what to do. Amen.

On Top of It All

You who bring good tidings to Zion, go up on a high mountain.
Isaiah 40:9

There is something inside humans that makes us want to climb to the top of the tallest mountain, go down into the deepest sea, fly to the moon and beyond, and excel in every possible way. If you have ever read stories about people climbing to the top of Mount Everest, the tallest mountain in the world, you know about the awful hardships they go through to make that climb. Many have even died on that mountain trying to reach the summit. Yet every year there is a new batch of people who want to go to the top, even if it costs them greatly to achieve their dream of climbing the mountain.

Worthy goals often involve risk and cost, which means courage is required. Thankfully, when God asks you to achieve something difficult he also supplies the courage. Maybe you need to be bold in standing up for your faith. Maybe you can practice some radical giving. Maybe you have a chance to stand up for someone who is being bullied. Maybe you need to trust God through difficult times. If you are ready to take on a challenge—or climb a mountain— remember Hebrews 13:6, "So we say with confidence, 'The Lord is my helper; I will not be afraid.'"

Dear Lord, Thank you for reminding me of your faithfulness. It reassures me that I can take on challenges with courage. Amen.

Captive Audience

*I was among the exiles by the Kebar River, the heavens were opened and
I saw visions of God.... There the hand of the Lord was upon [me].*
Ezekiel 1:1, 3

When God's people were taken by the Babylonians, God was with
them. Even far from their home surrounded by their captors, the
Israelites still heard his Word. There, under intense circumstances,
angels of the Lord gave the prophet Ezekiel spectacular visions that
declared God's holiness, glory and love.

When trials come into our lives, God isn't as far away as he may
seem. God doesn't waste any opportunity — even trials — which he
could use to reveal himself to his people in new, unexpected ways.
When you are captive to difficult, lonely or sad situations, what is
God saying to you? Spend time with him, with his Word, and with
wise teachers to find out.

Dear Lord, Reveal yourself to me. Remind me of your promises and
your character. Let me rest in you. Amen.

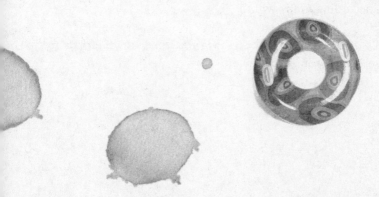

Nothing Is Too Hard!

Is anything too hard for the Lord?
Genesis 18:14

One day a religious leader came to Jesus. He was afraid. He was worried. His little girl was dying and there was nothing anyone could do about it. He found Jesus teaching and healing the sick and begged him to come touch his little girl and make her well. Jesus went with him, but on the way, there were a lot of sick people and he stopped and healed them. Then some men came and said to the man, "Your little girl is dead. Don't bother the teacher anymore." But Jesus ignored those men. "Don't be afraid; just believe," he told the father. When they got to the house, Jesus went into the little girl's room and said, "Little girl, I say to you, get up!" and she did, because nothing is too hard for the Lord.

What do you have in your life that might seem almost too hard for God? Does your mom or dad need a job? He can lead them to work. Do you know someone who is sick? God can heal that person. What have you been praying about that you are sure no one can do? What do you need fixed that you are certain no one can fix? Pray about it. God can do anything. He loves you and he wants to provide for you. He wants to give you what is best for you. Keep praying and keep believing he is working things out for you in his time, and according to his will.

Dear Lord, Sometimes it's hard to believe you can do anything. Help me believe. My hope is in you. Amen.

Is Discipline Good?

Those whom I love I rebuke and discipline.
Revelation 3:19

Do your parents ever discipline you for something you have done? Not fun, is it? Are your parents just mean or are they trying to accomplish something good when they give you time outs and restrictions? They are up to something good for you. Discipline is training that helps us learn self-control. When we learn how to control ourselves, our character grows stronger. We learn more about how to behave in ways that honor God and respect others.

Kids aren't the only ones who get disciplined. Athletes have to discipline themselves to complete their workouts day after day. They have to discipline themselves to push harder, to be more skillful in their sport, even when they'd rather do something that might be more fun. Musicians discipline themselves by practicing scales and doing other musical exercises so they can be even better at playing their instruments. And the need for discipline never goes away — we always need to discipline ourselves if we want to grow stronger or get better at something.

God's discipline is a sign of his love for his children. Hebrews 12:11 reads, "No discipline seems pleasant at the time, but painful. Later on, however, it produces a harvest of righteousness and peace for those who have been trained by it." Because he cares for us, our heavenly Father wants us to make decisions that give us freedom and security in him. With discipline he is building us up to be strong and have peace.

Dear Lord, Thank you that I am a child of yours, the King of kings. When I don't get my way or my sin produces consequences, I will remember you love me and want better for me. Amen.

Profit and Loss

But whatever was to my profit I now consider loss for the sake of Christ.
Philippians 3:7

Did you ever own something you just loved? You wanted it more than anything else you have in your house. Then, after a while, it wasn't so important anymore, and finally you got rid of that thing you once thought you had to have. Then something else became more important. As we learn and grow, we outgrow certain things.

Sometimes missionaries go to countries that are very hard places to live. They come home to talk with the churches and they are so excited about where they live. They don't mind the hardships. Why? Because these missionaries have given up what they once thought was important — like a pretty house in a nice clean town — to go far away and live among people who don't yet know or love God. Those missionaries have decided that the most important thing to them is being obedient to what God's has called them to do. Only God changes hearts like that so that everything they once thought they wanted doesn't matter as much as he does.

What God really wants is for you to love him more than anything else. What do you have that you just love and think you couldn't get along without? If God asked you to give it up, could you do it? You could only if God helped you. Keep your heart open to the things God thinks are important.

Dear Lord, Because you love me, I know you want the best for me. Because I love you, I want to follow you, even if it means giving some things up. Amen.

An Amazing Wake-Up Call!

As he was praying, the appearance of his face changed, and his clothes became as bright as a flash of lightning.
Luke 9:29

Sometimes Jesus talked to his disciples. Sometimes he taught them. They walked together from place to place and ate meals together. They were often with Jesus when he did miracles. But one day he chose three of his disciples for a very special experience. He took Peter, John, and James with him and went to the top of a mountain to pray. So far, not very exciting.

Of course, the disciples were very sleepy and soon were snoozing. But while they were sleeping, Moses and Elijah appeared in "glorious splendor." (That's what the Bible says.) They began talking with Jesus about his soon-coming death and resurrection in Jerusalem. About that time, the three disciples woke up and saw Moses and Elijah and Jesus talking together. Jesus looked different. His face had changed and his clothes were as bright as lightning. Just imagine what that would be like!

It would be wonderful if we were praying someday and suddenly Jesus all in shining clothes stood there with us. How exciting that would be! Jesus is with us when we pray and he is standing beside us listening to what we pray. The only difference between our prayer time and the one the disciples had is that we can't see Jesus. But he's right there. Getting to know Jesus better through prayer might change your life in an exciting way.

Dear God, I know you are nearby when I pray. Change me and change my life as I pray to you. Amen.

Almighty Strength

Men will dwell again in his shade. He will flourish like the grain. He will blossom like a vine, and his fame will be like the wine from Lebanon.
Hosea 14:7

If you are under a heavy burden or facing tough problems, you have someone in your corner—the same God who freed his weary children from slavery, fed them in a barren desert and led them to promised peace. He's the same God who rescued a drowning Jonah, nourished an exhausted Elijah, and sheltered Noah through the rain.

God watches over each and every one of his children. Get close to the one who sees you, loves you and hears you. He will strengthen you. Your relationship with him will get you through any problem that worries you.

Dear Lord, Let me draw near to you so I can unload all my anxiety. Guide me and strengthen me. I depend on you. Amen.

Never Give Up Hope

Against all hope, Abraham in hope believed and so became the father of many nations, just as it had been said to him, "So shall your offspring be."
Romans 4:18

If anyone had the right to give up hope, it should have been Abraham. God had promised to make him the father of many nations, but how on earth could that happen if he had not even one child? He waited and he waited and he waited and then he waited some more. He was almost 100 years old and he was still waiting. But what God says he will do, he will do. When Abraham turned 100, his little boy was born. It was a wonderful, happy time and Abraham was glad he had not given up hope.

What is the hardest thing you can think of that you want God to do? Is it something that would bring honor to God? Are you just about ready to give up hope that it can happen? Don't give up hope. If God doesn't answer your prayer the way you want him to, then go right on hoping that he has another idea and it could be a better idea than yours.

It's important to remember when we are hoping for something that God is a loving Father. He only wants what's best for us. In the New Testament Jesus said, "Which of you fathers, if your son asks for a fish, will give him a snake instead? Or if he asks for an egg, will give him a scorpion?" (Luke 11:11) Good fathers give only good gifts to their children because they love them. When you want to give up hope, remember that God loves you and he wants what's best for you.

Dear Lord, Sometimes I do feel like giving up, but help me to be strong and most of all help me to remember that you love me. Amen.

Growing Fruit

*He will be like rain falling on a mown field, like showers watering
the earth.*
Psalm 72:6

When you grow roses, trees and other plants, there are times when
it's essential to cut them back. Pruning involves removing leaves,
branches and even blossoms in order to increase the plant's fruit or
flower production or to improve its form. Even if a plant is blooming, the expert gardener knows that the plant will grow healthy and
more beautiful when skillfully trimmed first.

God prunes us in the same way—sharply making cuts to
increase our fruit and form. For example, if we let a sinful habit take
root because we have decided it's harmless, he might cut it away
so that our good fruit—patience, kindness, self-control, righteousness—can grow up instead.

When we have been disciplined or disappointed, it can feel like
we have been cut down instead of carefully pruned. But then the
love of God falls like rain on our fresh souls. Let it soak in. The fruit
is beginning to bud.

Dear God, You are the master gardener. Help me trust you. Amen.

Working for the King

They were the potters who lived at Netaim and Gederah; they stayed there and worked for the king.
1 Chronicles 4:23

Have you ever wondered what God could possibly do through you? Ever thought that if God is going to use you, it will be when you're older, smarter, stronger, or in charge of something? Have you put off a relationship with him until you're doing something dramatic or courageous?

Consider this: God's son started life on earth in a stable; Joseph spent years in prison before becoming the leader of Egypt; young David came in from the pasture to be anointed as the future king. If God can use people in these unlikely circumstances, don't you think he can use you?

The King directs his work in us and through us, no matter where we are, how old we are, what we do, or how much we have. Our hearts can always be transformed, and we can always serve Jesus out of love. So whether you're in the park, in the classroom or in a wheelchair, whether you're with your friends, teachers or the mailman, open your heart to the work that Jesus has for you.

Dear God, Thank you for being with me right here, where you have put me. Open my heart to the work you have for me to do, right where I am. Amen.

Good and Faithful Servants

For I have chosen him, so that he will direct his children and his household after him to keep the way of the Lord by doing what is right and just, so that the Lord will bring about for Abraham what he has promised him.
Genesis 18:19

In Exodus 3 and 4, when God called Moses to lead his people, Moses wavered. "Who am I, that I should go to Pharaoh and bring the Israelites out of Egypt?" he said.

"I will be with you," the Lord replied.

"But I am slow of speech and tongue," Moses said.

"Who gave man his mouth?" God answered. "Is it not I, the Lord? Now go; I will help you speak and will teach you what to say."

God knows the burdens you carry and he knows the burdens you *can* carry. He understands your fears, realizes your weaknesses, and knows your strengths. He never asks you to do more than you can. And just like he reminded Moses, God will be with you. He will help you.

So, servant of the living God, there's work to be done. Will you go with courage or will you shrink from the challenge?

Dear Lord, I am so glad you are always with me. Give me willingness and strength to be your faithful servant. Amen.

An Abundant Life

I tell you the truth, unless a kernel of wheat falls to the ground and dies, it remains only a single seed. But if it dies, it produces many seeds.
John 12:24

Can you imagine what the disciples were thinking the day Jesus died? They had loved and followed him but never really understood the coming cross. At that dark hour, they must have felt overwhelmed by sadness and confusion. After all, why would God allow the love, healing, and miracles Jesus brought to earth to end so soon?

The Bible shows us the truth. Jesus' three-year ministry on earth wasn't cut short by his death. Rather it ended at exactly the chosen time in God's perfect, loving plan. Jesus actually came to earth to die so we could live forever with him in heaven. Jesus' sacrifice on the cross means life for us.

Are you confused about something that doesn't seem "fair"? Are you sad about a loss or setback that seems to go against everything good? Remember God is the author of a broader, bigger story than you may see. Trust that even in the things you don't understand, God is good.

Dear Lord, I know your heart is good. Help me trust you through it all. Amen.

Strength in Weakness

But he said to me, "My grace is sufficient for you, for my power is made perfect in weakness." Therefore I will boast all the more gladly about my weaknesses, so that Christ's power may rest on me.
2 Corinthians 12:9

Abraham Lincoln once said, "I have been driven many times to my knees by the overwhelming conviction that I had nowhere else to go. My own wisdom and that of all about me seemed insufficient for the day." Although holding the most powerful position in the United States, our sixteenth president addressed such huge challenges that he felt small. He knew that he was too limited to handle the problems facing him and the country, so he continually prayed for guidance and strength.

Unlike Lincoln who was mindful of his weakness, many of us overestimate our importance and abilities. We believe we're independent and strong, so we rely on ourselves to control things instead of relying on God. Only when faced with the reality of our weakness and limits do we submit and allow him to work in all his power and glory. When you are self-sufficient, you give yourself credit. When you are weak, you recognize that God gets all credit.

So if you are weak, praise God you know where your real strength comes from. If you are burdened, praise God that you're learning to trust him. If you are in despair, praise God that you're discovering his saving grace.

Dear Lord, Thank you for my troubles and weakness because they help me remember to accept your grace, wisdom and power. Amen.

Overcomers

They overcame him by the blood of the Lamb and by the word of their testimony.
Revelations 12:11

What does it mean to "overcome" something? It means that after a long struggle you finally defeat something you've been battling. But defeating something is not as final as to "vanquishing" it. When you vanquish something, you completely overpower it. The enemy is done. It's the end of the war.

When Jesus died on the cross, our enemy, Satan, thought he had overcome Jesus. He thought that was the end of Jesus and his message. But he was in for a great shock. Jesus didn't stay dead. He rose from the grave after three days and he will never die again. He is alive to help us overcome whatever comes into our lives — no matter how difficult it is. He vanquished Satan.

What do you need to overcome in your life? Do you have a bad temper that takes over your emotions sometimes? You can overcome that bad temper because Jesus is alive to help you. Do you say bad words? Jesus would love to help you overcome that bad habit. Do you pick fights with people smaller than you are — like your brothers and sisters? Jesus came to bring peace to our families and he will help you stop fighting. No matter what you need to overcome, conquer, defeat, or vanquish in your life, Jesus is alive to help you.

Dear Lord, I sometimes forget you are alive to help me overcome my problems. Will you help me today with my needs? Amen.

With Justice for All

And the Lord said, "Listen to what the unjust judge says. And will not God bring about justice for his chosen ones, who cry out to him day and night? Will he keep putting them off? I tell you, he will see that they get justice, and quickly."
Luke 18:6–8

The world is not a fair place. Some people suffer great loss, while others do not. Some enjoy privilege that others do not. Some get opportunities that others do not. We yearn for fairness. We hope for truth. We fight for justice. But let's be clear: since Adam and Eve listened to the serpent, we have lived in a world that is fallen and damaged by sin.

But God is above the world. He is perfect truth and love, justice and mercy. Our hope isn't in the fairness of this world. Our hope is in the living God.

So what do we do while we wait for heaven but live in the world? With God's grace, we get to know Jesus and persevere. What if someone says something untrue about us? We endure and trust God's justice. What if someone's carelessness hurts us? We persevere and draw near to the all-knowing Comforter. What if God's timing doesn't seem to be fast enough? We wait and have faith in God's perfect plan.

Go ahead and tell God your hopes and share with him your disappointments. Ask in faith, wait for his answers, and press on. You'll get your peace.

Dear Lord, Thank you for being good and powerful. Thank you for caring about me while I live in this world. Help me trust you while I wait on your plan. Amen.

True Blessings

Blessed is the man who does not fall away on account of me.
Luke 7:23

As children of the King, can't we expect a life of comfort? As heirs of God, shouldn't we feel largely confident? As followers of the Savior, won't we always feel secure?

In a word: no. God has richer goals for us than our comfort, confidence, and security. He wants to bless us with an intensity of faith and a depth of relationship that rarely come with a life of ease. If we had all the comforts and pleasures that the world could offer at our disposal, would we remember to depend on God for everything? It is by leaning on God for our each and every need that we finally learn to follow him.

Here's another word: trust. God is faithful and trustworthy. So in the face of hardship, trust. In the midst of doubt, trust. In the middle of insecurity, trust. He is with us, helping us embrace an amazing life with him.

Dear Lord, Help me let go of expectations and hold on to you. Amen.

What God Gives

Though you have made me see troubles, many and bitter,
you will restore my life again.
Psalm 71:20

There is an old proverb that says, "The rain falls on the just and the unjust alike." That means that trouble comes to the good guys as well as bad guys. It's just part of being human and living on earth. The difference for believers in God is that God is the one who says what happens to us and how often trouble can come, and then he is right there in the middle of it to help us. Just remember when tough times come, God is with you.

Here's a poem that tells us no matter what God sends our way, he is with us.

> Though the rain may fall and the wind be blowing,
> And cold and chill is the wintry blast;
> Though the cloudy sky is still cloudier growing,
> And the dead leaves tell that the summer has passed;
> My face I hold to the stormy heaven,
> My heart is as calm as the summer sea,
> Glad to receive what my God has given,
> Whatever it may be.
> When I feel the cold, I can say, "He sends it."
> And His winds blow blessing, I surely know;
> For I've never a want but that He attends it:
> And my heart beats warm, though the winds may blow.

Dear Lord, I'm so glad to know you are near me every day of my life. Amen.

Waiting on God

Blessed is the one who waits.
Daniel 12:12

The Bible is full of believers who exercised patience and trust as they waited on God. King David prayed continually as he waited for an answer about his baby's health. Joseph drew near to the Father as he waited release from prison. The Israelites cried out to God while they waited to be rescued from slavery.

A journey with God involves adventure and excitement ... but not all the time. A fair share of the journey is waiting. This is not to be confused with aimless inactivity. Rather, waiting on God is filled with purpose — to deepen your faith and relationship with him.

As you wait for God's timing and purpose, keep talking to him. He is a master at work.

Dear God, It's hard to wait. Use this time to reinforce my faith and patience. Amen.

Friendly Advice

Commit your way to the Lord.
Psalm 37:5

The special bond between best friends doesn't happen overnight. A deep relationship like this takes time, give-and-take, and daily connection to build trust and closeness. A willingness to sacrifice for each other, spend time together, and confide in each other make the best friend relationship so meaningful.

You are invited to engage in a special give-and-take relationship with God. Knowing he cares, you can open your life to him and make sure it meets his approval. As best friends, you can both delight in meeting daily — continually — so you can commit your concerns to him and he can guide your way.

It is a chance of a lifetime to have a best friend in our loyal, loving God. Meet with him, commit your way to him and you will find yourself filled.

Dear God, I've never had a best friend like you, but I'm glad I do. Thank you for listening to me and caring about everything that happens in my life. Amen.

Nothing Is Impossible!

When he had gone indoors, the blind men came to him, and he asked
them, "Do you believe that I am able to do this?" "Yes, Lord," they replied.
Matthew 9:28

Jesus can do anything, and one of his specialties seemed to be
healing blind people. There is a prophecy written long before Jesus
was born that said: "The Spirit of the Lord is on me, because he
has anointed me to preach good news to the poor. He has sent me
to proclaim freedom for the prisoners and *recovery of sight for the*
blind, to release the oppressed ..." (Luke 4:18, emphasis added).
   Jesus healed many people: "At that very time Jesus cured many
who had diseases, sicknesses and evil spirits, *and gave sight to*
many who were blind (Luke 7:21, emphasis added). One of the blind
people Jesus healed was a beggar who was sitting by the road near
the city of Jericho. He called out, "Jesus, Son of David, have mercy
on me!" Jesus came up to him and asked, "What do you want me
to do for you?" The beggar answered, "I want to see." Then Jesus
said, "Receive your sight; your faith has healed you." The Bible says
that "immediately he received his sight." Wow! That's amazing! But
when we know Jesus, we are not surprised by the amazing miracles
he performs. Jesus can to anything—we just have to ask and believe.
   Maybe you don't need to be healed of blindness. Maybe you need
something else. Maybe you just need Jesus to open your spiritual
eyes so you understand something. Pray and expect God to help
you. He is close enough to hear your prayers.

Dear Lord, In my head I know nothing is impossible for you, but
sometimes in my heart, I am not sure. Please help me believe. Amen.

Tough Times

You have shown your people desperate times.
Psalm 60:3

One good thing about the Bible is that it tells the truth. It doesn't say everything in life is going to be wonderful. It doesn't say all Christians will be rich. There are thousands of extremely poor Christians all over the world who love God as much as Christians who have more than they do. It doesn't say that everyone with a physical problem will be healed. Even the Apostle Paul had a physical problem that he called a "thorn in the flesh" that wouldn't go away. The Bible says life can be tough, but the most wonderful thing is that God is with us no matter how tough it gets. He promised, and you know he cannot break his promises. He said, "I am with you always, even unto the end of the world (Matthew 28:20).

Why don't you make a list of the tough things you are going through right now? Then, find a promise in the Bible to help you understand that God is with you in that problem. Look for the promises and stories about Biblical characters going through the same problems you do. By the time you finish reading them, your heart will be encouraged that God is with you and wants to heal you.

Dear Lord, It is only your Word, the Bible, that encourages us when we are going through tough times. Thank you for your Word. Amen.

The Longest Minute

"Be still, and know that I am God; I will be exalted among the nations,
I will be exalted in the earth."
Psalm 46:10

Here's an experiment for you to try. Turn off the TV, radio, CD
player, iPod, Wii, and anything that makes noise and has an on-off
switch. Find a quiet place to sit perfectly still. Set a timer for one
minute and then wait for the minute to pass.

Did it seem like a long time?

Now try five minutes.

That's harder, isn't it? But if we are ever going to hear from God,
we have to learn how to be still. God is not going to track you down
and sit on you to get you to listen to him. And he wants to speak to
you and help you through life's hard times. So sit still and listen to
what God might tell you.

Here's a good thing to learn to do early in your life. At the end
of the day, before going to sleep, think of all the problems you had
during the day, questions you have, and anything else that makes
you feel sad or worried. Pretend that you are gripping them in
your hands. Now turn your hands over and open them. Let all the
problems go. Give them all to God. If you make it a habit to do this
every day, you will learn something that will help you have a more
peaceful life.

Dear Lord, My world is full of noise. Help me learn to be really quiet
and listen for your voice. Help me to turn all my problems over to you.
I can't fix them anyway and you can. Amen.

Three Strikes

Then he said, "Take the arrows," and the king took them. Elisha told him,
"Strike the ground." He struck it three times and stopped.
2 Kings 13:18, 19

There is an interesting and strange story in the Old Testament.
When the prophet Elisha was old and dying, the king of Israel,
named Jehoash, came to visit him. When he saw how sick Elisha
was he said, "My father! My father!" Elisha said to him, "Get a bow
and some arrows." When Jehoash had the bow and arrows, Elisha
told him, "Open the east window and shoot!" So the king did that.
Then Elisha told the king, "That was the Lord's arrow of victory,
you will completely destroy your enemy the Arameans." Then
Elisha said, "Strike the ground with the arrows." The king struck
the ground three times and stopped. Elisha was angry with him and
said, "You should have struck the ground five or six times; then you
would have defeated Aram and completely destroyed it. But now
you will defeat it only three times."

What that story teaches us is that we get from God what we
ask for and sometimes we don't ask for enough. Paul in the New
Testament said, "Now to him who is able to do immeasurably more
than all we ask or imagine, according to his power that is at work
within us ..." That means God can do things for us that are beyond
anything we can imagine. Wow! So think about what you need from
God today and ask a big request from God.

Dear Lord, Sometimes I don't know what to ask for, so I don't ask at all.
Help me to believe that you can do more than I could ever imagine.
Amen.

Plenty of Water

Caleb asked her, "What can I do for you?" She replied, "Do me a special favor. Since you have given me land in the Negev, give me also springs of water." So Caleb gave her the upper and lower springs.
Joshua 15:18, 19

Caleb had a daughter named Acsah and she was married to a man named Othniel. Caleb gave her a piece of land in the desert, but she knew that without water it was useless, so she asked her father for land with springs of water on it. And Caleb gave her what she asked for.

The Bible compares us to thirsty people who need God to fill up our lives with his living water. Once when King David was out in the desert he prayed, "O God, you are my God, earnestly I seek you; my soul thirsts for you, my body longs for you, in a dry and weary land where there is no water" (Psalm 63:1). And Jesus invited us, "If anyone is thirsty, let him come to me and drink" (John 7:37). Sometimes our thirstiness for God feels like restlessness. Sometimes our need for more of him makes us feel sad. All we have to do to be filled up with God's love, that is like living water to us, is to pray and ask him to fill us up.

God always provides springs of refreshment for us. He always helps us through our hard places. God loves us more than we can imagine.

Dear Lord, I feel restless and unhappy sometimes even when there is nothing to be restless or unhappy about. Fill me with your living water that will satisfy me on the inside. Amen.

Impossible — No Such Thing

For nothing is impossible with God.
Luke 1:37

Sometimes the dictionary is one of our best helpers in understanding the Bible. Today's verse says that nothing is impossible with God. Let's look up the word "nothing." Nothing means no thing; no part of anything. We sometimes use words like "zilch" which means zero, or "nada" which is Spanish for nothing. So if the Bible says "nothing is impossible with God" then it means that no matter how you stretch your mind, you couldn't even think of something that would be impossible for him.

All right, now let's look at the word "impossible" in the dictionary. It means "something that cannot be done" or it can mean "too difficult to do." Well, we can forget all about something that cannot be done because God can do everything. He made everything so he knows how it works and he wants us to ask him for his help when we feel like we are facing something impossible. He healed sick people, he raised people from the dead, and he is just waiting to hear from us about what we need.

So what do you need for him to do for you today? Does it seem impossible for him to do? It isn't. No matter how big our need is, nothing is impossible with God.

Dear Lord, I need you to help me with the things in my life that seem impossible. Thank you that you can do anything and that nothing is impossible with you. Amen.

Morning Songs

Where morning dawns and evening fades you call forth songs of joy.
Psalm 65:8

Have you ever gotten up before the sun comes up and gone outside? It is usually very quiet. A little later the birds begin to sing their happy song to say good morning to the day. And then little by little the sun comes up over the horizon and begins to warm up the day. It is a wonderful time that sleepyheads never get to see. God wants us to be hopeful and joyful every day — all day. It begins the first minute you climb out of bed. What do you do first when you get up? Are you grumpy? Grumpy kids in the morning aren't much fun. If you go to bed on time and sleep well, you should wake up feeling great. If you can train yourself to say good morning to God and think for a minute about all the possibilities he will give you throughout the day, you will be much happier. And so will everyone all around you.

So here are some guidelines for starting your day off right:

- *Go to bed on time the night before.*
- *Pray and ask God to give you good, quiet sleep.*
- *Thank God for another day as soon as you wake up.*
- *Get up and see if the sun is up yet.*

Dear Lord, Sometimes I'm grumpy in the morning. Help me be more cheerful for myself and for everyone. Amen.

Finding Peace

No discipline seems pleasant at the time, but painful. Later on, however, it produces a harvest of righteousness and peace for those who have been trained by it.

Hebrews 12:11

Think about well known people in the world and you will see those who have learned to discipline themselves. If they are sports figures, they have practiced their sports over and over. Basketball players shoot endlessly at the basket to improve their scoring. Dancers practice their steps again and again and again until those moves become automatic. Speakers and actors have disciplined themselves to learn everything they can about speaking and acting. No one achieves anything without training themselves through discipline.

Some people think discipline means punishment. But that's not always true. Discipline means being trained in the rules of an activity or exercise that develops or improves a skill. It means gaining control of yourself. It means resisting the desire to buy more and more when you don't need it. It means being careful with the earth's resources. It means taking care of what you have. So if your parents insist that you clean up after yourself and that you don't waste things, you are fortunate. They are teaching you how to discipline yourself. Be thankful and work hard to learn what they are teaching you. If no one is teaching you these things, you can learn to do them anyway. You can discipline yourself perhaps by making a chart to remind yourself to do those hard things you might forget to do such as cleaning your room. Discipline is a good thing to learn as it will help excel at what you do and it will also help you find peace in your life.

Dear Lord, Help me practice discipline because I know it will serve me well all my life. Amen.

Lighting the Way

Should you then seek great things for yourself? Seek them not. For I will bring disaster on all people, declares the Lord, but wherever you go I will let you escape with your life.
Jeremiah 45:5

Spelunkers, or cave explorers, often find themselves in tight spaces, surrounded by darkness and cold. If they get stuck or lost, there is one thing they must have to survive — and it's not food or water. It is light. It's so critical that spelunkers pack three sources of light, so that they won't be caught and find themselves lost in the darkness without a way to see out.

When we are in tight situations, lost in the dark, Jesus is our light. Even in the midst of great pressure and problems, we can endure them in his presence.

Remember that Daniel was safe in the middle of lions, that Noah was dry in the middle of the storms, that Shadrach, Meshach and Abednego walked in the middle of fire. The same God that sheltered them through their trials gives you security and fortitude in yours.

He's our light in the darkness, our refuge in pressure, our relief in great worry. Draw near to him.

Dear Lord, You know the problems that break my heart. Give me hope and peace even as you help me endure them. Amen.

Bigger Than You Thought

There remains, then, a Sabbath-rest for the people of God.
Hebrews 4:9

The Lord gave them rest on every side, just as he had sworn to their forefathers.
Joshua 21:44

In the book and movie *Prince Caspian*, one of the Chronicles of Narnia stories, Lucy says to the lion Aslan, "You're bigger." Aslan replies, "That is because you are older, little one." "Not because you are?" Lucy asks. "I am not," says Aslan, "but every year you grow, you will find me bigger."

That's how it is with God. The older you get, the more you understand that God can do anything. The more you appreciate he's bigger and stronger than any problems or worries you have. The more trust you build.

Some people worry about everything. They worry about a test even if they've studied well. They worry about looking too different and then they worry about looking too much the same. They worry that someone won't like them when that person has already told them they do like them.

Worry is the opposite of trust, and we are to trust God to take care of us. We learn to trust God by getting to know him better through prayer and Bible reading. As you do, you will find him bigger.

Dear Lord, I need you to help me to trust you. In my head I know you can do anything and take care of everything, but sometimes it takes a while for my heart to know. Amen.

In His Steps

God ... should make the author of their salvation perfect through suffering.
Hebrews 2:10

There was only one person who ever lived who was perfect, and that person was Jesus. He exactly fits the dictionary definitions of the word perfect:

He exactly fills a need. Long ago the people of Israel had to offer a lamb for their sins. When Jesus came, he became the offering for our sins. When he died on the cross he filled the need of a perfect offering.

He is correct in every detail. He was God and he was without sin.

He is pure. Only a pure, flawless lamb—Jesus—could be sacrificed for our sins.

Even Jesus, God's perfect, beloved son, suffered on earth. Before death on the cross, he endured 40 days in the desert with Satan. He grieved over his friend Lazarus' death. He experienced excruciating anxiety in the Garden of Gethsemane. Because he went before us, experiencing the same kinds of trials we face, we can find encouragement in the way Jesus trusted his father through it all. So through our own suffering, we can develop an enduring trust in God and good, sound character.

Dear Lord, Thank you for sending your perfect son Jesus to be our sacrifice for sin. Now I can have a daily, close relationship with you that will carry me through all the problems I face and will make me the person you want me to be. Amen.

A Lost Loved One

"Run to meet her and ask her, 'Are you all right?'"
... "Everything is all right," she said.
2 Kings 4:26

Almost everyone who has ever had a pet knows what good friends they can be. When something happens to them and they die, we are heartbroken to lose our best friends. We feel as if we will never have a pet as wonderful again. God knows when your heart is broken because you have lost a pet. He cares. Jesus said that not even a sparrow falls to the ground without God seeing it. If God knows when a small, common bird dies (while most of us don't pay much attention to sparrows), then he certainly sees when our pets die and he cares.

God also knows when a person you love dies. He cares about that too. The God of all comfort will be with you to help you through your tough time. Remember that the One who conquered death is the friend you can lean on for comfort, support, and peace. Jesus is near everyone who has a broken heart.

Dear Lord, Even when I feel alone, you are with me. Give me comfort. Give me strength. Amen.

Plug In

After he had dismissed them, he went up on a mountainside by himself to pray. When evening came, he was there alone.
Matthew 14:23

If you have an mp3 player, cell phone, or handheld game, you know you have to keep your eye on the battery. If the indicator light is green, you have enough power to play your game. A red light means you need to plug it in before it shuts down. Depending on how much you use it, you might plug in every night so it will be ready to go when you wake up.

Praying regularly is like plugging into God — recharging your batteries with the One who knows you best. Not only does daily quiet time give you strength, but it resets your focus on eternal things. You get to know him better and trust him more. And you'll find you look forward to your connection, just like Jesus did the many times he withdrew from people he loved to be alone with the Father he loved.

So get quiet and get plugged in.

Dear God, Thank you that I can come to you and you listen. Remind me to meet with you every day. Amen.

Follow On

I know, O Lord, that a man's life is not his own;
it is not for man to direct his steps.
Jeremiah 10:23

Jessica couldn't decide what to do. She knew she wanted to be a teacher, and two schools wanted to give her a job. One of the schools was in a very wealthy neighborhood. The students were intelligent and well-behaved and the salary was good. The other school was in a poor, dirty neighborhood. The children couldn't concentrate on their education because they were worried about where their next meal was coming from. Jessica's salary would be very small, but she thought God was leading her to the school where the children needed her more.

Living a Christian life means following Jesus wherever he leads. It means doing whatever he asks us to do. It means choosing to go his way rather than our own. Sometimes we are concerned that what God is asking us to do is too difficult, but God answers that when we get to heaven, it will all be worthwhile.

When we walk with God, go his way, and do as he asks, we cannot lose. God is on our side for our entire walk up into his kingdom.

Dear Lord, I am going to put my hand in yours and follow wherever you lead me. Amen.

Jesus Is Coming Again

I am coming soon. Hold on to what you have,
so that no one will take your crown.
Revelation 3:11

God promised that he would send a Savior to earth—and he did.
That Savior was Jesus. After Jesus died and came back to life, he
went up to heaven in a cloud. The disciples stood looking up into
heaven with their mouths hanging open at what they had just seen.
"As they were staring upward into the sky, two men dressed in
white stood beside them and said, "Why do you stand here looking
into the sky? This same Jesus, who has been taken from you into
heaven, will come back in the same way you have seen him go into
heaven" (Acts 1:10). And that is exactly what will happen.

How does it make you feel to think about Jesus coming back to
earth again? Does it make you feel excited or afraid? Some kids get
really scared when they think about Jesus coming back to earth.
They want life to go on the same way as it is now. They want to
grow up and get married and have jobs and houses and kids. It
scares them to think that if Jesus came back everything would be
different. God understands what you want to do in the future. God
put the desire to live and do great things inside of you when he
made you. He wants you to go on living your life every day the best
way you can by loving him and others, by serving him and others,
and by keeping your heart clean by asking his forgiveness when you
sin. The rest will take care of itself.

Dear Lord, I have given my heart to you and I want to be with you
forever. Help me to live my life as if you were coming today. Help me
not to worry about what happens next. Amen.

Faith in the Master

*This is what the Lord says: "Make this valley full of ditches. For this is
what the Lord says: You will see neither wind nor rain, yet this valley will
be filled with water, and you, your cattle and your other animals will drink.
This is an easy thing in the eyes of the Lord.*
2 Kings 3:16–18

The role of faith is not to question but to obey. Think of a dog with
her master. Their devotion to each other grows out of their time
together. Because the master loves his dog, he knows the needs she
has and takes care of each of them. Because the dog loves her
master, she trusts him completely, safe in her dependence. She waits
for his signal and then obeys.

Our relationship with God is rooted in faithfulness and love,
like the dog to her master. When we spend time with our Lord, we
know more about him and are better able to trust him. We develop
faith and confidence in his presence and plan. Just as a dog relies
on his master, we listen to ours, do what we're told, and trust the
results to him.

Nurture your relationship with God by talking to him, reading
about him, and reminding yourself of his good character. Practice active faith by giving your worries to him and then leaving the results
to him, confident that things will work out exactly as he designs.

Dear Lord, I know you are all powerful and at work. Help me act by
faith not sight. Amen.

Dressing Up

Therefore, as God's chosen people, holy and dearly loved, clothe yourselves with compassion, kindness, humility, gentleness and patience.
Colossians 3:12

Here's a fun challenge. When you get up in the morning, pretend you are getting dressed up in kindness, gentleness, patience, compassion, and humility. Then when you leave home — or even before you leave the house — see if you can bring a smile to the face of someone who is having a hard day. That doesn't mean being silly to make them laugh. It means being kind to them and being interested in them and their problems. Most people warm right up to kindness.

So who do you think you might meet today who is having a hard day? Do you ride a bus to school? School bus drivers have a tough job, mostly because some kids are unkind to them and to each other. Smile at your driver and see if you can get him or her to smile back. Then try it out on a classmate who is having a bad day. Maybe all your friend needs is a kind word. Next, see if the teacher is happy or sad today. Even if your teacher already seems happy and smiles, give your teacher a big smile back. Go all through the day smiling at people and being kind to them. And that includes your family. This kind of dressing up — in smiles and kindness — works. Try it and see.

Dear Lord, Help me be kind to everyone, no matter what problem they are facing or how cranky they are. Help me to think of others before I think of myself. Amen.

Turning Troubles into Beauty

For our light and momentary troubles are achieving for us an eternal glory that far outweighs them all.

2 Corinthians 4:17

When an oyster gets a grain of sand stuck inside it, it begins to cover the grains of sand with a substance to smooth it over. After time, it forms a pearl. The oyster has turned its trouble into something beautiful.

Some trees have huge burls growing on their trunks or their roots. A burl is a deformed mass of wood that has grown around something that has injured it. The tree tries to smooth over the injury by growing bark over it. People who work with wood seek out burl wood because of its beautiful circular and twisted markings. The most highly-prized burl wood looks as if an explosion caused the grain of the wood to grow in the way it did—out from the center. Burl wood is used in furniture, picture frames, or any other place where a truly beautiful wood is wanted.

Both oysters and trees are able to take something painful that happened to them and make something beautiful out of it. And that's a lot like what God can do with the painful things that happen to us. He can use the toughest, ugliest things that happen to us to make our hearts beautiful.

Dear Lord, I want you to take that hurtful things that have happened to me and make them into something beautiful. Amen.

Worthwhile Experience

If we are distressed, it is for your comfort and salvation; if we are comforted, it is for your comfort, which produces in you patient endurance of the same sufferings we suffer.
2 Corinthians 1:6, 7

If you lost your cat, who could best comfort you with understanding—a friend who has never owned a pet or one that has? If you were anxious about a move across the country, who could best help you with tender advice—a neighbor who has never relocated or one that has?

People who have shared your troubles can offer the sweetest support because they have been through it themselves. They know your sorrow firsthand so they can give the very encouragement you crave, even if just to let you know you're not alone.

So if you're suffering now, take heart—you are being prepared to help others. With the genuine empathy and patience you gain from difficulty, you will be richly equipped to give encouragement to others who are struggling.

Dear God, Give me the opportunity to use what I learn through my trials and support someone else. Amen.

It Happened at Night

Praise the Lord, all you servants of the Lord who minister by night in the house of the Lord.
Psalm 134:1, 3

One afternoon when a huge crowd of people had come to listen to Jesus teach, before he sent them home, Jesus fed them. A little boy had a lunch of two fish and five loaves of bread and Jesus multiplied that lunch to feed all 5,000 people and still have twelve baskets of food left over. Then he went to a mountain to pray. It was evening. His disciples waited beside the boats on the Sea of Galilee. Finally it was completely dark when they set off across the lake without him. A strong wind was blowing and the water became very rough. When they had rowed about three-and-a-half miles, they saw something, someone, coming toward them on the water. They were terrified until Jesus said, "It is I; don't be afraid." Can you imagine what that would have been like? They knew they had left Jesus on the shore. Yet there he was coming right at them in the darkness. There was lots of talking and questions as they helped him into the boat. In a short time they safely reached the shore. What an exciting nighttime adventure!

What do you do when you wake up in the night and are afraid? Do you hide your head under the covers? Do you call for your mom or dad? It's all right to do all of those things, but when you are afraid in the night remember that Jesus is right there. God said, "Never will I leave you; never will I forsake you" (Hebrews 13:5). So whether you are out on a cold lake in the dark in a storm or in your bed awake because you had a nightmare, Jesus is there. Remember that and thank him for it.

Dear Lord, I am so glad you are always with me whether it's day or night. Thank you. Amen.

Crossing the Finish Line

The time has come for my departure. I have fought the good fight,
I have finished the race, I have kept the faith.
2 Timothy 4:6, 7

There are several different kinds of runners. Some runners specialize in sprinting, and some are better at running long distances. The fastest man on earth might win a sprint, but that doesn't mean he could finish a marathon. And in any race, the goal is to finish well, not to lead only at the beginning.

When we first recognize what Christ did for us, it's exhilarating. But if we're running on an emotional high, mistaken that life as a Christian will always be this way, we will surrender at the first surprising disappointment. Our lifetime with Jesus resembles a marathon much more than a sprint. To persevere in faith until we cross the finish line is more important than starting out strong and quitting before we reach our goal.

Remember that the freeing love of Jesus is why you run the race. The journey can be long and difficult. But don't let a hard time make you lose sight of the goal. Remain faithful to the end.

Dear Lord, I want to be your faithful servant until I meet you face to face. Give me strength and help me persevere. Amen.

Light in the Darkness

I will give you the treasures of darkness, riches stored in secret places, so that you may know that I am the Lord, the God of Israel, who summons you by name.
Isaiah 45:3

If you are ever lucky enough to visit a huge cave, you will be amazed at the world below ground. Pillars of pale stone hang from the ceiling and grow from the floor. Veils of thin rock sweep across wide open spaces. Fields of crystals sparkle in water. Formed in complete darkness, these unexpected treasures can be appreciated only in the light.

Darkness in life is marked by feelings of despair and loneliness. But, even in darkness, God works beautiful treasures in you. Your capacity for patience, love and endurance will grow like the stately stalactites in a cavern.

If hopelessness is creeping in like a shadow, remember God's Word offers truth to hold on to:

- *You are my lamp, O Lord; the Lord turns my darkness into light.*
  2 Samuel 22:29

- *Even the darkness will not be dark to you; the night will shine like the day, for darkness is as light to you.*
  Psalm 18:28

- *I will lead the blind by ways they have not known, along unfamiliar paths I will guide them; I will turn the darkness into light before them and make the rough places smooth.*
  Isaiah 42:16

Dear God, Thank you for being with me, even in darkness. Help me go on in faith. I look forward to what you are working in me. Amen.

Teach Us to Pray

One day Jesus was praying in a certain place. When he finished, one of his disciples said to him, "Lord, teach us to pray, just as John taught his disciples." He said to them, "When you pray, say:

"'Father,

hallowed be your name,

your kingdom come.

Give us each day our daily bread.

Forgive us our sins, for we also forgive everyone who sins against us.

And lead us not into temptation.'"

Luke 11:1–4

Let's see what Jesus taught his disciples about prayer. He said:

Address God as "Father." We are all children of God and everyone who believes in Jesus can call God "Father."

"Hallowed be your name." "Hallowed" means "holy." Everything about God is holy, even his name. Ancient scribes bathed, changed their clothes, and got a new pen before they even wrote the holy name of God.

"Your kingdom come." That's what God wants most — for his kingdom to be established on earth and in heaven. His kingdom on earth is revealed when a person becomes a believer in Jesus.

"Give us each day our daily bread." God provides for us continually — not all at once — so it is natural that we come to him continually.

"Forgive us our sins, for we also forgive everyone who sins against us." We all do things that are sinful every day and we need to ask God's forgiveness.

"Lead us not into temptation." God sometimes allows us to be tempted, but he promised to be with us no matter how we are tempted and he will help us through it.

Jesus was not teaching the exact words to use. He was giving an example of a complete prayer, from praise to requests to forgiveness. Because he loves us, we can approach him about anything.

Dear Lord, You are my heavenly Father. Thank you that I can go to you for anything and everything, any time and all the time. Amen.

Yes, He Will

Commit your way to the Lord; trust in him and he will do this.
Psalm 37:5

The word "commit" means "to give something to someone for safekeeping." Moses' successor Joshua committed his way — his life, his daily choices — to the Lord. He knew the center of God's will was the safest place to be. So when there was opportunity to take the Promised Land, Joshua was ready to go. The same God who conquered Jericho would lead them in. But others were filled with doubt, seeing the giants as only one of the obstacles that stood in their way.

Joshua trusted God not only when it was easy to do so but also when it was tough. The more difficult the situation, the more trust is worth. When you rest in him even when you can't understand the timing or the circumstances, trust triumphs over doubt and there is peace.

Of course, your difficulty isn't conquering a new land, but God is the Lord of your problems as well. Whether you are feeling frustration over people or things, at school or at home, he is big enough and good enough for you to place your trust in him.

Dear Lord, I know you are God, but it is hard to rest in trust. I will be able to rest in you only if you help me. Amen.

Seeing God

There was also a prophetess, Anna, the daughter of Phanuel, of the tribe
of Asher. She was very old ... she spoke about the child to all who were
looking forward to the redemption of Jerusalem.
Luke 2:36, 38

The Bible is full of wonderful stories that only take up a paragraph
or so. This is one of them. There was an 84-year-old woman named
Anna. When her husband died she went into the temple and spent
the rest of her life worshiping, praying, and fasting. It is pretty
certain that one of the things Anna prayed about was asking God to
hurry the coming of the Messiah.

Then one day Mary and Joseph brought baby Jesus to the temple.
Anna saw them and began to give thanks to God out loud, saying
the baby was the redemption of Jerusalem that everyone had been
looking for.

Above all, Anna loved God. So she talked to him constantly,
sharing her heart with him. Not only did God answer her prayer and
send the Messiah, he gave her the gift of meeting Jesus herself.

You too can have heartfelt conversations with God that are
characteristic of a deep relationship. Persist with your requests.
Keep giving him your worries. Continue worshiping him. You will
find blessings you didn't even expect.

Dear Lord, Thank you for inviting me into a personal relationship with
you. I pray that our bond will grow every day. Amen.

Through and
Through

May God himself, the God of peace, sanctify you through and through. May
your whole spirit, soul and body be kept blameless at the coming of our
Lord Jesus Christ.
1 Thessalonians 5:23, 24

"Through and through" means something is completely and totally
in something else. For example, a sponge in a bucket of soapy
water is soapy through and through. Today's verse says the God of
peace will "sanctify you through and through." The word "sanctify"
means to purify something — to set it apart for a holy use. So God
makes us pure and holy through and through, and he does it so that
we can live out his will on earth and become the kind of people he
can use to help others.

When God cleans us up, there won't be any dirt, stains, or
anything that is not pure and clean. He'd like for us to live so close
to him that he can keep washing us clean every day.

Dear Lord, What a wonderful idea, to have a heart so clean that even
in the deepest, darkest part of it, there is no sin. What a wonderful,
free way to live! Amen.

An Amazing Victory

No, in all these things we are more than conquerors through him who loved us.
Romans 8:37

In C. S. Lewis's story *The Lion, the Witch, and the Wardrobe*, there is a wonderful story of Aslan the lion conquering death after first giving his life as a sacrifice for the sin of one of the children in the story, Edmund. Edmund had become involved with a witch who ruled over the country of Narnia. He betrayed his brother and sisters, thinking that the Witch would make him a prince. But he soon finds out that the Witch intends to make him a prisoner and soon kill him. Aslan, the great lion, rescues Edmund, who is sorry for what he has done. But it's too late. Someone has to pay the price for his sin. The children learn that Aslan had agreed to pay the price for Edmund by giving up his life to the witch.

The witch kills the lion Aslan and the children were devastated, until they discovered that Aslan had returned to life. He not only conquered death, but also defeated the Witch and all her evil. He made the children conquerors too, and soon all of them reigned as kings and queens of Narnia.

Jesus was like Aslan in that he died for the sins of others — for our sins. Then he conquered death and he lives forever to help us. One day we will reign with him just like the children ruled in Narnia. We are even more than conquerors because Jesus loves us.

Dear Lord, How exciting that not only are you an overcoming conqueror, but we will be too one day in heaven. Amen.

Don't Be Shy

This will result in your being witnesses to them.
Luke 21:13

The prophet Isaiah in the Old Testament saw some amazing things (see Isaiah 6:1–9). He had a vision in which he saw the Lord seated on a throne. The Lord had on a robe and the part that trailed behind — called a "train" — was so long that it filled up the temple. Then there were the amazing beings around him. Above him were seraphs. Seraphs are beings something like angels. They have six wings. With two wings they cover their feet, with two they covered their faces, and with the last two they were flying and hovering near the throne. They constantly called out to one another an amazing song of praise to God. They said, "Holy, holy, holy is the Lord Almighty; the whole earth is full of his glory." There is another Bible story in Revelation (see Revelation 4:8) that talks about beings that have six wings, and once again these creatures (probably seraphs) are spending all their time praising God. Some other amazing things happened in the story, but finally Isaiah said he heard the voice of the Lord says, "Whom shall I send? And who will go for us?"

If you saw what Isaiah saw and then had God himself ask you whom he could send, what would you say? Well, Isaiah said, "Here am I. Send me!" And God replied, "Go and tell this people."

When we see the Lord and understand how awesome he is, we too will want to share it — with people who don't yet know God's love as well as with other believers who may need encouragement and assurance.

Dear Lord, I want to be a living declaration of your good news. Encourage me so that I may encourage others who are just getting to know you or who haven't met you yet. Amen.

Never Alone

I am not alone, for my Father is with me.
John 16:32

David of the Old Testament was hunted and chased by King Saul's soldiers. He often felt alone and scared. But David knew that he was never alone. He wrote a beautiful psalm (song) that helps us understand we are never alone either. Here are parts of that song:

O Lord ... you know me. You know when I sit and when I rise; ... Before a word is on my tongue you know it completely, O Lord. You hem me in — behind and before; you have laid your hand upon me.... Where can I go from your Spirit? Where can I flee from your presence? If I go up to the heavens, you are there; if I make my bed in the depths, you are there. If I rise on the wings of the dawn, if I settle on the far side of the sea, even there your hand will guide me, your right hand will hold me fast.... How precious to me are your thoughts, O God! How vast is the sum of them! Were I to count them, they would outnumber the grains of sand. When I awake, I am still with you.

excerpts from Psalm 139

God is every place you go no matter where it is. That's because he is inside you — in your heart and mind. And the better you know him, the closer he seems, especially in the lonely tough times. When you are alone and frightened, stop and think about what David said. Think about how close he is to you. Then begin to thank him for being there and soon the loneliness will go away.

Dear Lord, I am sometimes lonely and sometimes scared. Thank you that David experienced that too and wrote about it. That is a great comfort to me. Amen.

I Can Do it with Jesus

He will see it, and I will give him and his descendants the land he set his feet on, because he followed the Lord wholeheartedly.
Deuteronomy 1:36

God didn't design us to live life on our own. We were designed to be in fellowship with others and above all to be in fellowship with him. To try to do everything on our own would be like sailing a boat that was designed for a crew. For awhile you might be able to pull it off, but if clouds started to build and storms closed in, you would find your own strength was dangerously incomplete. Thankfully we don't have to live life all by ourselves. Jesus comes alongside throughout our entire journey.

What storms are you facing? Are you trying to overcome them on your own? Remember, Jesus is with you in your life boat. Go ahead and let him take over. He's sailed before.

Dear Lord, Over and over you tell us that you are with us no matter what happens to us. Help me remember that the next time I feel alone and in trouble. Amen.

Valley of the Shadow

As the sun was setting, Abram fell into a deep sleep and a thick and dreadful darkness came over him.
Genesis 15:12

In the Garden of Eden Adam and Eve enjoyed the perfect relationship with God until darkness was introduced in the form of a serpent. Cunning liar that he is, Satan questioned God's goodness. God's children fell for it, embraced doubt, and rebelled against God. The rest is history.

What if Adam and Eve hadn't taken Satan's suggestion to heart but instead took it as an opportunity to clear it up with God himself? What if the darkness didn't blind them but instead drove them back to the Light?

Satan has not abandoned evil. Even today he whispers lies: "God has forgotten you.... If God really cared, he would have stopped this crisis...." Don't fall for it! Remember that God has revealed his perfect love on the cross so that you can never be separated from him. Instead of letting the darkness separate you from your Savior, use it instead to bring you nearer.

Dear Lord, Help me remember that my most discouraging times are the best times to cling to you with faith and trust. Amen.

Too Much

The angel of the Lord came back a second time and touched him and said, "Get up and eat, for the journey is too much for you.
1 King 19:7

Elijah was a man who lived a long time ago and who was a lot like us. He got hungry. He got tired. He was afraid. He didn't understand what was happening. He complained. Even though he was God's prophet, he was also human just like us.

A wicked King named Ahab, and his equally wicked wife, Jezebel, was furious with Elijah. He told them God was going to stop the rain on their land for three years, and it happened. He mocked their wicked priests and said their gods must be sleeping because nothing happened when the priests cried out to their gods. He made the priests look foolish, and then he killed them because they were false priests. When Jezebel found out what Elijah had done, she was furious. She told Elijah that he would be as dead as her priests by the same time the next day.

Elijah was afraid and he ran away as fast as he could into the desert. There he sat down under a tree and prayed that he might die. "I've had enough, Lord. Take my life." Then he laid down under the tree and fell asleep. It was all too much for him. Then God sent an angel to bake fresh bread for Elijah and give him some clean cold water. "Get up and eat," the angel told him, "for the journey is too much for you." So Elijah ate and drank and traveled on for forty days and forty nights until he was far away and safe.

God is tender and kind to us. He knows our needs. He knows our limits. When we've gone as far as we can go, he picks us up. So come near to him and rest in his provision.

Dear Lord, I'm so glad you love us and are watching out for us when we've had all we can take. I'm glad it is then that you take care of us the most. Amen.

Out in the Fields

He went out to the field one evening to meditate, and as he looked up,
he saw camels approaching.
Genesis 24:63

Some interesting things happen "out in the fields" in the stories
of the Bible. In the Old Testament, there is a story that describes
how Isaac was out in the fields walking around and meditating —
thinking. He looked up and he saw camels coming toward his camp.
He knew what that meant. His bride was coming. Several months
before this time, his father, Abraham, had sent a servant to look for
a bride for Isaac. The servant found the perfect girl, Rebekah, and
brought her home with him. Isaac just happened to be out in the
fields when the camel caravan arrived bringing home the servant
and Isaac's bride.

In the New Testament, there is another story about how
shepherds out in the fields one evening were watching their sheep
when they got the greatest news about Jesus' birth. An angel said,
"Do not be afraid. I bring you good news of great joy that will be for
all the people. Today in the town of David a Savior has been born
to you; he is Christ the Lord" (Luke 2:10 – 11). It just doesn't get any
more exciting than that.

You never know where you might be when God helps you or uses
you or tells you some earth-shaking news. It's always good to get
quiet with God "out in the fields" where you can meditate on him.
There you can pray and ask him to lead your life, and there you can
listen for him to speak to you.

Dear Lord, I am grateful that I get to have a close, personal relationship with you. Remind me to seek out quiet times with you. Amen.

God with Us

The virgin will be with child and will give birth to a son, and they will call
him Immanuel" — which means, "God with us."
Matthew 1:23

Once there was a preacher who had a dream. He dreamed that
Jesus had not come to earth — had never been born. In his dream he
found himself looking through his house. There were no
Christmas stockings hung by the chimney. There were no Christmas
bells or holly wreaths. There were no Christmas trees or beautiful
lights. He went out on the street, but there was no church where he
could worship. He came back in and sat down in his office. Every
book about Jesus was gone — vanished off the shelf.

At that point in his dream, the doorbell rang, and at the door was
a small boy who said that his mother was very sick and would the
pastor come and pray. When he got to the house, he opened his
Bible to read some comforting words of Jesus to the mother, but
his Bible ended at the book of Malachi in the Old Testament. There
were no gospels to tell the story of Jesus. And two days later he
stood beside this woman's coffin and conducted a funeral service.
Suddenly he realized that if Jesus had not come, there was no hope
of heaven. It was too much. That was when he woke up from his
dream. He was so glad to be awake and to realize that Jesus had
come. He is Immanuel — God with us — and that is the best
news of all.

Dear Lord, This Christmas day I want to say thank you for the best gift
of all, your son Jesus. I am so glad that Jesus is God with us forever
and ever. Amen.

Everyone Plays a Part

Then Jesus went with his disciples to a place called Gethsemane, and he said to them, "Sit here while I go over there and pray."
Matthew 26:36

Some people are leaders. They are the ones who make the plans and encourage others to follow. Jesus was a leader. In the verse above, he leads his disciples to a park called Gethsemane. With him are the disciples. He tells them to "Sit here" while he goes to pray. Then he chooses three disciples: Peter, James, and John, to go with him further into the garden. He wanted them to follow his example and pray and to help him in a difficult time.

In the Garden of Gethsemane each person had a different role to play. At Jesus' direction, some followed him closely to pray, and some waited at a distance. Without protesting, each disciple did what they were told. Similarly we are asked to listen to God's direction. Leading, following, or waiting come at his timing and his purpose. When we're called to take a role, we can be prepared to do our best.

Dear Lord, I trust that you have a plan. Prepare me for the roles you have a chosen for me. Amen.

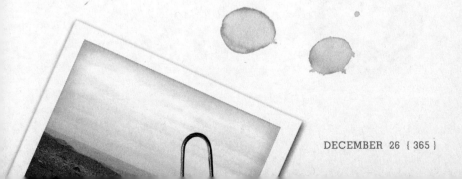

Growing Strong in Tough Times

They bruised his feet with shackles, his neck was put in irons.
Psalm 105:18

God uses suffering to strengthen souls. He shapes hearts through hard times.

Think of all of his beloved servants he carefully trained for their callings. David knew what it was to protect his flock from the jaws of a lion so he was ready to protect his country from a giant. How willing would Joshua have been to face the massive Canaanites if he hadn't first been refined in the desert? What if Noah had been sealed in the ark without any preparation? Instead, he first faced ridicule that strengthened his resolve and sharpened his focus on God.

Don't dismiss your hardships as wasted or excessive. Have faith that they are working together for his perfect purposes.

Dear Lord, I know you want me to be a strong, faithful follower. Help me draw especially near to you during hard times. Amen.

Hand Me
Some Joy

Rejoice in the Lord always. I will say it again: Rejoice!
Philippians 4:4

Do you know the story of Helen Keller? Helen Keller was a woman who was both blind and deaf. She couldn't see what people looked like and she couldn't hear their voices to know if they were speaking in a rejoicing way. But she knew lots of things by touch. She knew when people were happy or sad just by feeling their hands. She said:

The hands of those I meet are dumbly eloquent to me. I have met people so empty of joy that when I clasped their frosty fingertips it seemed as if I were shaking hands with a northeast storm. Others there are whose hands have sunbeams in them, so that their grasp warms my heart. It may be only the clinging touch of a child's hand, but there is as much potential sunshine in it for me as there is in a loving glance for others.

—Helen Keller

Of course, there are days when you feel like smiling and days when you don't. But regardless of feelings that go up and down, deep joy from a relationship with God is constant because he is constant — always loving, always faithful, always good. Let that knowledge sink in and warm your heart. A smile will follow soon enough.

Dear God, Your closeness comforts me and makes me happy. Amen.

Love Letter

We have seen that the land is very good.

Judges 18:9

When you pick up your Bible, remember that it is not merely a collection of stories about ancient times and ancient people. It is more than a guidebook meant to show Christ followers how to live.

The Bible is God's love letter written directly to you.

Hard to believe? Easy to forget? Try personalizing verses by changing the pronouns from us to me or from we to I.

For God did not send his Son into the world to condemn me, but to save me through him.

John 3:17

But I see Jesus, who was made a little lower than the angels, now crowned with glory and honor because he suffered death, so that by the grace of God he might taste death for me.

Hebrews 2:9

For great is his love toward me, and the faithfulness of the Lord endures forever.

Psalm 117:2

Without changing the meaning of the verses, reading them this way reminds you that your relationship with God is personal not distant. He had you in mind from the beginning. His words, his son's death, his love are for you. His promises are for you. Go claim them.

Dear Lord, Thank you for loving me. Thank you that I'm your child. Thank you that your promises are meant for me. Amen.

Prayer Changes Things

So Peter was kept in prison, but the church was earnestly praying to God for him.
Acts 12:5

When Peter was in jail, Christians prayed and God sent an angel to get him out. That angel just walked him right out the gate while the guards slept. Prayer can truly change circumstances.

Once a young boy was very ill. He had to go to a hospital where he was put in isolation. He had a disease that he could give to other people, so he had to stay away from everyone else. It was a very scary time for his family.

After he went to the hospital, his little brother and his big sister got down on their knees and prayed that God would heal him. That night his mom and his dad went to a church and the people there prayed for him too. The next morning when his family went back to the hospital, he was sitting up in bed and working a jigsaw puzzle. It was a miracle. He continued to get better from that day on and soon he was able to go home where he finished getting well.

There are times when no human power or influence can change a situation. An emergency that can't be helped by things on earth can be changed by power from heaven. Fervent, persistent prayer not only surrenders the power to the One who can actually change things (even through miracles), but it also reminds you who really is in control.

Dear Lord, Thank you for hearing me every time I pray. It's comforting to know that you actually want me to come to you for both big and small matters. Amen.

The End of a Year

Then Samuel took a stone and set it up between Mizpah and Shen.
He named it Ebenezer, saying, "Thus far has the Lord helped us."
1 Samuel 7:12

Once, long ago, God's people, the Hebrews, were fighting (for the umpteenth time) the Philistines — a terrible warlike people who seemed intent on destroying God's people. One day the Philistines were on the attack again and God's people were scared — really scared. They asked Samuel to pray to God to help them — and God did. That day when Samuel prayed, God sent a thunderclap so loud it scared the Philistines. They turned tail and ran for home. God's people chased them home. Then Samuel took a big rock and set it up as a memorial. He told the people this rock was to help them remember all the times when God had helped them. He called it the "Ebenezer Stone." The idea was that every time they looked at the stone, they would remember God loved them and had helped them, and he would help them in the future.

Picture your own memorial (or "Ebenezer Stone") and think of how God has loved you and helped you, even just in this last year. Through disappointments and triumphs, he is cultivating godly perspectives that you maybe didn't have twelve months ago. So you are better able to recognize how God has been faithful to you in the past and better able to trust that he will be faithful to you in the future.

Dear Lord, Thank you for loving me and never leaving me alone. Help me hold onto you in the New Year. I love you, Lord, and I want to serve you better in the future. Amen.

NIV Adventure Bible

Hardcover • ISBN 978-0-310-71543-6

In this revised edition of *The NIV Adventure Bible*, kids 8-12 will discover the treasure of God's Word. Filled with great adventures and exciting features, *The NIV Adventure Bible* opens a fresh new encounter with Scripture for kids, especially at a time when they are trying to develop their own ideas and opinions independent of their parents.

Available now at your local bookstore!

365 Days of Adventure

written by
Robin Schmitt

kidz

NIV Adventure Bible Book of Devotions

Softcover • ISBN 978-0310-71447-7

The *NIV Adventure Bible Book of Devotions* takes kids on a thrilling, enriching quest. This yearlong devotional is filled with exciting fictional stories about kids finding adventure in the real world. Boys and girls will learn more about God and the Bible, and be inspired to live a life of faith—the greatest adventure of all.

ZONDER**kidz**
.com

ADVENTURE BIBLE PURPLE BACKSACK
ISBN 978-0-310-82402-2

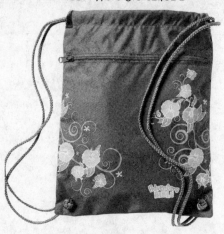

ADVENTURE BIBLE TAN BACKSACK
ISBN 978-0-310-82381-0

These versatile and sporty carriers feature a large pocket that holds the Adventure Bible and other stuff kids you may want to take along, an adjustable rope strap, and durable nylon material. These carriers will fit any of the Backpack Bibles, Adventure Bibles, as well as many other books and Bibles up to 6 1/8" x 8 13/16" (224mm x 156mm)..

Available now at your local bookstore!

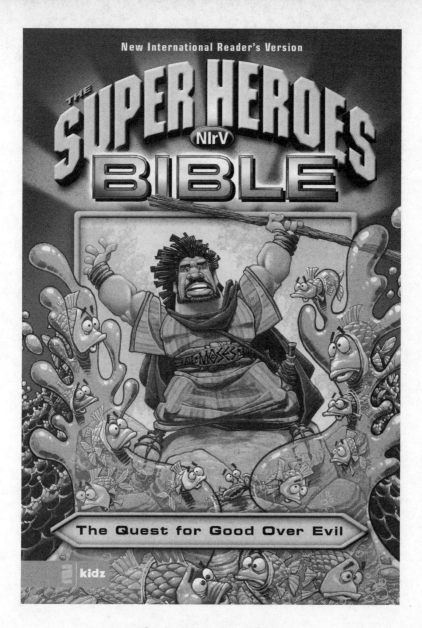

NEW INTERNATIONAL VERSION

Luke 2:52

Boys
BIBLE
THE ULTIMATE MANUAL

LUKE 2:52
AND JESUS GREW IN WISDOM AND IN STATURE,
AND IN FAVOR WITH GOD AND MEN.
-NIV

Boys Bible
Hardcover • ISBN 978-0-310-70320-4

Finally, a Bible just for boys! Discover gross and gory Bible stuff, find out interesting and humorous Bible facts, and apply the Bible to your own life through fun doodles, sketches, and quick responses. Learn how to become more like Jesus mentally, physically, spiritually, and socially. Part of the 2:52 series for boys.

Available now at your local bookstore!

Luke 2:52
365 DAILY DEVOTIONS

THE **ULTIMATE DEVO** for **Boys**

AND JESUS GREW IN WISDOM AND IN STATURE,
AND IN FAVOR WITH GOD AND MEN
LUKE 2:52 –NIV

ED STRAUSS

The 2:52 Ultimate Devo for Boys
Softcover • ISBN 978-0-310-71314-2

In the humorous, cheeky, and sometimes gross style that makes the 2:52 series so engaging and fun for boys, this year-long devotional combines important principles with practical messages, teaching lessons boys need to learn and helping them put this valuable knowledge into practice. Each devotion presents a Bible verse, explains it, shows how it applies to boys' lives, and offers tools to help boys live in a godly way.

ZONDER**kidz**™
.com

Available now at your local bookstore!

faiThGirLz!
the beauty of believing

Girl Talk
52 Weekly Devotions

Lois Walfrid Johnson

Girl Talk

ISBN 978-0-310-71449-1

This one-year devotional is filled with stories about girls who feel just like you. As you read their stories each week and fill in questions about how you think each girl should react, you'll learn new ways to deal with the pressures around you. There is someone out there who knows exactly how you feel. And he's more than ready to listen.

ZONDERkidz
.com

Available now at your local bookstore!

faiThGirLz!
the beauty of believing

Devotions

No Boys Allowed: Devotions for Girls

Softcover • ISBN 978-0-310-70718-9

This short, ninety-day devotional for girls ages 10 and up is written in an upbeat, lively, funny, and tween-friendly way, incorporating the graphic, fast-moving feel of a teen magazine.

Girlz Rock: Devotions for Girls

Softcover • ISBN 978-0-310-70899-5

In this ninety-day devotional, devotions like "Who Am I?" help pave the spiritual walk of life, and the "Girl Talk" feature poses questions that really bring each message home. No matter how bad things get, you can always count on God.

Chick Chat: Devotions for Girls

Softcover • ISBN 978-0-310-71143-8

This ninety-day devotional brings the Bible right into your world and offers lots to learn and think about.

Shine On, Girl!: Devotions for Girls

Softcover • ISBN 978-0-310-71144-5

This ninety-day devotional will "totally" help teen girls connect with God, as well as learn his will for their lives.

faiThGirLz!™
the beauty of believing

Bibles

Every girl wants to know she's totally unique and special. This Bible says that with Faithgirlz! sparkle! Now girls can grow closer to God as they discover the journey of a lifetime, in their language, for their world.

The NIV Faithgirlz! Bible

Hardcover
ISBN 978-0-310-71581-8

Softcover
ISBN 978-0-310-71582-5

The NIV Faithgirlz! Bible

Italian Duo-Tone™
ISBN 978-0-310-71583-2

The NIV Faithgirlz! Backpack Bible

Periwinkle
Italian Duo-Tone™
ISBN 978-0-310-71012-7

ZONDERkidz™
.com

Designed for tween girls!

Faithgirlz Messenger Bag
ISBN: O-310-82224-6

Faithgirlz Book and Bible Cover
ISBN: O-310-82036-7

We want to hear from you. Please send your comments about this book to us in care of zreview@zondervan.com. Thank you.

ZONDERVAN.com/
AUTHORTRACKER
follow your favorite authors